Dixie's Italians

Dixie's Italians

*Sicilians, Race, and
Citizenship in the
Jim Crow Gulf South*

Jessica Barbata Jackson

Louisiana State University Press
Baton Rouge

Published by Louisiana State University Press
Copyright © 2020 by Louisiana State University Press
All rights reserved
Manufactured in the United States of America
First printing

Designer: Laura Roubique Gleason
Typeface: Whitman
Printer and binder: LSI

Maps throughout this book were created using ArcGIS® software by Esri. ArcGIS®
and ArcMap™ are the intellectual property of Esri and are used herein under license.
Copyright © Esri. All rights reserved. For more information about Esri® software, please
visit www.esri.com.

Portions of chapter 1 first appeared in "Before the Lynching: Reconsidering the
Experience of Italians and Sicilians in Louisiana (1870s–90s)," *Louisiana History: The
Journal of the Louisiana Historical Association* 58, no. 3 (2017): 300–38, and are used by
permission of the editor.

Library of Congress Cataloging-in-Publication Data

Names: Jackson, Jessica Barbata, author.
Title: Dixie's Italians : Sicilians, race, and citizenship in the Jim Crow Gulf South / Jessica
    Barbata Jackson.
Description: Baton Rouge : Louisiana State University Press, 2020. | Includes
    bibliographical references and index.
Identifiers: LCCN 2019047626 (print) | LCCN 2019047627 (ebook) | ISBN 978-0-8071-
    7172-1 (cloth) | ISBN 978-0-8071-7376-3 (pdf) | ISBN 978-0-8071-7375-6 (epub)
Subjects: LCSH: Italians—Gulf States—History. | Sicilians—Gulf States—History. | Gulf
    States—Race relations—History.
Classification: LCC F220.I8 J33 2020 (print) | LCC F220.I8 (ebook) | DDC 305.800976—
    dc23
LC record available at https://lccn.loc.gov/2019047626
LC ebook record available at https://lccn.loc.gov/2019047627

The paper in this book meets the guidelines for permanence and durability of the
Committee on Production Guidelines for Book Longevity of the Council on Library
Resources. ♾

For Luca and Josh

Contents

Illustrations

Acknowledgments

When people learn of my research, they invariably ask if I am from Louisiana (I'm not) or if I am Italian (only my paternal grandfather was born there). I stumbled onto this project as a first-semester graduate student. Having taught history at the secondary level for a number of years, I had long been drawn to the cyclicality of immigration history and the shifting complications of race. I first thought of writing some version of how Italians "became white"; I quickly discovered that that book (and many others like it) had already been written. But, in an early America readings seminar, I encountered the complex and layered world of New Orleans; with encouragement to engage a transnational lens, to New Orleans were added migration studies, the racial history of the American South, and the unification of modern Italy. As questions abounded about race and violence, citizenship and identity, and immigrants and ethnicity, my inquiry began, leading to this book.

For this direction and focus, I am eternally indebted for my time and training in the history department at the University of California at Santa Cruz. I am grateful to everyone with whom I had the honor to work, particularly Alice Yang, Noriko Aso, Greg O'Malley, Lynn Westerkamp, and Vanita Seth, but especially my mentors, David Brundage, Kate Jones, and Cindy Polecritti—thank you for your perceptive critiques, challenging questions, and your fervent and enthusiastic support of this work. Many thanks to my graduate colleagues and my writing group—Melissa Brzycki, Stephanie Montgomery, and Kiran Garcha—who commented on early versions of this manuscript. And for my innumerable students over the years—from Ecuador to Italy to Santa Cruz to Fort Collins—thank you for challenging me and inspiring me to pursue this path.

I offer my sincere gratitude to the archivists who provided keen insights during my development of this project, notably those at the Louisiana and Special Collections at the University of New Orleans and Sal Serio at the American Italian Research Library. For financial assistance in conducting this research, thank you to the Conference of Presidents of Major Italian American Organizations, the UC Santa Cruz History Department, the UC Santa Cruz Humanities Institute, the University of Minnesota's Immigration History Research Center Archives, and the Summersell Center for the Study of the South. To the scholars around the country who took the time to answer a chance query from a graduate student, many thanks for pointing me in many fruitful directions.

In bringing this book to fruition, I consider myself abundantly fortunate to have found a home in the history department at Colorado State University. Thank you to all of my colleagues for your warm welcome, support, and encouragement, particularly my department chair Robert Gudmestad, Ann Little, my junior faculty comrades, and especially Sarah Payne, whose discerning eye to chapter drafts has considerably enhanced the final outcome. To CSU Writes and Kristina Quynn, to my accountability writing group Cate Dicesare, Ellie Moseman, and Cerissa Stevenson, and to my write-on-site group of scholar activists, OiYan Poon and Ricki Ginsberg—thank you for your time and space, your direction and advice, your collaboration and camaraderie. I owe a special debt to my graduate students Eric Newcombe and Jacob Swisher, whose research assistance was instrumental in the final stage of this project, and to Megan Clevenger for her last-minute on-the-ground help in New Orleans. My sincere appreciation to Joshua Reyling and the Geospatial Centroid at CSU for the creation of such stunning maps to accompany my research. From beginning to end, working with LSU Press has been an absolute professional pleasure—thank you to my editor, Rand Dotson, for believing in and championing this project; to my managing editor, Catherine Kadair, for shepherding this book through the finishing phases; to my copy editor, Gary von Euer, for his sharp eye and attention to detail; and to the anonymous reviewer whose incisive and constructive comments have helped to make this a better book.

Finally, this book would not have been possible without the love and support of my family and friends, too numerous to name. To my Fort Collins friends who have offered us a new home, to my Reedies near and (mostly) far, and to my California friends who will always be family—I am deeply thankful for your constancy and community. To my dad, Dennis Barbata, for his unwavering encouragement and for venturing with me to Italy to visit the ruins of our ancestral home in Ginestra degli Schiavoni. To my mother-in-law, Jean Jackson, who wishes we lived closer but still offers her steadfast and ever-willing assistance any way she can. To my mom, Judy Barbata, for her unfaltering dedication, who moved halfway across the country without so much as batting an eye to help our family and to care for our son. For my son Luca, who has been on this journey for longer than he realizes—I hope to make you proud. And for Josh, my best friend and partner in everything—thank you for believing in me, for challenging and sustaining me, for advocating for and empowering me, for listening to me read countless drafts aloud, and for being willing to go on this wild and unconventional journey; for this and for all the adventures still ahead.

Dixie's Italians

Introduction

The men and boys wore gray corduroy suits; the women and girls donned shawls of deep blue, red, and flaming yellow. The vibrant blue of their skirts and bodices appeared vivid in the twilight. From the crowded deck of the steamship in approach of the northeastern wharf, they called out "frantic and joyous" greetings to the crowds of friends and relatives who awaited their arrival behind a double line of ropes on shore. As the ship anchored and the gangplank lowered, seven hundred Sicilian passengers disembarked, seemingly en masse, a "swarming, struggling, seething, mass of humanity." With deep-toned cries and high-pitched shouts of anticipation, they danced and trotted, wriggled, and fought their way ashore, carrying huge sacks, canvas bags, sleeping infants, and wide-eyed small children. In their animation, they moved into the dock's maddened congestion like a "distracted and wildly-excited flock of variegated tropical birds." They gathered their inspected belongings and "dispersed helter-skelter" into the twinkling of the harbor's electric lights. It was October in 1901 New Orleans, and immigration season had begun.[1]

Such a scene depicts the massive fall arrival of Italian immigrants in the Gulf South, a regular occurrence in the late nineteenth and early twentieth centuries. Italians embarked for the American South as part of intense recruitment efforts by immigration agents to enlist European workers to replace emancipated slave laborers on southern plantations. By 1910, 45,000 Italians had entered through the Port of New Orleans; an average of 2,000 per year arrived between 1880 and 1898.[2] The largest contingent of Italian, predominantly Sicilian, immigrants settled in Louisiana. In 1910, 43,000 Italians (foreign-born and native-born) resided in Louisiana; by 1930, nearly half of all foreign-born families in Louisiana were Italian.[3]

Smaller but still noteworthy populations of Italians settled in Alabama and Mississippi. As of 1910, more than 4,000 foreign-born and native-born Italians resided in Alabama, where foreign-born Italians made up 14 percent of the state's foreign-born, white population. Italians made up 22 percent of the foreign-born, white population in Mississippi, with a total of 3,900 foreign-born and native-born Italians.[4]

Sicilians and other Italians arrived in a Gulf South attempting to negotiate an increasingly intractable post–Civil War social and racial order. On which side of the color line would Italians be consigned? After five Sicilians were lynched in Tallulah, Louisiana, in July of 1899, the *Times Democrat* of New Orleans published an article in defense of the lynching: "Citizens Plead Necessity for White Supremacy."[5] Just the year before, however, as Louisiana legislators disenfranchised black voters through the implementation of a literacy and property requirement for voting, they also passed a provision—subsequently dubbed the "Privileged Dago" Clause—that specifically protected the "foreign white vote" and Italian voting rights.

The paradox of Italians being lynched on behalf of "white supremacy" while at the same time securing their right to vote as "foreign whites" demands historical consideration: Where did they fit? What did it mean for Italians to be foreign "white" voters, yet susceptible to lynching? How could Italians fall both outside white supremacy's understanding of whiteness, and also within it? How would Italians be classified (and how would they position themselves) as southern states began imposing Jim Crow laws, like voting restrictions and interracial marriage bans? Animated by questions of identity and engaged with both official metrics of citizenship and unofficial constructions of belonging, *Dixie's Italians* recovers a history of immigrants in the Gulf South who were not totally "white" but who were not "black" either. Transporting their own complicated conceptions of identity and citizenship as emigrants from a newly unified nation, Sicilians and other Italians occupied a transitory place within prescriptions of southern white supremacy and confounded existing constructions of race, identity, and citizenship in the Jim Crow Gulf South between the 1870s and 1920s.

Many Italians who immigrated to the US in the late nineteenth century arrived with an obscured sense of nation and identity. Italy, the peninsula that was home to many countries, cultures, and distinctly different languages, had only conjoined under a constitutional monarchy in 1861, a political and territorial process that remained incomplete until 1871. National unification under the Piedmont royalty, promoted by the cultural and social Risorgimento, was less a popular movement and more an alliance between the propertied elite and the state—so much so that statesman Massimo d'Azeglio famously wrote in the 1860s (and posthumously published), "*l'Italia è fatta. Restano da fare gli italiani.*"[6] Colloquially translated, "We have made Italy, now we must make Italians."

Despite d'Azeglio's prescription, Italy's nation-building project failed to make Italians out of the *meridionali* (southerners). For those residing in the Mezzogiorno (Southern Italy), the territory that formerly comprised the Kingdom of the Two Sicilies and included those regions south of Rome and the former Papal States, unification exacerbated the "Southern Question."[7] Politically, the extremely restricted franchise meant that only 2 percent of Italian subjects were eligible to vote in the first parliamentary election.[8] Economically, Piedmont's protective tariff and free trade legislation aggravated the South's economic problems, which increased the economic disparity between the North and South.[9] Southern revolutionaries, in an effort to challenge the legitimacy of the Piedmont conquest, participated in a brutal civil war in the 1860s, dubbed by the Italian state the "Brigands War." The intense and bitter violence of the civil war, during which two-thirds of the Italian army were sent to subjugate the South, killed more Italians than all the combined wars of the Risorgimento.[10] Despite the accompanying propaganda campaign and the rhetoric of unification and annexation, the South was only annexed with the Italian nation through military conquest and political absolutism. The very act of naming a war against unification as the Brigands War explained the conflict to the new nation as a war for the purpose of subduing southern banditry, which conceptualized the entire South as a land of criminals. Consequently, Southern Italians resided outside the nation rather than within. Because of these efforts to unify Italy through the diversionary othering of the South, compounded by increased taxes, land hunger, environmental calamities, and fear of conscription, the Italian state effectively disenfranchised the southern peasantry. Accordingly, Italy's unification efforts were distinctly linked with the beginning of the large-scale emigration of Sicilians and Southern Italians.[11]

During the last quarter of the nineteenth century, Italians, accustomed to relocating for temporary work around Europe, extended their migrations across the Atlantic. Between 1880 and 1915, an estimated 13 million Italians left Italy; over 4 million made their way to the United States.[12] Italy as a cultural and linguistic unit did not exist for most of these emigrés, especially those from Southern Italy and Sicily. Instead, Italian identity was constituted by *campanilismo,* "a view of the world that includes a reluctance to extend social, cultural and economic contacts beyond points from which the parish or village bell could still be heard."[13] With this view amplified by regional differences in dialects, cuisine, and social practices, Sicilian and other Italian immigrants understood their sense of place and identity, at least upon their initial emigration, in terms of their region or village of origin—not nation or race.[14]

Official US policy, however, grouped and labeled Sicilians and Southern Italians as "Italian," which granted them legal access to naturalization and US citizenship. At the same time, nativist stereotypes consigned Italians, like other southern and eastern European immigrants, to an intermediary social status and hierarchically ranked their racial location.[15] Anti-Italian sentiment focused on Catholicism, their inclination toward seasonal migration and perceived unassimilability, and the presumed association between Italians and criminality.[16] Such nativism was further aggravated by a group of late nineteenth-century Italian positivist anthropologists who, as part of a nation-building project at the end of the nineteenth century, developed a new field of criminology and identified a scientific difference between "pure" Northern and "dark" Southern Italians.[17] Using skull measurements and other forms of "scientific proof," Italian criminologists like Cesare Lombroso claimed that Southern Italians, whose "inferior African blood" was responsible for "fomenting . . . insurrections and perpetuating brigandage," descended from "Arabs" and were "born criminals" predisposed to innate criminality.[18] Even as the Italian state made overtures toward fashioning a pan-Italian identity, Lombroso reasoned that Southern Italians were "racially distinct" and inferior to Northern Italians. Thus, biological determinism both explained the higher rates of murder, parricide, and poisoning in the South—Sicily was reported as having the highest homicide rate in Europe—and contributed to the Italianization of the peninsula by casting Southern Italians outside the new nation and defining them as a common enemy.[19]

Beyond the construction of a racial hierarchy in Italy, the transnational appeal of the criminologists' project—widely disseminated across popular as well as scholarly media sources—informed US perceptions of Southern Italians and directly influenced US immigration lawmakers.[20] As early as 1899, the US Bureau of Immigration began to officially record Southern Italians as a race separate from Northern Italians and classified the "North Italian" as "Keltic," while the "South Italian" was "Iberic."[21] US Immigration Commission reports fixed the geographic boundary that differentiated "North Italy" from "South Italy" at the southern edge of the Apennine Mountains, south of the Po River basin; in practice, officials cataloged those who arrived from regions south of Rome, inclusive of emigrants from Naples, Sicily, and Sardinia, as Southern Italians.[22] In addition to discriminating the "language, physique, and character" of Southern Italians, the Dillingham Commission's *Dictionary of Races or Peoples* went on to characterize Southern Italians by 1911 as "excitable, impulsive, highly imaginative, impracticable . . . [with] little adaptability to highly organized society."[23] As Edward Ross, a US social scientist, eugenics advocate, and immigration restrictionist, explained in 1914, Northern Italians were "more intelligent, reliable, progressive," while Southern Italians operated at a "primitive stage of civilization," were more "volatile [and] unstable," possessed an "inaptness . . . for good teamwork," and "lack[ed] the convenience for thinking."[24]

For the four million hierarchically ranked Italians who made their way to the United States, one of their main points of entry was the Port of New Orleans. In fact, a significant population of Italians—outpacing arrivals to New York—had already settled in New Orleans well before the Civil War and founded the Societa Mutua Benevolenza Italiana, the city's first Italian benevolent society, in 1846.[25] Following Emancipation, plantation owners in need of agricultural labor turned to European peasants; organizations like the Bureau of Immigration (1866) and the Louisiana Immigration and Homestead Company (1873) set to work distributing pamphlets to encourage and attract immigrants to the region.[26] In the contemporaneous wake of Italian unification, impoverished and disenfranchised Sicilians and other Southern Italians responded in great numbers.[27] While Sicilians generally made up 25 percent of Italian arrivals at the national level, as a result of these southern promotional and recruitment efforts and the existing citrus trade between New Orleans and Palermo, 90 percent of Italian immigrants in New Orleans were Sicilian.[28] This distinctly Sicilian immigrant population, identified by themselves and by other Italians as Sicilian rather than Italian, felt little allegiance to the Italian state, understood unification as having been imposed on Sicily, and migrated in large part because of their marginalized status in Italy. How did this predominantly Sicilian immigrant population establish a sense of belonging and negotiate the terms of nation, ethnicity, and citizenry in the post-Reconstruction Gulf South? At a time of prescribed southern white supremacy, to what degrees and in what contexts were Sicilians and other Italians included or excluded from categories and agendas of whiteness? How did they align themselves with white agendas and discourses? These are challenging but necessary questions for historians to analyze. Although the Jim Crow South is usually told as a story of the black/white color line, it is also an immigration story.

As both an act of historical recovery and a revision to whiteness studies, this book performs an in-depth analysis of the lynchings of Italians in Louisiana and Mississippi between 1886 and 1901, the impact of disenfranchisement efforts upon Italians in 1890s Louisiana, attempts to segregate Sicilian children from "white" schools in 1906–1907 Mississippi, and the inconsistent ways that Sicilians and other Italians were racially categorized in turn-of-the-century miscegenation statutes, especially in Louisiana and Alabama. Owing to the regional case studies of immigrant communities in northern cities such as New York, Buffalo, and Chicago, the historical focus of Italian immigration in the United States has been the urban North; this northern perspective (journalistic, historical, or otherwise) has since stood in for the prevailing national narrative on Italian immigrants and immigration.[29] In countering this slippage between the local and national, this book remains especially attendant to regional and local sources, which have enabled me to tell the specifically Gulf South version of the Italian immigrant story.

Beyond the limited scholarship on lynchings of Italians in the Gulf South, most of which focuses on the 1891 lynching in New Orleans, scholarly examinations of Italians in the South remain scant and limited in scope.[30] Recovering the unexamined Italian experience in the Gulf South—specifically Louisiana, Mississippi, and Alabama—*Dixie's Italians* broadens historical conversations of the Jim Crow South and introduces the Italian narrative into the scholarship on sex and marriage across the color lines, voter disenfranchisement, and school segregation. Moreover, by bridging previously disconnected, disparate histories and historiographies and engaging a transnational lens, *Dixie's Italians* amplifies the work on modern Italy and the development of Italian identity, restores Louisiana to southern studies, and expands on and remedies the limited scholarship on the lynchings of Italians and Italian Americans.

Critical whiteness scholars have provided a much-needed discourse to understand the intermediary racial status of arriving European immigrants at the end of the nineteenth century.[31] James Barrett and David Roediger consider Eastern and Southern Europeans as an "inbetween" people, meaning that Italians resided somewhere "inbetween" white and black.[32] Thomas Guglielmo counters this characterization of "inbetweenness" by suggesting that Italians, in terms of their "color status," were always white—"white on arrival."[33] Guglielmo contends that from the mid-nineteenth to the mid-twentieth centuries, color and race were two distinct and separate modes of classification. Color was not based on phenotypic signifiers or pigmentation; instead, it was a social category, derived from the nineteenth-century anthropological groupings of Caucasian, Mongolian, Ethiopian, etc., that granted its possessors certain legal privileges.[34] Race, on the other hand, subdivided the "color races" and was based on biological and geographic markers; for instance, Europeans could be Mediterranean, Alpine/Celtic, or Teutonic/Nordic.[35] Correlated to national identity, race carried certain assumptions about inherited characteristics and hierarchically ranked one's "color status." Italian "whiteness" was therefore qualified because Italians were Mediterranean, which fell below Teutonic/Nordic in dominant racial taxonomies of the era. Although Italians were granted significant legal privileges as a result of their "whiteness," they were simultaneously racialized and understood as a less-advanced and less-evolved "race."[36] Despite their being racially suspect, official and legal policy recognized Italians as "white," meaning their whiteness protected them from systemic legal discrimination and guaranteed them access to citizenship. According to the color/race schema, which proffers a valuable reading of the tempered whiteness of Italians, Italians could vote and be naturalized and, at least until 1924, immigrate largely without restrictions.[37]

Yet the multifaceted racial structure of the Gulf South requires a more nuanced and fluid concept for Italians' racial status than scholars have previously adopted. Both Barrett and Roediger's concept of Italians as "inbetween" and Guglielmo's theory of "white on arrival" provide too static an explanation for the lived experiences of Italians in the Gulf South, who were neither "in between" white and black nor always white.[38] I provide a new framework for understanding the liminal racial status of Sicilians and other Italians in the US South: racial transiency. This transiency, which highlights the instability of their racialization, meant that Sicilians and other Italians passed among and between racial communities; they moved (and were moved) as both "white southerners" and "people of color" back and forth across the color line. That Italians were lynched in defense of "white supremacy" but also possessed "unconquerable white blood" exposes this racial flexibility.[39] Italians secured voting rights as "faithful allies," "good citizens," and "foreign whites," but were still "degenerate monsters" and a "colony of vicious murderers and assassins [to whom] murder and blood were . . . what roses, moonlight and music are to poets and lovers."[40] An Italian could, on occasion, obtain a marriage license to wed a black partner without consequence, but be charged with miscegenation under other circumstances.

Racial transiency also meant that Italian racialization was available for transmutability, as Italian racialization was often an aftereffect of violence, disenfranchisement, and segregation efforts rather than its cause. Italians were depicted as contributors and "proper citizens" before the 1891 lynching, but then, in defense of their bloodshed, they were a "menac[ing] . . . gang of murderers," and yet later, when needed, "industrious, honest and peaceable" once again.[41] When Italians endeavored to contest Jim Crow conventions, they were racialized to dispense with their challenge. Italians were reduced to "ignorant [and] brutal" and "a disgrace to a civilized community" when they marched in the streets to protest disenfranchisement, and were "undesirable aliens" when they attempted to integrate a white public school.[42] Culture, ethnicity, and class contributed to these constructions of Italians as racially inferior. Still, to employ Barbara J. Fields's model, discourse and deed produced (and reproduced) their racialized treatment as ideology, through a "vocabulary of day-to-day action and experience . . . constantly created and verified."[43] Assessments of Italians were articulated in racial language and justified in terms of race; in this way, the discourse of Italian difference functioned racially and was, effectually, racial. The Mafia label was applied because of assumptions of criminality across the race of Italians, just as the anti-Italian commentary found in the 1890s lynching aftermaths constructed Italians in racial terms. Bringing the immigrant story into the Gulf South illustrates the extent to which the racial transiency of Italians, and their own efforts in navigating the southern racial structure, contributed to the construction of the South's color line in ways that mutually reinforced it and revealed its instability.

Race does not afford the only means to reconsider the narrative of Italian discrimination; citizenship also serves as a useful frame. The literature regarding conceptions of citizenship is vast but remains largely concerned with official versions of citizenship as defined by passports and identity documents and how the nation-state constructed definitions of and justified exclusions from citizenship.[44] Movement, migration, and the crossing of national boundaries further complicate formulations of citizenship, specifically with regard to how national identity was ascribed to arriving immigrants like Italians. Beyond the more common category of "formal citizenship," I offer "ascribed nationality" and "informal citizenship" as critical counter-categories. Ascribed nationality underscores moments when diplomatic officials invented and assigned a national identity that supplanted an individual's sense of their national identity. In the case of Sicilians, where the movement across borders resulted in the imposed nationalizing of migrating individuals, ascribed nationality exposes the tension between the initial superficiality of their named nationality as Italians and the potential for their ascribed national identity to be internalized (or at least exploited) in order to take advantage of the protections granted as rights of citizenship. Informal citizenship, which bridges Mae Ngai's "alien citizenship" with Bridget Anderson's concept of citizenship as a "normative moral status," signals the social and unofficial consideration of someone as foreign.[45] This informal citizenship includes those instances where bureaucratic actors, like marriage licensing agents and census enumerators, participated in constructing citizenship and where they policed the rights of citizenship through more subjective or extralegal practices of evaluating performances of citizenship and (racially) reading bodies.[46] Informal citizenship also includes those instances where immigrants themselves—as when Italians campaigned for voting rights as native, "white" southerners—navigated the strategies of exclusion, partook in formulating their own understandings of citizenship, and performed their roles as citizens.

In addition to recovering the racial transiency of Italians, *Dixie's Italians* reveals how official actors ascribed an Italian national identity upon Sicilians, how unofficial actors participated in constructing Italian citizenship, and how Italian immigrants themselves shared in formulating their understanding of citizenship and performed their role as deserving citizens. Even though Sicilians and other Italians may have been able to access formal citizenship, their rights to informal citizenship—whom could they marry? was their economic progress sanctioned? could they express political opinions openly and freely?—were fervently debated. While not resulting in their systematized or institutionalized Jim Crow segregation, Gulf South social convention and legal practice variously denied Sicilians and other Italians access to informal citizenship. Engaging Natalia Molina's concept of "racial scripts," which speaks to the discursive continuity of racial projects across time and space, exposes how southerners both advanced and denied Italians the privileges of citizenship by employing (or countering) the same racial scripts used to marginalize black southerners.[47] In this way, because of their racial mobility and transiency and through their efforts in navigating the southern racial structure, Italian immigrants in turn contributed to the codification of Jim Crow.

Similarly, transnational anti-Sicilian and anti–Southern Italian dialogue and northern anti-Italian nativism also operated as racial scripts, which communities in the Gulf South weaponized in various times and places to justify violence against and validate the subordinate status of Sicilians and other Italians. Focusing on scripts of citizenship incorporates the political and economic factors that underwrote contestations over Sicilian and Italian citizenship identities, while the Gulf South context highlights the duality that Sicilians and other Italians were both privileged as "white" Italians and marginalized—in violently real and racially discursive ways—as racially suspect "dagoes."

Finally, following this story in the United States and Italy demonstrates the transnational process of constructing immigrants' national and racial identities. While many of the Sicilians and other Italians arriving in the Gulf South lacked a coherent identity as Italian citizens when they immigrated, their status as either American citizens or Italian subjects became a source of intense diplomatic debate, and one in which immigrants themselves participated. Regularly, immigrants acted in ways that would entitle them to the privileges of US citizenship and participated in constructing their own citizenship. At the same time, despite their transported local fidelities as Cefalutana or Contessiotti, moments of crisis (like lynching or disenfranchisement) compelled Sicilians and other Italians, as a means of survival, to constitute their national identity as Italians.[48] Through this expansion of *Italianità* (an Italian-ness or Italian consciousness), *Dixie's Italians* shows how Sicilians in the Gulf South became Italian.

This book is organized chronologically into five chapters and an epilogue. Ranging from 1870s Louisiana through 1920s Alabama, each chapter centers on a particular case study. In chapter 1, I depict the oft-overlooked transnational history of the Italian and Sicilian diaspora in the Gulf South. The southern experience of Sicilian and other Italian immigrants, in contrast to their experience in the urban North, was originally characterized by a positive relationship with native-born southerners, which readily deteriorated over time. Chapter 2, which uses the March 14, 1891, mass lynching of eleven Italians in New Orleans as the primary case study, also addresses other lynchings of Sicilians and other Italians across Louisiana and Mississippi between the 1880s and 1910s. Chapter 3, focusing on the 1898 Constitutional Convention in Louisiana, chronicles the passage of Louisiana's "Privileged Dago" Clause, which worked to protect Italian voting rights over those of African Americans. Chapter 4, using 1907 Sumrall, Mississippi, as its central incident, investigates the efforts to segregate Sicilian children from local white schools. Chapter 5, using the *Rollins v. State* case in 1921 Jefferson County, Alabama, as its case study, examines the extent to which Sicilians and other Italians problematized marriage and miscegenation laws in the South. The epilogue follows federal and state immigration policies as they pertained to Italians up to 1924 and beyond and clarifies how debates regarding Italians and immigrants were configured within and by regional and transnational contexts. Close readings of these historical moments, when the meaning of race itself was in effect up for grabs, reveals both the racial transiency of Italians and the crucial character of context.

Defining the Gulf South

The Gulf South developed a distinctive identity and flexible social hierarchy as a result of its complicated historical legacies: French, Spanish, and

American colonial regimes and three different systems and histories of racial classification. From its early settlement under the French, the combination of Native American, European, and African cultural influences set
the region apart from other Anglicized colonies.[49] Along with competing
identities, imperial inattention, and environmental conditions that led the
Gulf territories to employ rather atypical slavery practices, the region was
marked by a certain "rogue colonialism."[50] Louisiana's large population of
free persons of color, or *gens de couleur libre,* typified the region's pecu-
liarity.[51] These competing groups, discourses, and dynamics complicated
race-making and contributed to a regional distinctiveness characterized by
a unique fluidity and flexibility. Even after the United States acquired the
Louisiana territory in 1803, this distinct regional identity persisted. The
Gulf South was an in-between region—neither fully American nor entirely
European, it exemplified a certain adherence toward color segregation,
while also contesting and subverting the doctrine of racial binaries.[52]

As a result of these historical legacies as well as historiographical debates, I use the term "Gulf South" to denote both cultural and geographic
conditions. The developing culture in the Gulf South was marked by a fluidity and hybridity similar to that of New Orleans, which would have allowed
for a more flexible racial experience for arriving immigrants. Therefore, I
term my region of study as the Gulf South because of the presence of a distinctive regional culture: French and Spanish cultural influences, proximity
to the Caribbean, the urban Creole tradition, a certain "frontier fluidity,"
and prevalent Catholicism.[53]

However, I also incorporate locations less culturally similar to the Gulf
Coast, traditionally more characteristic of the Deep South, such as Birmingham, Alabama, and rural Mississippi. In part, I have incorporated
those regions of the South that had large Italian immigrant communities; as
indicated in map 1, geographic sites of dispute generally contained a disproportionately large number of Italians. For example, in Birmingham, one of
the districts where Italians confounded marriage laws, Italians represented
nearly one-quarter of the foreign-born white population; and Italians made
up 72 percent of the foreign-born white residents in Bolivar County in
northwestern Mississippi, one of the locations that attempted to expel Italians from a local white school.[54] At the same time, despite Birmingham and
rural Mississippi's decidedly Deep South location, New Orleans remained

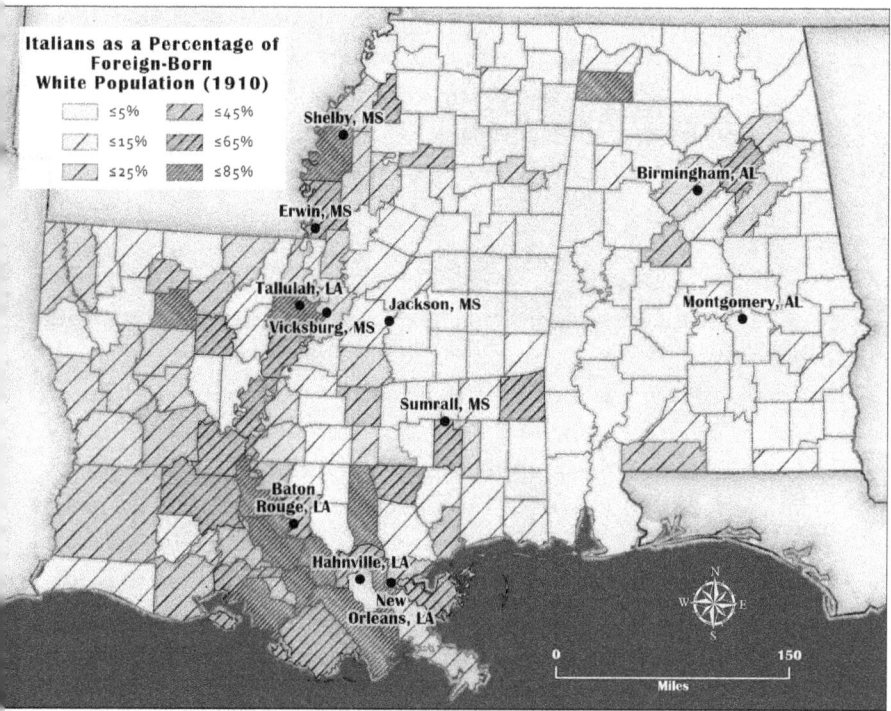

MAP 1. Density of Italian immigrant populations (as a percentage of the parish/county's foreign-born white population) in Louisiana, Mississippi, and Alabama in 1910. While Italian immigrants represented numerically small numbers in some locales, the geographic sites of conflict were generally parishes or counties with uncharacteristically large populations of Italians. Map by Joshua Reyling. Sources: US Census Bureau; ESRI.

a touchstone for these disparate immigrant communities, as Italians from Mississippi, Alabama, and surrounding areas still sought assistance from the Italian consulate in New Orleans in times of crisis. Moreover, on account of the presence of certain racial anomalies—blurred categories and regular boundary crossing—within other regions of the Gulf States (beyond Louisiana), I refer to the states (in their entirety) that border the Gulf of Mexico as the Gulf South in order to demonstrate the connectivity between Louisiana and the greater South. While the demographic and historical peculiarities of the Gulf South remain relevant to this book, demonstrating that Louisiana and the Gulf were part of a larger web of continental influences reveals the Gulf South to be more illustrative of southern race relations than has been previously understood.[55] The Italian narrative in the Gulf South, which represents the confluence of regional politics and national legislation, provides evidence to further support the notion of the Gulf States' comparability with their surrounding areas.

A Note on Sources

Most historical narratives of Italian immigrants in Louisiana begin with the lynching of eleven Sicilians in 1891 New Orleans, and they generally conclude that the lynching was the result of long-standing anti-Italian sentiment and racial animosity. Such easy interpretations are the result, however, of overlooking or misreading local sources. Therefore, while my archive included a broad collection of multilingual and multiethnic newspapers (including local, national, African American, and Italian-language presses), transnational governmental and legal records, census and marriage records, court records, church records, and ephemera of immigrant communities, my inquiry relied indispensably on analyzing the local and regional language of race and citizenship.

In addition to citing regional newspapers from around the Gulf South, my efforts converged upon the New Orleans press. The *Daily Picayune*, the *Times Democrat*, and the *Daily States* were the "big three of Newspaper Row," located on Camp Street in 1890s New Orleans. They enjoyed the highest circulation rates in the city (in that order), with a combined daily circulation of 49,488 and a combined Sunday circulation of 70,680 in 1891.[56] The rival *Daily Picayune* and *Times Democrat*, which merged to form the present-day *Times Picayune* in 1914, were known for maintaining objectivity in their reporting. Conversely, the editor of the *Daily States*, Major Henry James Hearsey, was notorious for his editorials blatantly supporting white supremacy.[57] In addition to editorial predispositions, print culture provides its own set of limitations, such as representing only a literate upper- and middle-class, and potentially government-influenced, perspective. Still, comparing patterns of public language across New Orleans, the rest of Louisiana, and the Gulf South gives insight into trends in characterizations of Sicilian, Italian, and other immigrants. Additionally, my focus on region and the local exposes a previously untold story.

In considering court rulings and legal decrees, I remained cautious against overstating the self-legitimacy of certain statutes and instead consider the permeability of statutory classifications.[58] The legal code, by definition, purported to represent precise categories such as "citizen" and "noncitizen" or "black" and "white," when, in reality, such groupings would have most certainly enjoyed varying degrees of instability. Even while contesting law as description and alert to the staticity of the resulting social relations, legislative moments informed and defined social operations— legal statutes expose how society thought its members ought to behave, and more specifically, the social values and attitudes of elites who made and shaped the law. Furthermore, considering law as a moving target requires recognizing that "unofficial" actors remained active in the implementation (or lack thereof) of legal statutes. Thus, the legal framework of the postbellum and post-Reconstruction Gulf South grants access into the very real and powerful behavioral instructions and prescriptive attitudes of the era.

A Note on Language

Historically (within press rhetoric and immigration records) and historiographically, the terms "Italian" and "Sicilian" were largely used interchangeably. Avoiding this convention, I complicate the language of "Italian" throughout this work in order to account for the fact that the majority of these historical actors were specifically Sicilian.[59] Because of these demographics, I refer to groups of actors in my study as "Sicilians and other Italians," while only specifying that an individual was Sicilian when I have definite evidence of his/her ancestry or place of origin. However, I do use the term "Italian" or "anti-Italian" to more generally reference attitudes, discourse, and legislation that impacted Sicilians as well as other Italians.

The term "dago," appearing in quotations throughout this work, is a pejorative slang term for an Italian-speaking (or even a Portuguese- or Spanish-speaking) person. According to nineteenth-century explanations, "We owe the word 'Dago' to the Spaniard, whose language furnished this slang name for the men of the Mediterranean countries who come to the United States" or for "dark-colored Europeans."[60] Contemporaries believed the term "dago" evolved from the prevalence of confusing Italians with Spanish or Portuguese sailors, who were universally referred to as "Diego" because "all of those nationalities looked much alike and the general sound of the language they spoke was similar."[61] As a commentary on the Italian propensity for violence, another explanation linked the meaning to an abbreviated version of "dagger-wielding."[62] Throughout, I use quotation marks with "dago" and "dagoes" to designate their origins in the source material.[63]

Finally, I use the terms "black" and "white" throughout in reference to the racial categories inscribed into law—via census records, naturalization papers, and marriage licenses—while cognizant of the fact that such groupings supposed fixed categories that operated with much less definitiveness in practice. In order to problematize the unqualified application of the category of "white" upon Italians and Sicilians, to historically account for the divergence between race and color, and to divest Sicilians and other Italians from the confines of a monolithic "whiteness," I put "white" in quotation marks when referring to Sicilians and other Italians. Although not without its shortcomings, I use "black" (without quotation marks) to denote freedpersons or black southerners in the Gulf South; whenever possible, I quote from the original source material or use a more precise racial category like *gens de couleur* to further deconstruct this historically fashioned legal and social category.

1

From "Proper Citizens" to "Alien Electors"

Reconsidering the Experience of Sicilians in Louisiana before and after the Lynchings

The Italian colony embraces some of the most worthy, respectable and highly esteemed citizens of New Orleans. They occupy prominent places in every business and profession, while the masses are industrious, honest, and peaceable.

—"Our Italian Fellow-Citizens," *Daily Picayune,* March 4, 1889

Mob led by members of committee of fifty took possession of jail; killed eleven prisoners; three Italians, others naturalized. I hold mayor responsible. Fear further murders. I also am in great danger. Reports follow.

—Italian Consul Pasquale Corte, March 14, 1891

On the morning of March 14, 1891, a mob of nearly 10,000 New Orleanians amassed outside the Parish Prison in search of Italians. Incensed by the court's acquittal of nine alleged Mafia members believed responsible for killing New Orleans police chief David Hennessy, an armed faction stormed the prison; they shot those Italians they could find and dragged out two others to be hanged in front of the crowd. Within hours, eleven Sicilians and other Italians were dead at the hands of vigilante violence in one of the largest mass lynchings in US history.[1] Contemporaries rhetorically grounded their justification for the lynching in the presumed criminality, unassimilability, and "undesirability" of Louisiana's Italian population. But the 1891 lynching was not the result of long-standing, anti-Italian sentiment and racial animosity.[2] Rather, the lynching and ensuing anti-Italian discourse within Louisiana were something fundamentally new.

It is precisely by removing the lynching teleology to understand the treatment of Italians in Louisiana that this new, unacknowledged narrative is revealed. Turning to overlooked historical documents and local accounts from before and after the 1891 lynching, this chapter chronicles the unexplored and specifically southern experience of Italian immigrants in Louisiana across a broader historical moment. Juxtaposing rhetoric concerning Sicilians and other Italians from the northern and national presses in the 1870s and 1880s with press reporting from Louisiana of the same era affords an alternative to the one-size-fits-all deterioration narrative long applied to the Italian immigrant experience throughout the United States and uncovers the regionally specific trajectory of Italian immigrants in the Gulf South.[3] In particular, this chapter clarifies hidden features of the Italian immigrant experience in America writ large: whereas northern press rhetoric characterized Sicilians and other Italians as unassimilable, undesirable, and largely criminal, commentary in Louisiana encouraged and gladly received Italian immigration. Motivated in large part by economic self-interest in the wake of the region's post–Civil War labor shortage, the Louisiana press clearly differentiated between the Italian and the criminal, and identified Italians as valuable and productive "fellow citizens." In contrast to the national narrative, Sicilians and other Italians enjoyed a more tolerant and congenial relationship with native-born white Louisianans in the 1870s and 1880s. Only later, and most detectable after the 1891 lynching, did Louisiana press coverage begin to fluctuate and adopt the virulent anti-Italian rhetoric that characterized the broader Italian immigrant experience at the end of the nineteenth century.

What is more, this revived account more fully exposes the unstable citizenship and racial status of Sicilians and other Italians in the Gulf South. In the aftermath of the 1891 lynching (and the lynchings of Italians in 1896 Hahnville, Louisiana, and 1899 Tallulah, Louisiana), the local press employed anti-Italian rhetoric to justify the violence. Even accompanied by this racialized rationale, US state officials rhetorically and legally constructed Italian lynching victims as American citizens—if Italian lynching victims were US citizens, state officials could avoid making indemnity payments to the Italian government for the wrongful death of Italian subjects. Meanwhile, Italian officials, as part of their own state-making endeavor, used these lynching crises and indemnity debates to claim Sicilians as Italians and enfold them within the Italian state. Combining US state officials' rendering of Italian lynching victims as American citizens with the increasingly vituperative anti-Italian press reporting conveys the transitory position of Sicilians and other Italians in the Gulf South, just as the transnational lens reveals that Sicilian and Italian citizenship status and subjecthood in the United States were inextricably linked to Italy's own nation-building project.

Meanwhile, Sicilians and other Italians participated in the construction of their own identity as citizens. In spite of their imported regional differences, moments of crisis made apparent their shared marginalization as "dagoes." Sicilians and other Italians in Louisiana began to reevaluate and realign their citizenship identity, dissolving the identity boundaries that once separated them. Demonstrating the emergence of *Italianità*, or Italian-ness, Sicilians and other Italians bound together in solidarity and forged transregional alliances, as Sicilians appealed to the privileges of their ascribed nationality as Italians. In the Gulf South, Sicilians and other Italians possessed civic and racial identities available for transience and transmutability.

Only 17,000 foreign-born Italians lived in the United States in 1870, making up less than 1 percent of the nation's foreign-born residents.[4] Yet, even in response to this fractional population, the New York press described arriving Italian immigrants in the 1870s as "ignorant and uneducated" "brigands from Southern Italy" who "belong to the criminal classes."[5] The *New York Times* considered Italian immigrants as "starving and wholly destitute," "wretchedly poor and unskilled," "professional beggars," and "a very degraded and ignorant population"; Italian children "were utterly unfit—ragged, filthy, and verminous as they were—to be placed in the public primary schools among the decent children of American mechanics."[6] In the 1880s, sanitary officers pronounced foreign-born Italians who resided in "squalid huts or noisome cellars" as "links in a descending chain of evolution."[7] The arriving Italian immigrants were the "filthy, wretched, lazy, ignorant, and criminal dregs of the meanest sections of Italy."[8]

Such considerations were not isolated to New York, as sentiment from Washington, DC, to Illinois to Colorado to California marked Italians as "ignorant scum" who contributed to the "deteriorating" state of immigration.[9] Dispatches in Chicago warned that Italians did not make good citizens because they posed a "severe tax upon the assimilative powers of the Nation," and that Italians were a "curse to themselves [and] a burden upon charity" who lived in "squalor and filth" and "contribut[ed] their quota to the filth, vice and wretchedness."[10] Another common trope described Italians as invading parasites: they were "locusts," "vile and filthy beyond description," "living like dogs" and bringing with them "contamination [and] pollution."[11] Such Italian immigration, the national press reported, put the United States in danger: "The body politic is threatened with dyspepsia from overloading and overtaxing the digestive organs."[12] Communities nationwide went on to suggest that the United States should increase its immigration restrictions, on par with Chinese Exclusion. Washington, DC's *National Tribune* proclaimed, "We did well when we prohibited Chinese immigration. We should go farther, and at once, and put an effectual stop to our country being made the dumping-ground for the ignorance, filth and the vice of Europe."[13] The *Los Angeles Times* highlighted the desirability of German immigrants, in contrast to Italians, because "Germans come to America to become Americans," and unlike Italians, they renounce their allegiances to their native lands and learn English.[14]

Well before the massive waves of Sicilian and other Italian immigration to the United States at the turn of the century, the question of the loyalty, allegiance, and inherent criminality of Italian immigrants contributed to the development of a nationwide anti-Italian discourse. In the wake of Italian unification, rumors began to circulate that the Italian government was purposefully sending Italian immigrants (especially Southern Italians) to the United States in order "to get rid of them."[15] Press reports in the 1870s and 1880s warned that the Italian state was "secretly stimulat[ing]" the emigration of "paupers" because of overcrowding and because immigrants "send back their savings to their native land."[16] Fearing that the influx of Italian immigrants who "depress wages" would be economically unsustainable and physically dangerous, people from around the country went as far as suggesting that

> we can no longer afford to overlook the evil of promiscuous immigration. . . . [Italians] are not a class of immigrants whom we can receive without danger to ourselves. In clannishness and persistent adherence to the speech, dress and mode of life of their own country the Italian and the Chinese immigrant are on a par, though the much-abused wearers of the pigtail are more cleanly in their domestic habits. But the Chinaman very rarely gives the Police or the courts any trouble, while it is notorious that no foreigners with whom we have to deal, stab and murder on so slight provocations as the Italians.[17]

Not only did Italians' unassimilable tendencies mark them as foreign, on par with other racialized immigrant groups like the Chinese, but the Italian habit of seasonal migration was also economically objectionable. The Immigration Investigation Committee of Congress of 1888, upon interviewing Italian immigrants with "unkempt" hair and "ill-fitting and slouchy" dress who could not speak English, could not read or write, and were not familiar with geography, disparagingly concluded that Italian settlement was only temporary, and that "Italians . . . come here to make their pile [but] they prefer to spend their money in Italy."[18] Indeed, Italians remigrated at a higher rate than any other immigrant group, with a likely 50 percent of Italian immigrants to the United States eventually returning to Italy.[19] This inclination toward temporary migration earned Italians the nickname "birds of passage."

Gilded Age protectionism meant that descriptions were not exclusively hostile, and northern newspapers offered the occasional friendly assessment of Italian immigrants. Much reporting on Italians critiqued the occurrence of forced labor and the "trafficking of Italian children" and expressed concern for "poor Italian" immigrants.[20] Another subset of articles dispassionately described Italian celebrations and festivals, with the periodic favorable mention of arriving Italians and the beneficial impact of the "Italianization of New York."[21] Such sympathetic remarks usually included reports that differentiated between previous immigrants made up of "industrious and honest people from Genoa and the towns of the Ligurian coast" and newer immigrants from Southern Italy "who are now so frequently guilty of crimes of violence . . . extremely ignorant . . . [and] miserably poor."[22] Even much of these more positive expositions described the need to help, protect, aid, and "improve [the Italian] condition."[23] Nativism against Sicilians and other Italians certainly intensified in response to increasing arrivals at the turn of the century—the number of foreign-born Italians in the United States quadrupled between 1880 and 1890 to 182,600, a figure that would increase nearly eightfold to 1.34 million by 1910.[24] Nonetheless, national discourse in the 1870s and 1880s already identified Sicilian and other Italian immigrants as helpless and transitory sojourners predisposed to violence and criminal activity.

* * *

At the same time, public perception and press accounts in 1880s Louisiana challenged the archetypal and national stereotypes of Sicilians and other Italians.[25] For instance, the Louisiana press conveyed a contrasting and relatively sanguine response to the practice of return migration. One article, entitled "Homeward Bound: Members of the Italian Colony Going Back with their Savings," described the departure of an Italy-bound ship transporting Italians who had resided in Louisiana for several years and had "earned enough money to enable them to return and spend the remainder of their lives in their native land, sunny Italy."[26] Unlike the national commentary, the tone of this regional response evoked neither contempt for the eastward flow of US currency, nor disdain for Italians who resided only "temporarily" in Louisiana before ultimately returning "home." Motivated by both a social disinterest in permanently integrating foreigners and an economic need for cheap labor, this was distinctly more encouraging than northern and national press assessments of the same seasonal migration phenomenon.

In general, New Orleans newspapers described Italians as fitting in, contributing to the "prosperity of the city and state," "falling in line," behaving like "proper citizens," and being an "industrious, honest and peaceable" people.[27] New Orleanians went as far as acknowledging the obligation they owed to "Italian enterprise and capital" that had stimulated "phenomenal growth" in the region's economy.[28] Having steadily moved into commercial endeavors, Italian immigrants had, in fact, contributed to the local economy; by the 1890s, Italians controlled New Orleans's fruit-importing trade, and members of the city's elite included a number of Sicilians and other Italians. As the *Daily Picayune* reported, the Italian population in New Orleans included "many prominent professional and business men and tradesmen of all sorts, representing a very large aggregate of wealth. Many of them are American citizens, but they still preserve a strong attachment to their native land and cherish a warm admiration for its king."[29] Noticeably absent from the *Picayune*'s commentary was a demand for Italians to "assimilate" or "Americanize." Rather, Italians were "an industrious and thrifty people [who] make up an important and picturesque element of our city's life."[30] Not only did native-born New Orleanians respect Italians' cultural ties with Italy, they encouraged and welcomed their immigration and invited them to naturalize as American citizens.

In direct opposition to the negative tropes found within national reporting, opinions within the regional press around the state of Louisiana advocated the "advantages of an influx of immigrants" and explained, "We have room for immigrants, who will meet with a cordial reception and find a genial climate."[31] These advocates argued that increased immigration would lead to "prosperity, wealth and refinement" for Louisiana, and that "the future prosperity of our State depends to a great extent upon immigration."[32] Accounts from the cotton and timber parish of Alexandria in central Louisiana suggested "open[ing] the doors of Louisiana wide to the best class of industrious immigrants," while the local paper for St. Martinville in south central Louisiana urged the organization of a society to advertise its region and to encourage immigration.[33] Testimonies explained that "immigration is the present need of our parish" since "thousands of acres of the most fertile land of the state is idle, anxiously waiting for the tiller's plow to break its surface, and yield luxuriant and abundant crops of all kind."[34] Even in Jackson, Mississippi, some fifty miles from the Louisiana border, reports described Southern Italians as "industrious [and] economical" people who would add to the "wealth and prosperity" of the country; they would make good laborers and bring valuable industries to the region.[35] Ultimately, the unique labor demands of the region, along with economic self-interest, influenced this promotion of immigration and more welcoming public discussion.

Louisiana newspapers did acknowledge and participate in perpetuating certain negative stereotypes about Sicilians and other Italians, especially regarding their violent tendencies. The very occasional unfavorable depiction described the "dark dago who creeps stealthily down a back alley and buries his stiletto in the bosom of an enemy, is dark and bad all the way through," and explained that "every Sicilian carries a long, sharp knife for family purposes, as he generally has a vendetta or two on hand."[36] Yet these types of overtly denigrating mentions and deleterious descriptions remained exceedingly scarce, as the statewide press did not racialize Sicilians and Italians in the same manner as the northern and national press.[37] While northern and national rhetoric regularly likened Italians to parasitical "scum," vermin, or "pests," characterizations of Sicilians and other Italians in Louisiana papers, beyond the singular reference to the "creep[ing] dago," did not employ this type of animalistic, dehumanizing language.[38]

The press offered categorically few instances of applying negative "racial" characteristics to Sicilians and other Italians as a group.

Discourse in Louisiana assumed a correlation between Sicilians and other Italians and the Mafia. Articles made reference to an awareness of the Mafia dating back to the 1870s, although few implied that the Mafia existed *in* Louisiana before 1890.[39] Reports regularly commented on the Italian or Sicilian practice of "vendetta" and "blood vengeance" and eventually interpreted all Sicilian and Italian violence as the work of the Mafia, though more accurately factional violence rather than syndicated organized crime.[40] Such accounts still differentiated between the Italian community at large and the criminal element. While an 1874 article termed the "Sicilian vendetta" as "deplorable," the same piece also described Sicilians as "frugal, industrious and hard-working."[41] When grisly homicides headlined local papers, like the killing of a Sicilian husband whose neck was found slit and body half burned by "his wife and her paramour" in 1889, the press still maintained that "the Italian colony embraces some of the most worthy, respectable and highly esteemed citizens of New Orleans," and therefore, it would be "a gross injustice to cast reflections on their good name for the crimes of a few of their race."[42] The "evil-doers" in this case were both the criminals themselves and those who failed to differentiate between the Italian community and the criminals who happened to also be Italian. Despite the propensity of the "dago population" to engage in "blood vengeance," the "dagoes" overall were still a "respectable and hard working class of citizens."[43] On occasion, the press even wrote favorably about the violent habits of Sicilians and other Italians, agreeing with the "eminent wisdom of the Sicilian gentlemen" that the method of assassination was "infinitely safer" than a duel.[44] Unlike northern and national press descriptions that considered reports of Italian-on-Italian crimes as evidence of the violent tendencies of Italians, the Louisiana press did not capitalize on these criminal stereotypes. Certain individuals engaged in vendettas or were prone to violence, but as a group, Sicilians and other Italians were not altogether dangerous nor unwelcome.

Even alongside discussions that explained the criminal element as the result of the "influx of foreigners," the New Orleans press continued to encourage an open-door immigration policy.[45] Rather than discouraging further immigration or advocating increased immigration restrictions, as did the northern and national press, New Orleanians advocated that criminality should not impede Italian immigration. In a description of an arriving ship of Italian immigrants in December of 1888, the *Daily Picayune* used the opportunity to speak out against an impending head tax that would require immigrants to pay a security of 60,000 francs and effectively reduce the numbers of Italians who could immigrate: "Italians ought to be allowed to better themselves by emigrating if so desired."[46] Another report, though describing Italian immigrants as provincial—bringing "boxes of ugly, ill-smelling cheeses" and not being "over-intelligent"—declared the arrivals to be "earnest," "strong," and "enduring."[47] Similarly, as shown in figures 1 and 2, an October 1888 *Times Democrat* article, entitled "From Sunny Italy, Arrival of a Shipload of Immigrants," included several sketches that depicted uncaricatured versions of Italian emigrés.[48] Such representations—one image in particular portrayed an Italian in culturally specific attire bearing a heavy load—spoke to the perception of Italian immigrants as hard-working and economically necessary laborers in Louisiana. These friendly depictions, conceivably a public relations campaign intent on welcoming the much-needed immigrant labor to Louisiana, overlooked Italian criminality as a point of concern.

Moreover, the New Orleans and Louisiana press used the term "dago," generally understood as a derogatory slur or moniker, in a less charged, less racially disparaging, and more neutral manner than the northern and national presses. Countless references to "Dago Joe," "Dago Dave," "dago fishermen," "dago sailors," and "dago populations" indicated that Louisiana newspapers regularly used "dago" as a means of racially describing or identifying, not slandering.[49] Even in those cases where articles used "dago" in connection with a negative description of an Italian, such reports did not apply their negative assessments to the Italian "race" as a whole. For example, an 1870s *Daily Picayune* article wrote of "dago hucksters" whom they noted as "reeking with odors of every vile description," but this depiction referred to a specific area in New Orleans and to two specific individuals, not Italian immigrants in general.[50] Even positive and sympathetic illustrations of Sicilians and other Italians used "dago" as an identifying synonym interchangeable with the categories of Italian and Sicilian: New Orleanians owed the "valuable discovery" of the red snapper to a "Dago"; a poor "young Dago" in 1886 was robbed and "cruelly" beaten by a "crowd of negro base-

FIGURES 1 AND 2. Sketches, "From Sunny Italy, Arrival of a Shipload of Immigrants," *Times Democrat,* October 18, 1888. Although the Italians depicted in these images are represented in culturally specific attire, ethnic caricatures are notably absent. The image to the left portrays Italians as hard-working and economically necessary laborers in Louisiana.

ball players."[51] At least within Louisiana press rhetoric, Italians, Sicilians, and even "dagoes" occupied a relatively unthreatening place in Louisiana's social and cultural landscape in the 1870s and 1880s.

As seen in figure 3, *The Mascot,* New Orleans's weekly scandal sheet, did print a contemptuous and unabashedly anti-Italian cartoon in 1889; however, this singular depiction challenges the supposition of widespread anti-Italian attitudes in 1880s New Orleans press accounts.[52] *The Mascot* regularly ridiculed all groups in New Orleans—immigrants, prominent citizens, politicians, and law-enforcement officers alike—which meant that no one was safe from *The Mascot*'s mockery, gossip, and political muckraking. Based on their history of contrarian reporting as well as their circulation numbers, *The Mascot* was not representative of New Orleans press

FIGURE 3. "Regarding the Italian Population," *The Mascot*, September 7, 1889. This blatantly anti-Italian cartoon and accompanying article, which described Italians as "dirty, lazy, ignorant and prone to violence," was not characteristic of New Orleans rhetoric of the 1880s.

coverage. Self-reported and estimated circulation numbers in 1887 place *The Mascot*'s weekly distribution at 4,000–5,000, while the *Daily Picayune* distributed 10,000–12,500 issues daily (at least 70,000–87,500 weekly) and the *Times Democrat* distributed 15,000–17,500 issues daily (at least 105,000–122,500 weekly).[53] Additionally, and in contrast to other local papers, *The Mascot* was the only paper in New Orleans to print a scathing critique of the lynch mob in the days following the 1891 attack; although intended to disparage the strike leaders, the front-page story also served to sympathize with the lynching victims. While the September 1889 issue of *The Mascot* did describe Italians as "dirty, lazy, ignorant and prone to violence," such a description was neither characteristic nor all-encompassing of 1880s New Orleanian rhetoric.

The Mascot did occasionally critique immigrants and immigration more generally. Another 1889 issue printed a caricaturized image of an Italian with a hooked nose and dirty beard, as seen in figure 4, but conversely, this depiction did not actually serve as a critique of Italians as a group or Italian immigration in general.[54] Rather, the caricature was intended, as explained

FIGURE 4. "Encouraging Italian Immigration," *The Mascot*, January 5, 1889. The characterized image of an Italian with a hooked nose and dirty beard was not evidence of widespread anti-Italian sentiment but was intended to criticize Governor Nicholls for appointing an "undeserving" Italian to a government position.

by the accompanying editorial, to criticize Governor Francis T. Nicholls for appointing an allegedly "undeserving" Italian to the position of "Inspector of Weights and Measures for the First District." *The Mascot* offered a marked critique of increased immigration in an April 13, 1889, issue, as seen in figure 5, although they explained that the specific immigrant group

RESULT OF ENCOURAGING EMIGRATION.

Paupers, Vagabonds, Murderers and others of the European and Asiatic Scum Refused Admission elsewhere, are Readily Landed Here.

FIGURE 5. "Result of Encouraging Immigration," *The Mascot*, April 13, 1889. While clearly advocating a more restrictive immigration policy, *The Mascot* specifically targeted "Austrian gypsies" and still notably welcomed the arrival of "honest and industrious foreigners."

they caricatured and targeted on the front page were "Austrian gypsies." The article went on to admit, "Honest and industrious foreigners are always welcome and always will be, for they and their descendants make useful and respectable citizens and improve the condition of the community. We don't want the paupers."[55] Despite certain moments and occasional misgivings, anti-Italian sentiment was far from ubiquitous in the New Orleans press in the decades leading up to the 1891 lynching.

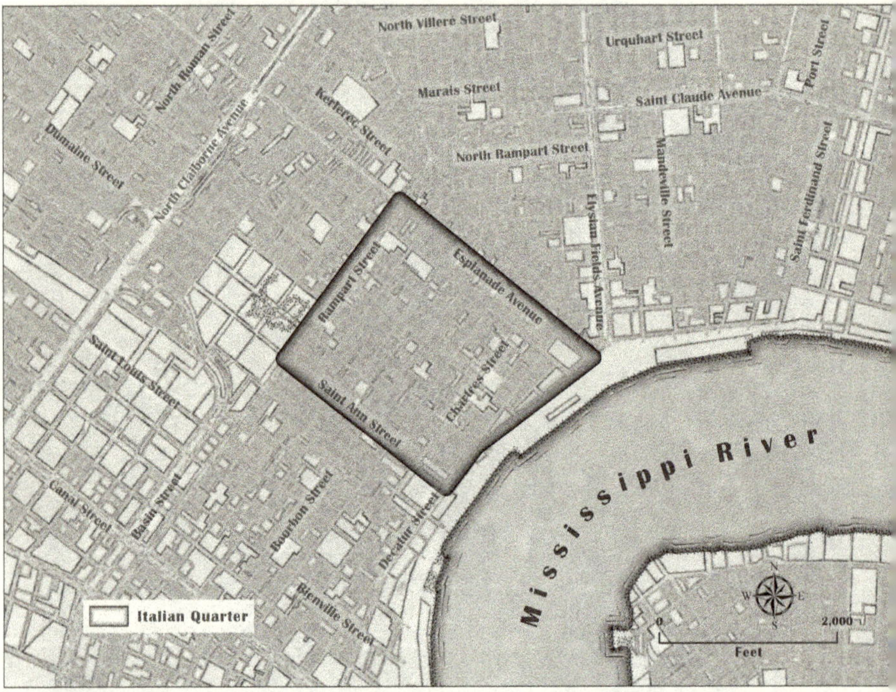

MAP 2. Sicilian and other Italian immigrants settled in decentralized patterns throughout New Orleans. By the turn of the twentieth century, the "Italian Quarter" occupied portions of the French Quarter. Map by Joshua Reyling. Sources: "A Morning Tour in Little Italy," *Daily Picayune*, July 30, 1899; USGS; US Census Bureau; City of New Orleans.

Louisiana's uniquely tolerant discourse toward Italian immigration resulted in part from the distinctive demographic and migratory patterns of the Sicilian majority to the region. Postbellum Sicilian migrants, unlike the earlier wave of educated and urbanized Italian migrants of the 1850s, worked seasonally, arriving with the citrus fleets in early fall and departing after the *zuccarata,* or sugarcane harvest, in the spring.[56] Initially, these Sicilians disproportionally settled in the rural sugar parishes of southern and south-central Louisiana. In addition to sugarcane, they labored in strawberry fields, on cotton plantations, and in lumber and railroad yards. Difficult to enumerate without precise remigration figures, Sicilian and other Italian sojourners eventually settled in the Gulf South: 11,000 foreign-born and native-born Italians lived in Louisiana in 1890, and that population increased to nearly 29,000 by 1900, at which point Italians made up one-third of the state's foreign-born white population.[57]

By the turn of the century, Sicilians had resettled from rural and agricultural areas to more urban areas like New Orleans, where they opened businesses as fruit vendors and grocers and moved into the ranks of local businessmen and professionals. In New Orleans, Sicilians and other Italians settled primarily in the lower city around the French Market, dubbed "Little Italy" by the late 1890s (see map 2).[58] Unlike in northern cities, there were no large-scale tenement constructions; by settling in fairly decentralized and dispersed patterns, Sicilians and other Italians avoided ethnic segregation and established ties and relationships with various parts of the community.[59] Such settlement patterns facilitated integration, since Sicilians and other Italians were obliged to learn English, adopt non-Italian customs, and communicate and interact with non-Italians more regularly than they would have had they been isolated in an "Italian ghetto."[60] As Sicilians and other Italians established themselves in the local fruit trade and joined the ranks of the city's elite business owners, a shared prestige not present in northern cities developed between the native-born white and Italian communities. The elevated class status of certain Sicilians and other Italians garnered them less hostility from native-born whites and contributed to their ability to more easily incorporate into higher levels of New Orleans's class and power structures.

The distinctive cultural particularities of New Orleans further influenced the successful integration of Sicilians and other Italians in the region.[61] New Orleans was a cosmopolitan city with a mixed population that included locally born French Creoles, free blacks, and European, Caribbean, and Latin American immigrants.[62] New Orleanians who practiced culturally Mediterranean traditions—such as Creole, Spanish, and Irish Catholics—did not consider Italians especially foreign nor discriminate against Sicilians and other Italians because of their religion.[63] Due to their shared Catholicism and the cultural fluidity of the region, Sicilian immigrants enjoyed a kindred kindness with the culturally and religiously similar New Orleans community. This tolerance, and even kinship, directly contrasted with the experience of Italians elsewhere in the more rural Gulf South and northern, largely Protestant cities, where one of the central factors that generated anti-Italian sentiment was anti-Catholicism.

Of course, some anxieties still developed with regard to Italian immigrants in 1870s and 1880s Louisiana. The abundance of Italian-owned businesses in New Orleans and neighboring rural communities, signaling their economic advancement, triggered a certain amount of apprehension about Italians' upward mobility.[64] Nonetheless, the significant number of "colored saloon licenses" that Italians held in Louisiana's sugar parishes meant that Italians specifically targeted some of their enterprises for African American customers and black neighborhoods.[65] Establishing businesses in historically black communities allowed Sicilians and other Italians to participate in available and untapped markets, which made such ventures less directly threatening to the commercial pursuits of native-born white business owners. In this regard, native-born whites did not view Italians, acting as a sort of "middlemen minority," and their businesses as directly competing with native-born interests.[66]

Owing in part to these economic pursuits, the relationship between Italians and the black community in Louisiana was not particularly hostile. Italians lived in neighborhoods (and even apartment buildings) integrated with black New Orleanians, established businesses that catered to black clienteles, cooperated and interacted with black laborers as fellow wage earners, and participated in "interethnic unionism."[67] Additionally, several accounts reported evidence of interracial solidarity and sympathy from black southerners for the Italian lynching victims—black neighbors were present at the burial of the Hahnville lynching victims, while two black brothers provided names of the members of the lynch mob to Italian diplomatic investigators following the Tallulah incident.[68] Generally, native-born white southerners would have considered those who "intermingled" with blacks as challenging southern racial imperatives, leading contemporaries to understand Italians through a distinctly southern lens as inferior and suspect by association.[69] However, at least in the 1880s, the press was silent when it came to what appeared to be Italians racially intermingling and defying the color line; such behavior may have been understood as less problematic than it would be in later decades.

By 1890, these spatial, cultural, demographic, and economic factors had contributed to a well-established, distinctly Sicilian, and physically integrated community of Italians living in Louisiana and especially New Orleans. Except for the occasional negative press mention and even despite certain anxieties regarding Italians' propensity to violence, their economic mobility, and their habits of racial intermingling, the general press discourse welcomed and encouraged Sicilian and Italian immigrants in 1870s and 1880s Louisiana as "fellow-citizens." The New Orleans press praised their contributions to the region and credited them with having expanded the profitability of the fruit industry in the city. But this changed in the last decade of the nineteenth century.

In March of 1891, thousands of New Orleanians charged the Parish Prison and lynched eleven Sicilians and other Italians; lynchings of Italians followed in Hahnville (1896) and in Tallulah (1899). Overturning the positive discourse of Italians circulating in the Louisiana presses, the lynchings and increasingly violent treatment of Italians in the 1890s represented a distinct departure from the approbation that Italians had earlier received. Still, increased acrimony that informed where and how native-born whites discursively and racially located Italians in Louisiana did not neatly map onto spikes in Italian immigration. Anti-Italian nativism intensified independent of the number of Italian immigrants arriving through the Port of New Orleans. For instance, the ship *Entella* arrived from Palermo with 841 Italian passengers (which accounted for more than one-third of the year's Italian arrivals) weeks after Italians had been rounded up en masse for Chief Hennessy's murder in October 1890; likewise, the March 1891 lynching took place just a few weeks before the beginning of the massive influx of Italians that year—800 arrived aboard *Olympia* and *Plata* in April and May, and 1,600 debarked from *Stura* and *Italia* in October and November.[70] Despite Italians' generally upward arc toward whiteness within US racial taxonomies, fluctuating assessments of Italians in Louisiana, which did not explicitly correlate to their arrivals, demonstrated the racial and civic transiency of Italian immigrants in the Gulf South.

In the days, weeks, and even years following each of the lynchings, international debates arose regarding the citizenship status of the lynched victims. Citing an 1871 treaty between Italy and the United States that guaranteed "the protection of the subjects of a friendly power," Italy requested that the United States pay indemnities to the families of the victims for the "killing of [Italian] subjects without due process of law."[71] Complicating the matter, according to an 1879 clause in the Louisiana Constitution, a foreign person could vote in local and state elections simply by taking out their first set of naturalization papers and declaring their intent to naturalize.[72] The ambiguity-inducing statute required intense investigations to evaluate which of the victims were in fact Italian subjects and thus owed indemnities, and which individuals were naturalized American citizens. This resulted in a series of diplomatic crises.

Following the 1891 lynching, for example, officials severed diplomatic relations between the United States and Italy, which continued well into 1892.[73] In asserting the victims as subjects of Italy, Italian diplomats claimed that many of those individuals who had "declared their intention" were not actually aware of the ramifications of the local policy: "They were still Italian subjects and desired to remain so, and had no idea that registering they were surrendering their allegiance to the King of Italy. . . . They did not know that in registering they abandoned their Italian citizenship."[74] Italian Consul to New Orleans Pasquale Corte even suggested that this manipulation was the result of Louisiana politicians who "coerce[d]" Italians into registering as soon as they arrived in New Orleans; he additionally noted that Italians did not knowingly give up their Italian citizenship when they registered to vote, because in Italy anyone could vote, regardless of one's naturalization status.[75] Claiming a conflict between federal and state power and alleging the victims had declared their intent to naturalize, thus making them US citizens, US officials initially refused to make indemnity payments. Consequently, Italy severed diplomatic relations with the United States and recalled Baron Fava, the Italian ambassador, from Washington, DC, in March 1891. At the same time, Albert Porter, American ambassador to Italy, returned to the United States. In turn, Corte claimed that the safety of Italians in the United States was at risk and requested that an Italian war vessel be sent to New Orleans. Although the ship was never sent, the request led to a lingering threat of war between the United States and Italy.[76] The following year in April, the United States eventually paid indemnities in the amount of $25,000 for three victims of the lynching who were determined to be Italian subjects. Officially, the United States admitted no wrongdoing and insisted that the payment was simply its "solemn duty" in restoring "old and friendly relations"; in turn, King Umberto of Italy lifted the ban on US pork products and ordered the resumption of diplomatic relations.[77]

The citizenship debates galvanized legal efforts by administrators in the United States to conceptualize Italians as Americans citizens. Take, for instance, the Hahnville case, in which three men—Lorenzo Salardino, Salvatore Arena, and Giuseppe Venturella—were lynched in Hahnville, Louisiana, on August 8, 1896.[78] The US State Department claimed that the three men were citizens of the United States because they "had taken out their first naturalization papers," and had resided and voted in Louisiana without a "fixed intention to return to their native country." In addition, they did not contribute to the "prosperity and wealth of Italy," avoided military duty in Italy, and actively participated in Louisiana politics; indeed, they were "citizens of the State."[79] The state of Louisiana claimed that the lynching victims had "acted" like citizens by voting, obtaining naturalization papers, and expressing no intention to return to Italy.[80]

In their efforts to prescribe citizenship to Sicilians and other Italians, American state actors emphasized a performative concept of citizenship rather than a strictly legal definition—one could "act" like a citizen and thus be considered one. Rather than requiring evidence of a completed formal naturalization process, the US State Department noted that by voting and not returning to Italy, the Hahnville victims behaved like American citizens and thus should be considered naturalized US citizens.[81] This more informal concept of citizenship was in the best economic interests of the US, freeing the government from paying indemnities for victims determined to be (or having declared their intention to become) American citizens. Moreover, marking Italian lynching victims as US citizens ultimately limited their rights and privileges since, as US citizens, they could be indiscriminately lynched without the intervention of the Italian state. Less than an actual claim for informal citizenship, the US State Department advanced a utilitarian application of this broader definition of "citizen" since it served the economic and diplomatic needs of American statesmen. Just as the racial status of Italians was transient and available for manipulation, their citizenship status was transient.

Conversely advocating a more narrowed view of formal citizen, Italian ambassador Fava disputed the assertion that the three Hahnville victims were US citizens. According to several sworn affidavits, Salardino had resided in Louisiana for twelve years and may have voted but had never taken out papers, Arena had arrived in Louisiana in 1891 and taken out his first papers but had not proceeded further, and Venturella, who had been in Louisiana for three years, had neither voted nor taken out papers.[82] Fava noted that only federal law, not state law, could grant naturalization, and that "a mere declaration of intention [did] not confer citizenship."[83] As Fava derided the US Secretary of State, "The federal laws having prescribed a uniform rule of naturalization being exclusively in Congress, the Italian government is entitled to think that the laws of Louisiana, however peculiar they may be in respect to citizenship, cannot be recognized by a foreign power."[84] Furthermore, since the Louisiana Constitution stipulated that "any foreigner may vote who has taken out his first papers," Fava presented this as "conclusive proof that any foreigner who does so vote, is still an alien."[85]

Fava proceeded by insisting that the three victims had only been residing in the United States temporarily. Venturella's wife and seven children, Arena's wife and four-year-old son, and Salardino's elderly father were all still residing in Italy. Fava claimed that had the three victims intended to relocate more permanently, "they would have sent for their families . . . whom they supported . . . by their labor." Sworn statements attested to the fact that Salardino "refused" to take out his naturalization papers because "he hoped to return home soon," and that he had always expressed "his intention to return as soon as he could to his folks in Italy." Fava went on to stipulate that the victims had always aspired to return to their families in Italy, and that more specifically, just a few days before his arrest, Venturella had purchased a ticket from New Orleans to Palermo. Fava additionally countered the claim that the victims had refused to comply with military service in Italy and provided additional sworn statements that Venturella had completed his service and that Arena and Salardino were both only sons, which meant they were in the "third class" and exempt from service.[86]

Fava insisted on the Italian citizenry of the three victims and placed tremendous emphasis on the necessity of securing "just and adequate compensation . . . to the families of the victims."[87] Citing the New Orleans and Walsenburg, Colorado (1896), lynchings as precedents, Fava implored that "a just and suitable indemnity will speedily be granted to the eleven persons who have been left without means of subsistence by the murder committed with impunity of those who were their sole support. . . . The members of these families are numerous and have been left wholly without means."[88] As the debate dragged on, Fava bemoaned the following March, "Nothing has been done as yet on behalf of the destitute families of the victims."[89]

Fava's emphasis on the impoverished nature of the victims and their dependents in Italy likely obscured more practical motives. In line with other post-Risorgimento policies on the part of the Italian government, like suppressing and othering Southern Italians in the Brigands War of the early 1860s, demanding indemnity payments could have been part of the larger unification project intent on reunifying the (Italian) North and South against a "foreign" enemy. Just as Italian officials explained the Brigands War (in reality a civil war against unification) to the newly unified nation as a war for the purpose of subduing southern banditry, Italian diplomats' defense of Sicilian lynching victims and their demands for indemnity payments served as a rallying point for the fledgling Italian state. The citizenship status of Sicilians and other Italians in the United States was additionally available for exploitation and manipulation by the Italian state. As the Italian state maintained a central role in shaping the civic status of Sicilians and other Italians in the United States, the way in which their citizenship operated there remained intimately linked to Italy's own domestic nation-building project.

By the following July, nearly a year after the Hahnville lynching, the United States did eventually pay out indemnities on the three victims in the sum of $6,000.[90] This was a declining price tag, as Italy was unable to continue its diplomatic strong-arming and risk permanently alienating a major trading partner. Although $25,000 was paid out on three 1891 lynching victims determined to be Italian subjects, only $1,900 was paid for two Sicilian victims in Tallulah in 1899.[91] Embroiled in international power plays and attendant financial consequences, US officials grew impatient with paying indemnities to Italian families while under pressure from the Italian government. Willing to instead invoke the obligatory evasions to maneuver themselves out of making indemnity payments, American statesmen proffered Sicilians and other Italians access to the rhetoric of US citizenship.

In the aftermath of the indemnity crises, the New Orleans press hypothesized that Italian criminals would be even less likely to become citizens, since they could simply turn to the Italian government for help and support: "Probably nine-tenths of the Italians who hold political rights in Louisiana voting and holding office, are not actual citizens, but only prospectively so. At any time they can claim Italian protection and demand indemnities out of the United States treasury. They enjoy so many privileges without becoming citizens that they have every inducement to remain foreign subjects, enjoying all the rights and benefits of citizenship which they do not possess."[92] Even while American statesmen attempted to categorize Italians as American citizens, likely an economic means to avoid paying indemnities, public opinion continued to believe that Italians resided outside the community. These estimations cited anxieties regarding Italian loyalty and the ability of Sicilians to exploit diplomatic pressure from the Italian state.

Such presumptions regarding the ability of Sicilians to utilize the Italian state may not have been entirely misplaced, since the lynching and indemnity crises worked to reconceptualize Sicilian citizenship status and identity, and restructured alliances between Sicilians and other Italians. In part the result of transported *campanilismo* (regionalism) and despite being referred to as the "Italian Colony," Sicilians and other Italians in the Gulf South comprised an incoherent community. With 90 percent of Louisiana's Italian immigrants originating from Sicily, Louisiana's "Italian" population did not identify as Italian. Such divisions between Sicilians and other Italians were most directly evident in the development of Italian benevolent societies in New Orleans. The city's oldest Italian society, established in 1843, Societa Mutua Benevolenza Italiana or the Italian Mutual Benevolent Society, prohibited Sicilians from joining. Because of this membership restriction, by the 1880s Sicilians founded a number of benevolent orders in New Orleans. The most prominent were the Congregazione di San Bartolomeo Apostolo (1879), Societa Italiana di Beneficenza Mutua Contessa Entellina (1886), and Societa Italiana di Mutua Beneficenza Cefalutana (1887). Not only were these societies all Sicilian-based, they were founded to support immigrants to New Orleans from particular Sicilian towns or villages (see map 3). The Societa Italiana di Mutua Beneficenza Cefalutana restricted affiliation to Cefalutana, that is, immigrants from the small

Map 3. Origins of Italian benevolent associations in New Orleans. Benevolent societies were founded for Sicilians from Ustica (A), Contessa Entellina (B), and Cefalù (C). Map by Joshua Reyling. Sources: Benevolent Society Papers, American Italian Research Library, East Bank Regional Library, Metairie, LA; ESRI.

fishing village of Cefalù and their descendants; the Societa Italiana di Beneficenza Mutua Contessa Entellina limited membership to Contessiotti, or the "direct male descendants" of the mountain commune of Contessa Entellina; and the Congregazione di San Bartolomeo Apostolo was founded by and offered aid to Usticesi immigrants from the island of Ustica, forty miles off the coast of Sicily.[93] While the New Orleans press referred to these organizations as "Italian societies" and immigration officers listed their arriving members as Italian, Sicilians and other Italians in Louisiana identified themselves as distinctly different, just as Usticesi were unique from Contessiotti.

The citizenship identity of Sicilian immigrants—an imposed and ascribed nationality activated by their movement across borders—contributed to a regionally fragmented community of Sicilians and other Italians in New Orleans. As early as 1884, at a celebration of the unification of the state of Italy, certain Italian community members endeavored to "unite the Italian residents" of New Orleans across their ascribed nationality as Italians.[94] Present at the banquet hosted by the Societa Mutua Benevolenza Italiana was the president of at least one Sicilian organization, the Congregazione di San Bartolomeo Apostolo, and one of the evening's speeches congratulated the gathering on the "unification of the Italian colony in this city." Yet, while enjoying a cake "crowned with a bust of the immortal poet Dante," decorated with miniature Italian and American flags and "inscribed with the name of Garibaldi," a transregional alliance between Sicilians and other Italians in the city remained more or less superficial. While toasting the "President of the United States and the American nation," efforts were more focused on depicting the Italians of the city as respectable members of the community, not on incorporating the city's Sicilians within the larger Italian community.

However, during moments of crisis, such as the lynchings of Sicilians in the 1890s in the Gulf South, *Italianità* expanded, and Sicilians' ascribed nationality as Italians began to further consolidate. After the mass arrests of Sicilians and other Italians in New Orleans in 1890, the "Italian colony" in New Orleans provided a unified response. The "leading Italians of the city" proposed the establishment of a "federation of the Italian societies of New Orleans" in order to "more fully protect and advance the interests of the

Italian colony in Louisiana."[95] When the *Gazzetta Cattolica,* New Orleans's Italian-language Catholic press, revealed that the prisoners held at the Parish Prison were being beaten, robbed, and generally mistreated, the editor Father Manoritta rose to defend the persecuted Sicilians: "I must and I am willing to give up my life, if necessary for the defense of the oppressed and outraged *countrymen* of mine."[96] Likewise, Italian-language newspapers around the country printed daily accounts of the collections they were raising for the defense funds of the accused New Orleanian "Italians," just as Italian communities in cities around the country would subsequently organize mass meetings to protest the lynching.[97] Furthermore, despite any transported feelings of disenfranchisement from the Italian state, Sicilians in New Orleans in the wake of the lynching violence flocked to the Italian consulate to seek aid, to demand indemnities, and to file suit against the city.[98] Regardless of regional differences transported from Italy or regional separation in the United States, the Italian immigrant community offered a unified response to the arrests and lynchings of Sicilians and other Italians in New Orleans as Italians rallied behind their Sicilian "countrymen."

Something had shifted within the New Orleanian Sicilian community in the aftermath of the 1890s lynching. While Sicilians still honored with parades and feasts their regionally specific saints, as in the Cefalutana celebration of San Salvatore, Sicilians and other Italians presented a more unified front as Sicilians demonstrated evidence of "Italianizing."[99] When the Societa Italiana di Mutua Beneficenza Cefalutana hosted a celebration to honor and commemorate Cristoforo Colombo in 1904, members of the city's Italian benevolent society sat alongside members of the city's various Sicilian benevolent societies, beneath both American and Italian flags, toasting both the president of the United States and the King of Italy.[100] In 1906, "members of every Italian society in the city" contributed to the purchase and dedication of a statue of Giuseppe Garibaldi, the revolutionary hero of Italian unification who had famously invaded and conquered Sicily in 1860.[101] Significant not only because Sicilians and other Italians acted in tandem, but because Garibaldi remains *the* iconic figure of the Italian Risorgimento and a key symbol in the process of nationalizing the peninsula and conquering the South. Sicilian participation in celebrating Garibaldi demonstrated that Sicilian immigrants in New Orleans were adopting the nationalistic imagery of the Italian state, further revealing their developing *Italianità,* and marking their participation within their ascribed nationality.

The perspective of a broader historical moment, and a specifically regional lens, challenges the conventional version of the Italian immigrant experience and exposes the overlooked and unique trajectory of Italian settlement in the Gulf South. In contrast to widespread anti-Italian disparagement found elsewhere in the United States in the 1870s and 1880s, New Orleanians initially encouraged and welcomed Italian immigrants. The core of this embrace resulted from the Gulf South's Reconstruction-era labor shortage and the fact that immigrant labor was in such high demand. The new 1890s anti-Italian rhetoric represented a change from how Italians were originally and less prejudicially perceived in New Orleans in the previous decades. Attendant to local sources, the regional focus offers a nuanced and previously hidden narrative, one that highlights the transitory racial and citizenship identity of Italians in the Gulf South.

Not only were Sicilians and other Italians racially transient, their citizenship status was additionally in flux. This fluidity resulted from being manipulated by state actors (both Italian and American) as well as immigrants' participating and performing as citizens. Just as plantation owners initially encouraged Italian migration because of the demands for inexpensive labor, economic mandates propelled US state officials to categorize Italian immigrants as American citizens to avoid paying indemnities. Meanwhile, Italian officials, as part of their own state-making project, utilized these lynching crises and indemnity debates to discursively enfold Sicilians within the Italian state. Irrespective of the efforts of state-makers, immigrants themselves participated in the construction of their own citizenship identity, appealing to the Italian state in certain moments and attempting to present themselves to others as "white" Americans. Sicilians appealing to the Italian consulate in New Orleans claimed their Italian citizenry and participated in formulating their understanding of and performance of citizenship. When Sicilians "declared [their] intent" to become US citizens while also appealing to the Italian government to intervene on their behalf, they operationalized their ascribed nationality. So too, the citizenship status of Italians was also unstable and transient.

2

The Lynchings of Italians in Louisiana and Mississippi (1880s–1910)

Gentlemen, do you wish to kill me? I have always thought
that you were my friends.

—Francesco Difatta (lynching victim), August 1, 1899

On the misty evening of October 15, 1890, while making his way home, Police Chief David Hennessy was gunned down in the streets of New Orleans. Hennessy's friend Captain William O'Connor responded to the shots fired and rushed to the chief as he lay bleeding in the street beneath a flickering street lamp.

"Who gave it to you, Dave?"

Hennessy replied, "Dagoes did it."

Lying in a hospital bed hours later, the popular thirty-two-year-old police chief succumbed to his injuries. As a result of his declaration, local law enforcement rounded up dozens of "suspicious" characters throughout the city, including a Polish Jew and a Romanian, both of whom were released when they were discovered to be non-Italian. Eventually, nineteen Italians were indicted and imprisoned, including a fourteen-year-old boy named Gaspare and a "fool" named Emanuele Polizzi.

When the trial began the following February, a carriage containing the prisoners rumbled to the district courthouse each morning from the Old Parish Prison. For nearly a month, nine defendants charged as principals in Hennessy's assassination or accessories before the fact assembled before the courtroom, where they were confronted by sixty prosecution witnesses and eighty defense witnesses. Finally, on March 13, 1891, the jury reached a verdict. Citing reasonable doubt and contradictory and insufficient evidence, the jury declared six of the defendants not guilty, including the fruit peddlers Antonio Bagnetto and Antonio Marchesi, Marchesi's son Gaspare, wealthy and influential importer Joseph Macheca, Macheca's associate Charles Matranga, and laborer Bastian Incardona; the judge ruled a mistrial for the remaining three—Antonio Scaffidi, a fruit peddler, Pietro Monasterio, a cobbler, and Polizzi, a street vendor. Almost immediately, the native-born white community in New Orleans unleashed accusations of bribery and jury tampering. Officially explained as a temporary measure, the court remanded the exonerated defendants back to the Parish Prison amid throngs of hissing New Orleanians who threw rocks at the passing carriage of prisoners.[1]

The next day, the following announcement headlined the *Daily Picayune, Times Democrat,* and *New Delta:* "Justice. Do the Good People of New Orleans Want It? All good citizens are invited to attend a mass meeting . . . at Clay Statue to take steps to remedy the failure of justice in the Hennessy Case. Come prepared for action." Far from being anonymous, the notice was signed by the Committee of Fifty, made up of some of the city's most well-known citizens and prominent business figures. As dawn broke, a mob of thousands assembled to answer the call.[2] The young Democratic lawyer William Parkerson, perched on the pedestal of the Henry Clay statue, bellowed over the crowd, "Murderers must be given their desserts. The jury has failed."[3] "Kill the Italian," the horde chanted in return.

Following the rousing speeches, the amassed mob, brandishing Winchester rifles, made their way to the prison.[4] Armed with a battering ram, they burst through the barricaded prison doors. They killed the Sicilians and any other Italians they could find—eleven in total, six of whom had already been acquitted or granted a mistrial; the remaining five had yet to have their day in court.[5] The body of James Caruso was discovered with forty-two bullet wounds; Antonio Marchesi's wounds were not immediately fatal, but after being denied medical attention, he succumbed nine hours later. The mob spared Gaspare, but dragged Bagnetto and Polizzi outside to be hanged and shot in front of the crowd. Parkerson dispatched the assembled with the words, "You have acted like men: now, go home like men."[6] Some members of the mob made their way toward the Italian-inhabited Poydras Market; according to the Italian consul of New Orleans, the scene left behind at the prison was a butcherous massacre with "dead bodies hanged in trees."[7]

The infamous 1891 lynching was not the only lynching of Sicilians and

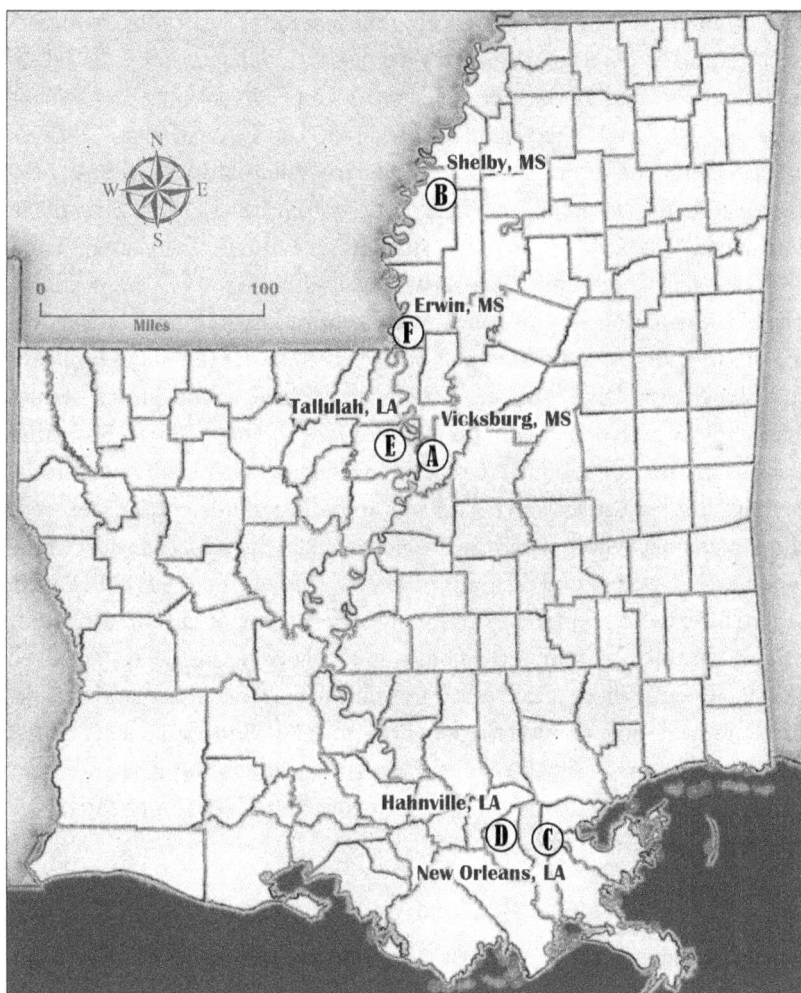

MAP 4. Locations of lynchings of Sicilians and other Italians in Louisiana and Mississippi between 1886 and 1901. (A) Vicksburg, MS (March 28, 1886): Federico Villarosa. (B) Shelby, MS (June 11, 1887): "Dago Joe." (C) New Orleans, LA (March 14, 1891): Antonio Bagnetto, James Caruso, Loreto Comitis, Rocco Geraci, Joseph P. Macheca, Antonio Marchesi, Pietro Monasterio, Emanuele Polizzi, Frank Romero, Antonio Scaffidi, Charles Traina. (D) Hahnville, LA (August 9, 1896): Salvatore Arena, Lorenzo Salardino, Giuseppe Venturella. (E) Tallulah, LA (July 22, 1899): Giovanni Cerami, Carlo Difatta, Francesco Difatta, Giuseppe Difatta, Rosario Fiducia. (F) Erwin, MS (July 11, 1901): Giovanni Serio, Vincenzo Serio. Map by Joshua Reyling. Sources: Webb, "The Lynching of Sicilian Immigrants in the American South, 1886–1910," 175–204; US Census Bureau; ESRI.

other Italians in the Gulf South during the late nineteenth and early twentieth centuries. In an act of historical recovery, this chapter presents a comprehensive account of the more than two dozen Sicilians and other Italians who were lynched in this region between 1886 and 1910 (see map 4). Those lynched included an Italian named Federico Villarosa in Vicksburg, Mississippi (1886), "Dago Joe" in Shelby, Mississippi (1887), three Sicilians in Hahnville, Louisiana (1896), five Sicilians in Tallulah, Louisiana (1899), and a Sicilian father and son in Erwin, Mississippi (1901).[8] Unquestionably, black lynching victims immeasurably outnumbered nonblack lynching victims. And yet, Sicilians and other Italians were the only Europeans to be lynched in large numbers. Moreover, no other ethnic group, besides Mexicans, were lynched with greater frequency.[9] That Sicilians and other Italians in the Gulf South were subject to lynching, a punishment typically perpetrated against African Americans and other non-Europeans, exceeds the explanatory power of existing frameworks. By providing a history of the lynchings of Italians and Sicilians across the (broadly defined) Gulf South, where little to no scholarship exists, and offering historical correctives for others, this chapter shows the continuity of how victims were racialized (especially after the fact) as well as the contingency of context and the specific circumstances that led to each incident.[10] Furthermore, the lynchings of Italians underscores the unfixed racial identity of Sicilians and other Italians, which, if Italians' whiteness was contestable, complicated race relations throughout the Gulf South.

Lynching, the extralegal killing of someone by "a group of three or more persons . . . under the pretext of protecting justice or tradition," derived its power from its attempt to make meaning through violence.[11] Predicated upon vengeance and the punishment of an alleged crime and through a conscious rejection of law, these systemized and ritualized acts of terror possessed both a discursive afterlife and an ability to mark space with violence.[12] Capitalizing upon community approval and communal complicity to intimidate predominantly black victims—six out of seven lynching victims were black or mixed-race men or boys—lynching operated as violence against race.[13]

Still, the existing scholarship on black lynchings does not adequately

explain why certain "white" individuals fell victim to lynching, in part because evaluations of the causes of lynching have relied on historical and
contemporary data inventories with a number of well-known limitations.[14]
The most evident oversight in these inventories is the means by which
lynching victims have been racially classified. The three main historical inventories, compiled by the *Chicago Tribune,* the NAACP, and Tuskegee University, all focused primarily on collating the lynchings of African Americans in the US South; in so doing, they identified lynching victims solely
as either "black or white," and categorized Chinese, Latino, Sicilian, Italian, and indigenous victims all within the category of "white."[15] This geographic and binary racial focus has resulted in flattening, compressing, and
ultimately discounting "white" lynching victims. Incorporating a critical
consideration of the atypical, nonblack victims contributes to the existing literature on lynching, presents a more varied lynching culture in the
Gulf South, and demonstrates how the same racial scripts that validated
the lynchings of black victims were employed to justify the lynchings of
nonblack victims.[16]

Given the history of lynching as race-based violence, and the abject dis-
avowal of citizenship and community standing that conveyed, this chapter
uncovers what made Italians lynchable, meaning, what circumstances were
in place that made it possible for racialized vigilantism to victimize Italians. Certainly, assumptions about race, ethnicity, and exceptionality, and
Italians' racially understood status as "outsiders," criminals, and potential
Mafia members, marked Italians as being at risk for lynching. Yet Italians
were not lynched *because* they were Italian; the racialization of Italians was
a consequence of the violence, not its cause. Instead, close readings of these
historical moments reveal how select economic and political implications
served to unfix the racial identity of Italians—rendering them racially transient—and to construct Italians as justifiably subject to lynching.

Between 1882 and 1930, 352 people were lynched in Louisiana; of those,
301 were black, 48 were categorized as "white," and three as "other."[17] During the same time period, 537 people were lynched in Mississippi; of those,
508 were black, 22 were categorized as "white," and seven "other" or unknown. The majority of victims identified as "white"—more than half in

Louisiana and 40 percent in Mississippi—were lynched for violent actions such as murder or "murderous assault."[18] Only two "white" victims were accused of rape or attempted rape in Louisiana (as compared with 68 black victims), and five "white" victims were lynched on charges of rape in Mississippi (as compared with 144 black victims). These statistics confirm previous assessments regarding certain racial stereotypes—while black men were characterized as sexual predators, this stereotype was not systematically applied to "white" men.[19] Only about 5 percent of black victims in Louisiana and 7 percent of black victims in Mississippi were lynched for "challenger" or race-based offenses—including miscegenation, "improper attention to a white girl," incendiary language, "biting a man's chin," or "insulting a white man"—whereas over 12 percent of "white" victims in both Louisiana and Mississippi were lynched for challenger offenses such as "anger[ing] klan," "political causes," interfering with an overseer, and "being a foreign worker."[20] Black southerners may have been more thoroughly conditioned than non-native whites to conform to the racial hierarchy in the Gulf South, which would explain why white men were twice as likely as black men to have been lynched for violating the "prevailing racial and economic hierarchies." But if anything, these figures indicate that black victims in Louisiana and Mississippi were lynched for generally and comparatively the same reasons as white victims.

Efforts to extrapolate larger patterns and claims from these statistically small samplings of "white" lynching victims—only 14 percent of total victims in Louisiana and only 4 percent of total victims in Mississippi—are not without their limitations. Previous explanations have suggested that "white" men were lynched because of their lack of "social embeddedness" and because of a particular "outsider" status.[21] One specific reading offered the "eleven Italian immigrants rousted out of jail in New Orleans on March 14, 1891" as direct evidence that "many of these [white, male lynching victims] . . . were easily identified as outsiders."[22] Yet such an assessment presumes an outsider status of immigrants; especially given the international and highly mobile environment and Creole culture of New Orleans, an individual born outside the state (or even the country) would not have automatically been "unembedded." Such numerically small statistics challenge a sociological conclusion, because the contextual contingency of time and place requires more systematic parsing.

Sicilians and other Italians in Louisiana and Mississippi were not lynched because they were "easily identified as outsiders" or socially un-embedded. Their outsider status—either a perceived status as foreigners or the ability to ascribe an outsider status to them—was certainly a condition that made lynching possible, but it was their exceptionality, interpreted through race, that informed why these "white" victims were lynched. This was seemingly consistent with explanations for black lynchings, since black lynching victims were also more likely to be lynched because of ex-ceptionality. Theirs was an exceptionality of circumstance, not a specific characteristic or crime: successful black men were only more likely to be lynched if they lived in an area with few successful black men; if an indi-vidual was born out of state, he or she was more likely to be lynched only if the community in which they lived contained few out-of-state residents.[23] The exceptionality that marked Italians for lynching, however, was less about demographics, since the lynchings of Italians generally took place in parishes or counties where Italians made up a considerable proportion (not a marginal fraction) of the foreign-born white population. In Madi-son Parish and St. Charles Parish, Louisiana, and Washington County and Bolivar County, Mississippi, Italians made up more than two-thirds, even upwards of three-quarters, of the foreign-born white population.[24] Rather, the economic and political exceptionality of certain Sicilians and other Italians—which requires turning to the historical particularities of each instance—explains what marked these "white" Italians as lynchable. Fur-thermore, these lynchings of Sicilians and other Italians, in their discursive afterlives and through the production of race as an aftereffect of the vio-lence, shaped concepts of race and citizenship throughout the Gulf South between 1880 and 1910.

The most infamous lynching of Sicilians and other Italians followed Police Chief Hennessy's murder, the account which opened this chapter. Local opinion in New Orleans at the time presumed that Chief Hennessy's murder resulted from his work to crack down on the violence in New Orleans and his entanglement in a feud between two rival groups of Sicil-ians: the Matrangas, who had secured control of the citrus trade importa-tion contracts and employed the stevedores/dockworkers; and the Proven-zanos, who had previously managed the fruit-unloading contracts. As the two Provenanzo brothers awaited trial for the attempted assassination of

Charles Matranga in the early summer of 1890, Hennessy apparently sympathized with the Provenzanos over the Matrangas, which led contemporaries to conclude that Matranga and his associates had orchestrated the conspiracy to assassinate Hennessy.[25] The *Daily Picayune* did offer an alternative explanation that if Italians were responsible for killing Hennessy, it was "at the instigation of persons outside that race"; however, this theory was never systematically investigated at the time.[26]

Instead, based only on circumstantial evidence, Sicilians and other Italians throughout New Orleans were detained and arrested. Of the nineteen indicted, most were not in fact "unembedded" or community outsiders. One of the accused, Joseph Macheca, was a native-born New Orleanian, a veteran of the Confederate army, and one of the wealthiest, most influential, and well-respected members of New Orleans's Sicilian community. He organized Sicilian immigrants into the paramilitary *Innocenti*, who carried pistols and knives and donned white and red caped uniforms as they joined other New Orleanian Democratic clubs in assaulting black supporters of Republican candidates in the 1868 election campaigns.[27] Macheca led a band of Italians in the White League's insurrection against the Reconstruction government in Louisiana at the Battle of Liberty Place in 1874, organized the city's fruit wholesalers as the New Orleans Fruit and Produce Association, and later went on to found the United Fruit Company.[28] Beyond Macheca, the purported conspiracy to assassinate Chief Hennessy spanned the class structure of New Orleans's Sicilian community. Other members of the city's ethnic elite, Charles Matranga, Matranga's foremen James and John Caruso, and former council member and merchant Charles Patorno, were indicted on conspiracy charges in the killing of Hennessy.[29] Working-class individuals were also indicted on charges of shooting Hennessy or on suspicion of their participation in the conspiracy: Pietro Monasterio, since the gunfire reportedly came from the direction of his home and a shoe print matching his was found at the scene of the crime; Antonio Scaffidi, on association, since it was his uncle's fruit stand where the assassination plot was supposedly hatched; Antonio Bagnetto, the night watchman at Scaffidi's fruit stand, later absent from work and found with a loaded pistol; Antonio and Gaspare Marchesi, charged as accessories after being found with a suspicious amount of cash; Charles Pietzo, a grocer, later seen with two guns; and Pietro Natali, just arrived from Chicago in reportedly ill-fitting clothing and dubbed a "suspicious character."[30]

When the jury handed down their not-guilty verdict, the foreman explained that after having been taken to the actual scene of the crime to evaluate the plausibility of eyewitness testimony, given the late hour of the attack and the distances required to positively identify the perpetrators, the lack of visibility was a key factor in finding "reasonable doubt."[31] Identifying the not-guilty verdict as evidence of the failure of the court system and the citizens charged with upholding it, the New Orleans press blamed the Mafia. Applying a Mafia identity upon all Sicilians and Italians because of racial assumptions of criminality, they accused the defendants of being "a gang of assassins who had escaped the penalty of their damnable crime by the bribery of a jury and the perjuring of hired witnesses"; it was "owing to the money and the machinations of the Mafia they were enabled to walk through our courts and laugh at justice."[32] Similarly, national press interpretations of the verdict suggested that even though "everyone knew" that the Italians were guilty, jurors had been "terrorized" by the Mafia into acquitting.[33]

The accusation of Mafia interference—that the Mafia had tampered with and bribed the jury—was part of a long-standing misunderstanding and misuse of the term in both Italy and the United States. Like the process of othering Southern Italians by naming their opposition to unification as the Brigands War, as early as 1865, Italian officials employed *mafioso*, which meant bold, prideful, and self-confident in Palermitano dialect, in reference to anyone who opposed the Republic or disagreed with the unification government.[34] Consequently, organizations of Sicilian peasants earned the designation Mafia, whether such conspiracies were in fact bands of criminals or self-defense groups. Likewise, the American press by the 1890s began to categorically refer to all Italian violence as Mafia-related vendettas when much was simply semi-organized factional gangland-style violence.[35] While there is little evidence to suggest that the Mafia as syndicated organized crime existed in New Orleans in the nineteenth century or was responsible for Hennessy's assassination, the accusation of Mafia was a potent means of salvaging the sanctity of the local court system and discrediting the subversive power of immigrant organizing.[36]

In addition to the belief in the Mafia, the severity of the local uproar increased with regard to (mis)interpretations of the local Italian response to the verdict: "Much boasting was indulged in by the Dagoes who largely congregate there. . . . Joyous enthusiasm . . . which shows how little respect these people entertain for the country which gives them a home and prosperity, or its government which protects and shields them."[37] In reality, the Italian community was preparing for the celebration of King Umberto of Italy's birthday on March 14 and for the Sicilian celebration of St. Joseph's Day on March 19. But native-born, white New Orleanians interpreted these national and cultural celebrations as evidence of the Sicilian community's unpatriotic roots and their willingness to celebrate injustice. Marking the Italian community at large as suspect, the misreading of these celebrations conspicuously unincorporated the local Italians from the larger native-born community in New Orleans. The ensuing violence was not directly reacting to these cultural performances, nor were the victims killed because of their participation here, but these cultural displays contributed to interpretations of the Italian community as "socially unembedded" outsiders.

The morning following the verdict, the Committee of Fifty brazenly broadcast their invitation across the city's newspapers and summoned city residents "to take steps to remedy the failure of justice in the Hennessy Case."[38] Allegations of the Mafia's involvement in the Hennessy trial verdict and misinterpretations of the Italian Colony's cultural celebrations roused thousands to make their way through the early-morning pockmarked streets to the Clay statue. As the smiling and laughing crowd swelled, the gathering initially felt like a jubilant affair; were it not for the jostling of rifles, one might have mistaken the assemblage as one awaiting a Mardi Gras parade. Despite the show of force, even members of New Orleans's black community were present: "Nearly every negro man or woman to be seen (and there were hundreds of them) wore a broad grin, while laboring men elbowed their way through the crowd shrieking and applauding as if wild with delight. . . . The neutral ground was quickly swarming with humanity of varied colors and nationalities, high and low, rich and poor."[39] The Committee of Fifty had instigated a city-wide, anti-Italian hysteria; spread across class and racial lines in 1891 New Orleans, the diverse mob had come "prepared for action."[40]

As the mass made their way to the Parish Prison, "Men, women and little children stood on doorsteps and galleries watching the passing of the solemn procession, joking, laughing and cheering as though it had been a circus parade."[41] Upon arriving at the Parish Prison, a throng of men laid siege to the barricaded doors. The prison wardens, having received word of the approaching mob, unlocked the Italian prisoners from their cells; some of the prisoners sought hiding spots in the women's part of the prison, others in the latrines. Once the prison doors collapsed from the force, the armed horde burst through the shattered frame in search of Italians. Amid the bedlam, but with carefully orchestrated precision, they executed eight Sicilians and three other Italians.[42] When the fevered pitch broke, the lynch mob dispersed. While *The Mascot* critiqued the employ of "lynch law" in the slaughter (as shown in figure 6), the headline in the *Daily States* the following day read, "Retribution! The Citizens Wipe Out in Blood the Blot on the City . . . and the Red-Handed Assassins of Our Chief of Police are Visited with Condign Death."

The eleven Italian victims crossed class and citizenship status. Some had declared their intention to naturalize and had voted in local elections, others planned to return to their families in Italy. Marchesi, a widower, and

LYNCH LAW.

FIGURE 6. "Lynch Law," *The Mascot*, March 14, 1891. *The Mascot's* postlynching reporting criticized the use of "lynch law" in its depiction of unarmed and defenseless Italians being slaughtered by the armed mob.

Polizzi had declared their intent to naturalize just days before their arrests. Monasterio, of "good character," had left his wife and five children just the year before in Caccamo, Sicily, thirty-two-year-old Rocco Geraci forsook his wife and children in Monreale, and thirty-six-year-old Vincenzo Traina was survived by his mother and father in Contessa Entellina; a resident in Louisiana since age thirteen, James Caruso had previously served as the commissioner of elections in the fifth ward.[43] Some of the victims had been found not guilty; others had yet to be tried. Their single shared trait was having been imprisoned for Hennessy's assassination and being Italian. Other members of the ethnic elite, like Patorno and Matranga, did manage to walk out of the prison unharmed; persons of the laboring and working class also survived, including John Caruso (James Caruso's brother), Bastian Incardona, Gaspare Marchesi, Pietro Natali, Charles Pietzo, and Salvatore Sinceri. Mere happenstance separated victims from survivors.

In contrast with the secrecy and *extra*legal elements of "traditional" lynchings, the New Orleans event was organized by city leaders and committed in broad daylight; a trial had already taken place and the accused had been found not guilty. The victims were not "easily identified as outsiders," as the victims in this case were not unfamiliar to or with the native-born white community. Macheca was both a native of New Orleans and represented the city's fruit-importing elite; others, like, Bagnetto and Caruso, were natural-born or naturalized US citizens and had spent nearly their entire lives in New Orleans. Yet their status as Italian or Sicilian rendered them all more plausibly culpable. Natali's manner of dress marked him as "suspicious" and thus arrestable; several of the New Orleans Italian victims were killed simply because of their physical, personal, and ethnic proximity to other accused Sicilians. Ultimately, the Italian-ness of the accused provided an opportunity to map an outsider status upon them regardless of the extent to which they were in fact integrated into the social and economic workings of New Orleans. Their lynching may not have been predicated on their being Italian or Sicilian, but their racialized ethno-nationality provided a convenient justification for it.

The 1891 lynching was by far the largest and most well-documented lynching of Sicilians and other Italians, but it was not the only act of vigilante violence against them in the Gulf South at the end of the nineteenth century. Evaluating other cases offers insight into both the continuity of causes as well as the historical particularities behind these atypical lynchings.

Take the case of Federico Villarosa, a Sicilian fruit dealer from Palermo who had resided in Vicksburg, Mississippi, for at least four years. In March of 1886, Villarosa "indecently" assaulted the ten-year-old daughter of the native-born white postmaster.[44] The victim "found herself in the grasp of the burley Italian who attempted to commit an outrage upon her. . . . His hellish purpose was only frustrated by the screams of the child attracting attention."[45] A "negro boy" passing by heard the girl's screams, intervened, and rescued her. This was Villarosa's third assault, as he had previously served time in Baton Rouge for attempted rape—his previous two victims were the daughter of a "worthy colored carpenter" and a "little negro girl about eleven years old."[46] This was the first time he had assaulted a white victim. According to the *Weekly Commercial Herald*, Villarosa did not deny committing the crime, but "the course of law was too slow and tedious to deal with cases of this character."[47] Awaiting trial, Villarosa was removed to a neighboring town for "safe-keeping"; the sheriff dispersed one lynch mob, and Villarosa broke his leg trying to escape a second. Ultimately, the "scoundrel" was "severely dealt with," and Villarosa was lynched on a third attempt in Vicksburg on March 28, 1886.[48]

In response to the lynching, Italian ambassador Fava admitted that the alleged assault "arouses a feeling of horror in the minds of all right-thinking men," but that Villarosa was lynched on "mere suspicion" of the crime. According to the consul's report, Villarosa had been wrongfully accused and executed, and the "unfortunate man" had not in fact committed the crime with which he was charged.[49] Whether this was a case of a mistaken assassination or an instance of diplomatic posturing, Villarosa's Italian-ness made him accusable and marked him a plausible perpetrator.

Villarosa's case is somewhat of an anomaly in comparison with the other lynchings of Italians. Of those Italians who were lynched in the Gulf South, this is the only case of an Italian accused of a crime with "sexual overtones."[50] Only five "white" men in Mississippi were lynched because of crimes with "sexual overtones," intimating that sexual deviancy was not a stereotype ordinarily applied to "white" lynching victims. If Villarosa's race did not mark him as a likely sexual predator, his suspected sexual assaults of relatively young girls, especially with a third victim who was white, certainly spurred his lynching punishment. Additionally, based on press reports that Villarosa served time in Baton Rouge and had only resided in Vicksburg for four years, it remains likely that Villarosa was not a native to Vicksburg but a newer arrival. Such a demographic valuation would mark Villarosa as less socially embedded in Vicksburg. Villarosa's Italian-ness, while mentioned in the press accountings, was not a factor in why the lynch mob considered him plausibly culpable. Whether or not Villarosa was wrongfully accused, as Ambassador Fava claimed, his lynching was grounded more in his personal reputation, the perceived atrocity of his purported crimes, and his particular living pattern, rather than because of a proclivity associated with his race or ethnicity.

Even though Villarosa may not have been lynched because of a presumed correlation between his Italian-ness and a tendency toward sexual deviancy and criminal transgressions, public discussion in the Gulf South was certainly beginning to observe a link between Italian-ness and (nonsexual) criminality. The lynching of "Dago Joe" on June 11, 1887, in Shelby, Mississippi, both highlights and obscures this developing association. Throughout the late spring of 1887, local papers reported on the latest news concerning "the dago who killed young Mr. Walter Haynes."[51] "Dago Joe," the press proclaimed, was aiming at a station agent who had expelled him from a depot building, when he "accidentally" and "without provocation" shot the "innocent" and "popular" Haynes; a statewide manhunt promptly ensued.[52] The *Greenville Times* reported on various attempts to capture the "dago," including one instance in which a local citizen shot himself in the foot "endeavoring to creep up" on someone mistakenly believed to be "Dago Joe."[53] By June, the *Daily Picayune* reported that "Dago Joe," the "murderer," had been lynched: "From last reports Dago Joe was still swinging."[54] However, despite his moniker and despite the fact that "Dago Joe" is included within existing tabulations of Sicilian lynchings, he may not have actually been Italian.[55]

A singular reference laid claim to Joe's Sicilian origins, proclaiming him a "half-breed . . . son of a Sicilian father and mulatto mother."[56] But the *New York Times* report remains inconsistent with a more comprehensive reading and broader sampling of press reports of Joe's racial identity. According to most accounts, Joe was a "negro," "a young half breed," and a "colored man."[57] One report branded Joe a "desperate half-breed between negro and creole."[58] The *Memphis Daily Appeal* explained that Joe was well known along the Mississippi River from New Orleans clear up to Cairo in southwestern Illinois, a "desperate character, evil and treacherous as half breeds generally are."[59] The *Daily Picayune* went on to report that local "negroes [were] raising some trouble about the lynching" and were threatening to kill the group of men responsible for guarding Joe. As the *Picayune* warned, "Should the negroes attempt this, the citizens of Australia, [Mississippi,] have ordered a lot of Winchester rifles and will be prepared."[60] Across the dozen articles that mentioned "Dago Joe," the singular *New York Times* report made the only claim to Joe's Sicilian origins, indicating that Joe cannot be unequivocally included within this compilation of Sicilian lynchings.[61]

Several possibilities exist for the vernacular flexibility that dubbed a plausibly non-Italian a "dago." Joe could have been, given his characterization as a "half-breed," part Italian or Sicilian. However, since the local black community in Australia, Mississippi, rose to Joe's defense, it remains unlikely that Joe lived among the Italian or "dago" community or necessarily identified with his Italian heritage. If not Italian, what then did "dago" mean? In the context of 1887 Mississippi, the press employed the "dago" moniker as a pejorative synonym for criminal. Even if it is not possible to assess Joe's background and his "social embeddedness," he clearly possessed a particular reputation within the community. His ambiguous depiction as a "half-breed" marked him as capable of criminal activity, though his lynching was not predicated on his Sicilian-ness. In this case, Italian-ness or Sicilian-ness was less relevant than an invocation of a label that established the victim's outsider-status and a discursive construction of identity that legitimated the violence against him.

While the Sicilian-ness of the victims was not an appreciable factor in the violence in Vicksburg and Shelby, the events in Hahnville, Louisiana, in 1896 reveal the susceptibility of Sicilians to lynching because they were Sicilian. One muggy August evening, Jules Gueymard, a wealthy white planter and merchant, leisurely awaited the arrival of a friend's river boat; out of the twilight and from close range, a "heavy load of slugs and buckshot" rained down upon the esteemed planter. As he lay mangled in the gallery of his home, witnesses heard him call out, "What does this mean?"[62] Straightaway, local officials proceeded to the boarding home of the agricultural laborer and barbershop keeper, Lorenzo Salardino, a thirty-six-year-old Sicilian native of Campo Fiorito. Gueymard had testified against Salardino to creditors in New Orleans, after which Salardino publicly threatened Gueymard. Given the threat and his "freshly fired shotgun," Salardino was arrested and taken to the parish jail. Despite Salardino's "red and ill-looking countenance" that demonstrated his "inborn brutality," locals insisted the case would go to trial and began collecting a fund to aid in the prosecution.[63]

Two months earlier, another murder had transpired in St. Charles Parish—Don Roxino, an elderly, quiet, and humble Spaniard, was beaten to death with clubs, his body dragged and abandoned in the woods. Law enforcement arrested two Sicilian laborers, Salvatore Arena and Giuseppe Venturella, for the "cowardly" murder on account that they had competed with Roxino in the moss-gathering trade and were "known to have a strong grudge against him."[64] Arena and Venturella were imprisoned in St. Charles Parish along with three other Italians who happened to be incarcerated there for unrelated crimes at the time that Salardino was arrested and jailed. On August 9, despite protestations that the parish had "decide[d] against a lynching," a mob overtook the jail and "barbarously" put Salardino, Arena, and Venturella to death.[65] Proclaimed as justice against "high-handed murderers" and the result of a "defective and inefficient administration of the law," three Sicilians fell victim to lynching in Hahnville.[66]

In the aftershocks of the lynching, the belief in the Mafia—or the purported Mafia label—justified the violence. The *Daily Picayune* explained that the lynching was the result of a "mafia conspiracy," that the victims "deserved their fate," and that "the Italian Government should know that the lynching of a few Italians in various parts of the United States is directly due to the practice of cowardly assassination which some of the Italians resort to so often."[67] The *Picayune* justified the lynching as a means of "teach[ing] the lawless Italians a salutary lesson."[68] The idea of the Mafia was dangerously destabilizing; it challenged local, white elites' monopoly on extralegal violence, which explained why certain Italians could be lynched for their perceived Mafia associations. The specter of the Mafia also offered a convenient after-the-fact explanation that served to discredit Italians and justify the lynching verdict. In fact, no tangible evidence connected the lynched Hahnville victims to any kind of organized Mafia society.[69] Furthermore, later in the month, a notorious New Orleans criminal, the "murderous . . . wretch" Antoine Richard, "otherwise known as the Creole," came forward and claimed responsibility for killing Don Roxino, which confirmed the actual innocence of at least two of the lynched Sicilians and further discredited the Mafia-conspiracy theory.[70]

More so than either Vicksburg or Shelby, the Hahnville case confirms Sicilian-ness as an inciting factor in the lynchings of Arena, Venturella, and Salardino. Local press accounts originally misidentified the victims, meaning that Arena and Venturella were not widely known within the community where they were killed.[71] Additionally, Arena and Venturella, posthumously exonerated by Richard's confession, were killed for a crime they did not in fact commit. The Hahnville case remains consistent with the pattern that Sicilians who were lynched were almost always killed in "multiple lynchings." All three were lynched because of a presumption of guilt based on "trivial, insufficient," and circumstantial evidence; even Salardino may have been able to explain the "suspicious circumstances alleged" against him had he been given the opportunity to defend himself in court.[72] Without any substantive evidence to suggest that an actual conspiracy existed among the three victims, the explicit references to a "mafia conspiracy" illustrate that Arena and Venturella were lynched because of their physical proximity to Salardino. Sicilian-ness marked them as plausibly criminal and conceivably associated with the Mafia. Because of this available Mafia label and emerging premise that linked Sicilians with "criminal conspiracy," assumptions could be ascribed to and assumed of their race, for which Sicilians could be justifiably lynched.

Being Sicilian also remained a causative factor in the violent events that transpired in Tallulah, Louisiana, in 1899, where trouble began over a goat. The surrounding area of Madison Parish was home to several thousand African Americans, several hundred whites, and six Sicilians, three of whom were the Difatta brothers. The popular and vivacious Difatta brothers owned two grocery stores in Tallulah; because of their financial success, certain members of the community "regarded [them] with secret animosity," but otherwise, they often caroused with prominent community members, drinking and playing cards.[73] Wednesday, July 19, began like any other day. In the humid midday heat, a goat belonging to Francesco Difatta wandered onto the property of Dr. J. Ford Hodge. It was not the first occasion that Difatta's goats had trespassed on Hodge's estate. But having grown impatient from the repeated intrusion, on this particular sweltering day, Hodge drew his revolver and shot the interloping goat. The following day, Francesco, aggrieved for his goat, called to Hodge across his property; they quarreled, exchanging a barrage of animated words, but with "no serious consequences." Less willing to dismiss the incident so easily, when Difatta's brother Carlo encountered Hodge later that day, Carlo "spoke harshly" with Hodge. As the conversation grew increasingly heated, Carlo struck the doctor with his fist. Although Carlo was unarmed, Hodge drew and fired his revolver, grazing Carlo on the forehead; as Carlo collapsed, Hodge placed his boot on his chest, holding him to the ground. Giuseppe, the third Difatta brother, witnessed the fray from the gallery of their home. While Hodge worked to clear the chamber of his jammed revolver, his boot still lodged on Carlo's chest, Giuseppe fired upon Hodge from the balcony with a pistol loaded with birdshot. Word spread swiftly through Madison Parish that "the Italians had killed Dr. Hodge," and the three Difatta brothers were hastily arrested.[74] The sheriff rounded up Giovanni Cerami and Rosario Fiducia, two Sicilian friends supposedly in cahoots with the "cold-blooded foreigners," the Difatta brothers, on charges of conspiracy.[75]

Within hours, hysteria over Hodge's shooting enveloped the parish. Disquieting murmurs and anxious broadcasts reported that in an act of premeditated homicide, Hodge had been shot fifty to seventy-five times.[76] With the five Sicilians confined in the parish jail, a crowd "intoxicated with blood" multiplied outside.[77] After constructing a makeshift gallows from a device used to hoist livestock for skinning, the throng stormed the jail. They first dragged out Carlo and Giuseppe, then Francesco and Rosario, and finally Giovanni, making three separate trips from the jail to the swine slaughterhouse. In three separate acts, the frenzied mob lynched five Sicilians to enact "vengeance upon the guilty" and to "teach the Italian and his gang a lesson."[78] The *Weekly Messenger* went on to describe the shooting of Hodge, not the lynching, as a "tragic" and "dastardly" event.[79]

Meanwhile, Dr. Hodge survived the shooting and was declared "out of all danger" three days later.[80]

In the aftermath of the lynching, newspaper reports declared that Tallulah had "emptied their town of Italians."[81] Residents had issued a pronouncement warning "all others of the race within the parish lines had three days to leave under penalty of death," at which point the one remaining Sicilian reportedly fled Tallulah.[82] Despite the fact that the members of the lynch mob were well known in the community, and two "Negro brothers" who witnessed the lynching even provided a list of names to the Italian diplomatic investigators, the Madison Parish Grand Jury concluded that they were "wholly unable to discover the names of the perpetrators of the lynching."[83]

Similarly to several of the victims in the New Orleans lynching, the Tallulah victims enjoyed a marked degree of social embeddedness within the community and were not simply lynched because of their exceptionality or outsider status. Popular community members who frequently socialized with their native-born, white neighbors, the Difatta brothers had lived in the area for at least six years, while Dr. Hodge had only resided in Madison Parish for a year and a half.[84] Diplomatic correspondence noted, "Nothing could be said against [the Difattas]; they never had difficulty with any one . . . the behavior of these men had always been good."[85] But Francesco Difatta, a recognized participant within the business community, had obtained commercial success independent of the elite white power structure. Not just his economic mobility, but the Difatta brothers' successful grocery businesses marked them as potential threats to certain members of the Tallulah community. Certain press reports described the accused as having "fierce and quarrelsome dispositions" and "bad reputations"; they were "violent men, easily excited—thrown into a perfect furry [sic] at the least cause," with "no love lost between them and the other inhabitants of the place."[86] The success of the Difatta brothers made it necessary to find ways to portray them as disreputable residents in an effort to justify the lynching. The behavior of the Difatta brothers in their interaction with Dr. Hodge, more legally recognizable as self-defense, was not criminal in and of itself. Yet owing to their Sicilian-ness and the fact that they had overstepped their place, the local native-born, white community read the Difattas' actions as criminal and disregarded their right to defend themselves. Furthermore, like two of the victims in Hahnville, Cerami and Fiducia were lynched in Tallulah not for having participated in the attack on Dr. Hodge itself, but because they were the "wrong" ethnicity in the wrong place at the wrong time.

Postlynching press accounts employed an unequivocally racialized discourse, which affords the impression that Sicilians and other Italians were lynched because of their racial ambiguity. Though true that Sicilians and other Italians were at risk for being lynched because of their race and ethnicity, evidence of such prejudice and racialized stereotypes has obscured other instrumental factors. The various lynchings of Sicilians and other Italians—in spite of the particularities of each incident—resulted from a continuity of causes, such as economic and political competition.[87] In the aftermath of the violence, community members employed race to defend the killings in racial terms, even if race was only tangentially related to the conditions that instigated the lynching.

For instance, the dispute that unfolded between Dr. Hodge and the well-liked, well-embedded, long-term Tallulah resident Difattas was not explicitly economically motivated. Dr. Hodge was not in any sort of direct commercial competition with the Difatta brothers' successful grocery stores, nor did he shoot Francesco's goat because of fiscal resentment. Still, even though Dr. Hodge's wounds were not in fact life-threatening and he made a full recovery within days, local townspeople were exceedingly quick to form a lynch mob. Parish residents took the Hodge/Difatta dispute as an opportunity to "dispose of the Italians who had lived in their midst."[88] The fact that certain members of the community subsequently ordered the expulsion of the remaining Italians from the parish following the lynchings intimates that the mob instigators held preexisting views about the local Sicilians as economic competitors; wanting to get rid of Italians, they used Hodge's shooting to do just that.

In the meantime, the press protested that "the same punishment would have been vented upon any set of men, no matter whether they were Italians, Englishmen, Germans or natives of the United States," but ultimately justified the lynching in explicitly racial terms. The *Times Democrat* entitled their piece "Citizens Plead Necessity for White Supremacy" and defended the lynching on the grounds that it was necessary for "white supremacy." The native-born, white community in Tallulah felt "obliged" to commit the lynching, since the "complicity in the conspiracy . . . could never have been proven legally, and that to insure white supremacy, no other course was possible than the course pursued." The *Times* went on to explain that of the "several lynchings" in Madison Parish in the past eighteen months, "the result is that Madison Parish is never the scent now of any race troubles. The negroes have come to the realization of the fact that lawlessness on their part will not be tolerated."[89]

The explicit awareness that the lynching of these five Sicilians contributed to a culture of fear coerced compliance from the "negro" community and functioned to reduce Italians to the position of nonwhites. Suggesting that "white supremacy" would otherwise be in jeopardy, and identifying the reasons for the lynching of these five Sicilians as comparable with the motives behind the lynchings of African Americans, indicates that Italians could be, when necessary, consigned outside a larger category of whiteness. Relegating Italians to a position outside of "whiteness," which confirmed their racial transiency, presented a popular means to validate the lynching and to insure the legitimacy of violence that would otherwise undermine white and nativist respectability. Ultimately, this process of racializing Italians was an aftereffect of the violence, rather than its cause.

Sicilians and other Italians had enjoyed a relatively sanguine relationship with the native-born white population in the 1870s and 1880s. But long-building factors—a growing concern over Italian and Sicilian economic competition, resentment over their commercial success, and ambivalence regarding their intermingling with the black community—contributed to the surging virulence of anti-Italian rhetoric most immediately evident in the aftermath of each of the lynchings in the 1890s. As nativist rhetoric intensified, Gulf South negotiations challenged Italians' access to "whiteness" and unqualified citizenship. In New Orleans, for instance, attitudes toward Sicilians and other Italians began to harden as a consequence of Chief Hennessy's murder, the ensuing trial, and the subsequent lynching. Initially, while Italians were being rounded up, arrested, and indicted for Hennessy's murder, the press still differentiated between the Italian community at large and the criminal element.[90] The *Daily Picayune* continued to refer to Italians as "our fellow citizens," urged the city to avoid "anti-Dago" action, and reminded New Orleanians that Italians possessed "honesty, probity, public spirit, patriotism and useful citizenship."[91] Even while reporting on Hennessy's assassination and the impending trial, the press still publicly credited the Italian community with developing the region's fruit industry and contributing to the region's commercial prosperity.[92] After the lynching, echoes of these proclamations noted, "Some of the most respectable, orderly, order-loving and law abiding people in this city are Italians," as certain members of the New Orleans press still attempted to distinguish "law-abiding" Italians from criminals.[93]

At the same time, in contrast to depictions from the 1880s, press rhetoric following Hennessy's murder did begin to include elements that spoke more directly to anxieties about Italians' potential for criminal activity. Certain voices from the New Orleans press began to emphasize the negative potential of these arriving Italians, since "many of them are criminals" and "paupers."[94] The Times Democrat, in a clearly derogatory tone, explained that the accused Sicilians' "low, repulsive countenances, and slavery attire, proclaimed their brutal natures . . . They were as dumb as clams."[95] Describing the clothing of the prisoners as "slavery attire" categorically transposed the jailed Sicilians outside the native-born, white mainstream community, just as reading the brutality as part of their "nature" implied the characteristic as intrinsic to their race. Partially motivating this shift in tone, Hennessy was not just a member of law enforcement but the chief of police, in an era when white southerners interpreted the killing of a police officer in the South as an attack upon the region's racial order.[96] Enabling New Orleanians to apply a similar and extant logic to the accused Sicilians and other Italians, they operationalized antiblack racial scripts, which read African Americans as innately criminal, against Sicilians and other Italians.[97]

As debate within the New Orleans press ensued, both anxieties and language progressively intensified. Around the country, Italian-language newspapers like Il Progresso and Cristoforo Colombo in New York printed daily accounts of the collections—upwards of $50,000—that they were raising for the defense funds of the imprisoned Italian defendants in New Orleans.[98] The perception of transregional Italian solidarity contributed to a growing divide between Italian and native-born communities in New Orleans, as public discussions began to more unequivocally collapse Italian criminality with the Italian community at large. Just a week before the lynching, the *Daily States* reported:

> Our gates are open to all who seek entrance, conditioned only upon their be-
> coming Americans in the truest sense of the terms when they cast their lot
> among us. . . . Unfortunately, the most inconsiderate of these we have found
> to be the Sicilian. In numbers they are a dangerous proportion among us. No
> people, probably by instinct and education are more foreign to American ideas
> than they. Generation after generation they live among us and to the last they
> remain Sicilian still. . . . Few among them are producers. They rarely follow la-
> borious occupations. . . . one can suspect that therefore, the majority who seek
> our shores are of the criminal class.[99]

As the trial ran its course, no longer were Italians well-meaning and contributing citizens in New Orleans. Instead, Sicilians had become the most
"inconsiderate," the most resistant to "becoming American," and the most
universally criminal among immigrant groups.

In the aftermath of the lynching, only *The Mascot* came out against the
violence; their critique, as shown in figure 7, however, had less to do with
their sympathy for Italians and more to do with their disparagement of
specific members of the lynch mob.[100] Beyond *The Mascot*'s critique, by
and large, the New Orleans press condoned the lynching because of what
they perceived as a presumed criminal element (newly) present within
the Italian "race" at large. The press described the Italians as "undoubtedly
guilty" since the victims were "assassins," "criminals," and members of the
"Mafia."[101] Such arguments claimed that the lynching resulted from a need
for self-defense: "The safety of our citizens was menaced and the peace of
the great city of New Orleans was in the hands of a gang of murderers—
when justice fails, the responsibility falls into the hands of the people, and
it becomes their duty to establish law and order."[102] Because of the need to
protect themselves, the Committee of Fifty suggested the total prohibition
of immigration from Sicily and lower Italy.[103]

The anti-Italian rhetoric espoused across New Orleans was not entirely
new, but it did represent a salient move regarding how the press had written about Italians across Louisiana in the previous decades. In order to explain the lynching in publicly consumable terms, the New Orleans press
adopted the available and existing anti-Italian vernacular already in the

FIGURE 7. "A Bad Easter Egg: The Bloodiest Carnival and Lent in the State of Louisiana," *The Mascot*, March 29, 1891. In contrast with mainstream press depictions in New Orleans, *The Mascot* remained critical of the 1891 lynching in this and subsequent issues.

employ of northern and national newspapers. Despite the particularities of the victims, at least several of whom were well-integrated into the social and economic domains of New Orleans, such racialized rhetoric constructed the Italian lynching victims as "outsiders," subverted their social embeddedness and community connectedness, and marked their lynchings as defensible. For the racially transient Italians in the Gulf South, discourse could validate an otherwise racialized form of punishment and racialize Italians after the fact.

But the social order and racial landscape in the Gulf South at the turn of the century were fluctuating; even while certain parlance in 1891 could racialize Italians as criminal and foreign, discourse could also consolidate Italians as part of the native-born, "white" mainstream. The lynching in 1901 in Erwin, Mississippi, which departs from the pattern of the previously discussed lynchings, illustrates this restructuring. In November 1900, a horse belonging to the young Vincenzo Serio, a native of Cefalù, Sicily, wandered onto the property of the plantation manager G. B. Allen. The incursion devolved into an animated dispute, whereby a convergence of armed men shot and injured Vincenzo. Vincenzo escaped to nearby Greenville, but upon recovering, returned to the township of Glen Allan, some forty miles south on Lake Washington, to rejoin his father Giovanni. On his return, citizens in the community issued an order giving Vincenzo thirty days to leave the village, an order he disregarded.[104]

During the evening of July 10, 1901, incensed by Vincenzo's blatant insolence, Allen made no secret of gathering together an armed contingent to finish what he had begun eight months beforehand. On three separate occasions, friends of the Serios attempted to contact Vincenzo, who was staying in neighboring Erwin, to warn him of the impending threat; they were prevented by both force and fear from using the parish telephone.[105] Under the impression that the trouble had blown over and not "suspecting danger," Vincenzo and his father, along with two other Sicilian friends, went to sleep that same night in hammocks hung in the gallery of their home. After midnight, a "volley of rifle and pistol bullets were poured into them."[106] Father and son, Giovanni and Vincenzo, were shot to death, and

Salvatore Liberto took a bullet to the groin, while a fourth man escaped unhurt.

Press reporting of and public reaction to the Erwin episode employed a tone in contrast with that which followed the previous lynchings of Sicilians and other Italians. Much of the reporting called the incident an "assault" or "assassination" rather than a lynching—uniquely, this was the only lynching of Italians wherein the victims were not taken while imprisoned and were not murdered in punishment for a specific (alleged) crime. Both the *Shreveport Caucasian* and the *Pascagoula Democrat-Star* referred to the incident as a "carefully planned assassination."[107] The *Greenville Times* "deplore[d]" the killing and referred to the lynch mob as the "Erwin assassins."[108] If the "assassins" were not "denounced," the *Times* explained, "it would stand as a barrier to the advancement of any improvement in the county."[109] The Young Men's Business League of Greenville submitted a resolution, which passed unanimously, "denounc[ing] the cowardly assassination of [the] two helpless Italians."[110] Pointedly critical of the killing, Governor Andrew Houston Longino of Mississippi, one of only two Italian American governors to have ever been elected in a southern state, ordered a careful investigation; Longino announced that he would "do everything in his power to have the assassins apprehended and punished," and personally offered a $100 reward for the arrest and conviction for each of those "guilty of the murders."[111]

Not only did the rhetoric surrounding the incident deviate from that employed after previous lynchings, but commentary concerning the subsequent investigation to discover the parties responsible for the lynch mob additionally included a more hopeful tone. Italian diplomat Francesco Carignani implored the US secretary of state that the Erwin incident end more "nobly" than previous cases. After all, Carignani explained, one of the victims survived and his testimony would provide a "powerful means to detect the murderers."[112] Even the press spoke favorably of the likelihood that the men responsible for the lynching would be held accountable: "If talk can mean anything, the men who killed the three Italians are known and unless they leave the country, will be arrested."[113] *Le Meschacebe* reported that authorities were hopeful and the State of Mississippi had adopted a resolution "condemning the outrage."[114]

Despite this promising departure from previous accountings of lynchings of Sicilians and other Italians, the grand jury report found that "after a careful and rigid examination and investigation of all the witnesses to find sufficient evidence as to who were the perpetrators of this assassination,"[115] the jurors concluded that the Serios "came to their death by the act of God in that they died from gunshot wounds at the hands of unknown parties to this jury."[116] Though unable to "ascertain the guilty parties," the grand jury still resolved: "We deplore and denounce the cowardly midnight assassination of two helpless Italians."[117] Official lynching statistics identified the alleged crime of the Serios as "unknown."[118]

Without considering the divergence in diction of one incident as evidence of a wholesale adjustment in the manner in which southerners racially located Italians, the Erwin lynching does hint toward a new pattern of racial construction. Confirming the racial transiency of Sicilians and other Italians, the lynching of the Serios in Erwin, Mississippi, exposes the fluidity and available transmutability of Italian racialization. While the 1899 rhetoric considered the lynching of Sicilians as necessary for "white supremacy," 1901 rhetoric questioned the validity of "cowardly assassinat[ing]" Sicilians. The Erwin case denotes an ebbing of Italian or Sicilian lynchings in the South; only one other Italian lynching in the Gulf South occurred, when two Sicilians were lynched nine years later in a labor dispute in the Ybor City neighborhood of 1910 Tampa, Florida.[119] A dearth of subsequent Italian lynchings—and accompanying racializing justification—indicates that southerners were increasingly subsuming Italians within the white mainstream. Both the rhetoric of the Erwin lynching and the larger context in which it occurred mark a progressive restructuring of the racial location of Sicilians and other Italians within the Gulf South.

From 1891 to 1910, the lynchings of Sicilians and other Italians in the Gulf South reveal both the significance of contextual specificity as well as the presence of shared characteristics. In terms of continuity across these various incidents, after each lynching, press rhetoric began to employ an increasingly hostile anti-Italian and anti-immigrant sentiment. Additionally, within each postlynching moment, a citizenship and indemnity crisis ensued in which the Italian government requested payments for the wrongful deaths of Italian subjects. Despite these shared patterns, chronicling the backgrounds of the victims and the particularities in each case illustrates the limitations of a strictly statistical or sociological assessment of Sicilian and Italian lynchings. Historically accounting for time and place reinforces the contextual contingency of Italian racialization. Moreover, while press accounts of Italian lynchings in the 1880s and 1890s readily referred to those events explicitly as lynchings, by 1901, press accounts described the deaths of the Serios in Erwin, Mississippi, as an "assassination." Changing the way the public read and processed the killings of Italians, this shift in language indicates that southerners were beginning to more readily incorporate Sicilians and other Italians into the white, native-born community.

Southerners did not lynch Italians *because* they were Italian, but Italian-ness, read and applied in racial terms, made them susceptible to being lynched. Race and ethnicity offered the means to prescribe an outsider status upon Sicilians and other Italians, thus designating them (and perceiving them) as unembedded or foreign even when they were not. Economic, class-based, and political competition performed by and mapped onto Sicilians and other Italians—such as the economically mobile Italian—further contributed to each of these lynching episodes. As violence consolidated *Italianità,* or an Italian identity, southerners racially categorized Italians differently, sometimes as white and sometimes not, in different moments and for different reasons. Bound by these distinct contextual characteristics, qualified temporality, and geographic conditions, the lynchings expose the commutability of racial construction. Demonstrating the victims' transiency, Italian racialization advanced as an aftereffect of the violence. The racialized and abjectly anti-Italian discourse in the aftermath of each lynching operated racially and functioned as a discursive means to legitimize the violence. Foremost, if race was not the cause of the Gulf South's vigilante violence, the lynchings of Sicilians and other Italians contested their unqualified whiteness and drew into question Italian access to the protections of whiteness in a Gulf South governed by white supremacy.

3

"Electoral Freaks and Monstrosities" in Louisiana's Disenfranchisement Debates (1896–1898)

The Privileged Dago Voter . . . enjoys the right to vote because he was
born abroad, whereas had he been so unfortunate as to have been born under the
Stars and Stripes he would be disqualified. . . . We can crow over our sister States
very much like the circus man of having the most extraordinary collection and
aggregation of voters in the world, electoral freaks of all kinds, voting
through their wives, their children and their grandfathers.

—*Times Democrat*, March 6, 1898

In March 1898, legislators at the Louisiana Constitutional Convention passed an ardently debated suffrage amendment, which was carefully calculated to disenfranchise the state's black residents, poor whites, illiterate and landless citizens, and foreigners, naturalized or otherwise. The amendment included a residency requirement, a literacy provision, a property (with a valuation of at least $300) ownership requirement, and a poll tax, all designed to limit the political power of the impoverished masses. Besides adding stringent literacy and property requirements, the final iteration of the divisive Section 5 of the amendment included a "grandfather" clause, a stipulation that granted a voting right exception to any "male person . . . [or] son or grandson" who was eligible to vote in 1867, and also made the following allowance: "No male person of foreign birth, who was naturalized prior to the first day of January 1898, shall be denied the right to register and vote in this State by reason of his failure to possess the educational or property qualifications prescribed by this Constitution."[1] Referred to as the "Privileged Dago" Clause, Section 5 specified that a "foreigner," even if he did not meet the amendment's education or property requirement, still possessed the right to register and vote in the state of Louisiana. While the suffrage amendment effectively disenfranchised Louisiana's black population, the "Privileged Dago" Clause protected Italians' voting rights.

Louisiana's suffrage debates represented a confluence of class-based opposition to universal voting rights by marking a parallel development between Jim Crow disenfranchisement deliberations and efforts to narrow the voting rights of immigrants.[2] Yet in spite of this convergence and even though Louisiana legislators ultimately safeguarded the foreign-born right to vote in 1898, disenfranchisement efforts still affected Italian immigrants and their standing in the Gulf South; in what ways and to what degrees is the focus of this chapter. What were the lasting impacts of Italian enfranchisement on Louisiana governance and racial politics? In what ways did Italian voting protections shape Louisiana discourses of racial difference? And in what ways did Louisiana's later nineteenth-century voting debates reflect regional particularities as well as larger nationwide trends toward voter constriction?

This chapter details the imposition of voting restrictions in 1890s Louisiana, which were driven by the mounting contestations within the state's divided Democratic Party. Beginning with a historical overview of party politics complicated by geospatial, class, and ethnic conflicts, this chapter describes two particular moments: the 1896 "Dago Parade," in which Italians marched under an Italian flag in opposition to the proposed amendment that would have eliminated the "foreign vote," and the 1898 Constitutional Convention, which passed the "Privileged Dago" Clause and enfranchised "foreign" Italian voters.[3] The negotiation of voting access for the state's "electoral freaks and monstrosities" reveals the racial and civic repercussions of expanding Italian voting rights within the disenfranchisement efforts of post-Reconstruction Louisiana. Ultimately, by the close of the 1898 debates, Italians retained their right to vote owing to their political utility to the (Regular) Democratic Party and their functionality as useful constituents in the "white" political machine. The preservation of Italian voting, therefore, was not necessarily prompted by their own elevated status. In their attempt to wrest political control away from Republicans and Populists, Louisiana legislators affirmed the racial acceptability of Italians, protected the Italian franchise, and discursively enfolded Italians into the white mainstream.

The suffrage debates reconstructed Italian place and identity within the

Jim Crow racial order. Participating in contestations over voting rights, Italians strategically aligned themselves on the side of native, white "southerners" rather than allying themselves with black southerners, who were historically the victims of political disenfranchisement. This configuration divided what could have been a potentially united political coalition to oppose suffrage restrictions and instead promoted the progressive articulation of Louisiana's legal and racial categories in terms of a more binary, less fluid structure. As Italians moved out of their "inbetween" racial status—their transiency enabling them to be made (and to make themselves) as white— Louisiana's employ of an intermediary racial category steadily disappeared in both law and practice. Meanwhile, these voting debates demonstrate moments in which the political organizing of Sicilians and other Italians as "Italian voters" produced a fledgling *Italianità* that increasingly erased their transnationally imported (from Italy) regional factionalism and turned Sicilians into Italians.

Louisiana party politics were a complicated affair in the 1880s and 1890s.[4] While planters historically voted Democrat, geospatial regionalism contributed to an intense divide among elites across the state. The region's bifurcated commercial agriculture—cotton parishes and sugar parishes— comprised different demographics and economies, which demanded diverging political ends.[5] Since sugar planting required a great deal more capital than cotton, northern investors became the primary financiers of Louisiana sugar in the postbellum era, receiving $30 million in sugar subsidies from a Republican federal government. As a result, sugar planters encouraged (and pressured) their workers to vote Republican because of the party's support of sugar subsidies.[6] Backland cotton parishes (in northern and central Louisiana, home to a majority of small, white subsistence farms) and black belt alluvial cotton parishes (in northwestern and northeastern Louisiana along the Mississippi River, made up of large plantations and a coercible black laboring majority) generally all voted Democrat. But the state's divided Democratic Party further confounded party politics in Louisiana.

With the elimination of the common enemy that had bound them together under radical Republican and military rule, the Democratic Party was no longer a monolithic force in the post-Reconstruction era and defied easy categorization. Under a variety of different names, Louisiana's Democratic Party splintered into two main factions: Reformers and Regulars.[7] The Regulars, made up of Bourbon reactionaries and prolottery urban politicians, negotiated changes in leadership and constituents by adopting different names in different moments, including: the Ring, the Choctaw Club, the Regular Democratic Organization, and the Old Regulars.[8] By the 1890s, the Ring represented the Regular Democrats and Bourbons; by and large professional politicians, they practiced classic urban machine politics and controlled municipal politics. Through a well-established system of patronage in exchange for votes, ethnic ward bosses, traditionally of German and Irish descent, secured local allegiances and funneled votes to the Ring tickets.[9] The Ring rewarded their constituents—New Orleans's working-class, immigrant populations, and French-speaking Creoles—for their votes with jobs, social services, and community assistance.

The primary opposition to the Regulars was the Reformers, also referred to as the Reform Democrats, the Independent Party, or the Citizens' League by 1896.[10] The Reformers, composed of antilottery forces and fiscally conservative patrician planters and merchants, were founded to combat municipal corruption and voter fraud.[11] Known as the "party of wealth," the Citizens' League was comprised of socially prominent, affluent, predominantly Anglo-Americans who represented the city's businessmen and commercial elite.[12] They won the occasional election, but as political amateurs and without an extensive constituent base, their influence, at least in New Orleans, was generally limited, especially since their "reform" efforts meant cutting jobs and attacking the patronage system.

Despite representing distinctive social backgrounds, classes, ethnic groups, and political agendas in Louisiana, certain elements and practices developed as mainstays for both Regular and Reformer Democrats. Both preserved ties to the White League, offered patronage for votes, and engaged in undisguised election fixing. Bourbon planters in the rural cotton parishes of northern and central Louisiana maintained control of the Democratic nominating conventions by fraudulently manipulating black voter rolls and regularly voting on behalf of their black employees.[13] If patronage in New Orleans failed to secure the necessary votes, the Ring sanctioned and utilized violence, intimidation, and economic threats, whereby workers and tenants were only hired if they voted the Regular Democratic ticket.[14] Similarly, and evincing signs of an anti-Republican Reformer/Regular alliance, Reformers resorted to falsifying returns in Louisiana's gubernatorial election of 1896. When antilottery reformer Murphy Foster defeated the Republican/Populist candidate John N. Pharr, returns in some parishes surpassed the number of registered voters, and Foster's campaign was credited with transporting Italian voters by train to New Orleans to fraudulently vote in the election.[15]

On account of such flagrant ballot rigging and election tampering, a combined force of Democratic legislators began to consider proposals as early as the Constitutional Convention of 1879 to drastically limit voting qualifications.[16] The stated objective was to circumvent the "obstacle" of the Fourteenth Amendment and "to forever rid the state of the possibility of negro domination."[17] Not wanting to risk federal intervention or a mass exodus of freedmen from the state, since both their labor and presence for the purpose of congressional representation were needed, Louisiana legislators did not move forward with constitutional disenfranchisement in 1879.[18] Likewise, Bourbon Democrats resisted disenfranchisement efforts because of their capacity to compel the votes of their black laborers. Yet, with growing fears about the possibility of an alliance between the state's illiterate and propertyless poor white farmers and urban laborers, Regulars and Reformers agreed that severely restricting the franchise—and forfeiting the (manipulable) black vote—would be preferable to class conflict and Republican/Populist rule.[19] By the 1890s, Bourbon/Ring Democrats and Reformers ultimately united over the concept (but not the means) of ballot reform.

By 1896, Louisiana Democrats began their concerted attempt at ballot reform, proposing a suffrage amendment that included a literacy test as a prerequisite for voting. Public opinion favored the move based on the open discussion that Louisiana had the highest rates of illiteracy in the United States—in 1890, 20 percent of Louisiana's white population was illiterate (compared to 7 percent nationally) along with 70 percent of its black population.[20] Reflecting fears that the state's large population of illiterate voters might wield political influence through their very presence as a majority, the ensuing suffrage debate made an appeal not only to disenfranchise the "negro vote" but also to disqualify the "hundreds of illiterate, unemployed, thriftless bums and tramps who are permitted to vote."[21]

The class of illiterate voters included the relatively new category of "declarant aliens," noncitizen immigrants who had made known their intention to naturalize. The 1879 "declarant alien" clause, which allowed "declarant" foreign-born persons the right to vote in state elections after residing in the state for one year, surfaced as a central issue in the suffrage debates.[22] Proclaiming the declarant clause was a means of "prostituting the rights of citizenship," the *Daily Picayune* worried that continuing to allow unnaturalized foreigners the right to vote created the impractical category of "inbetween" citizens who could vote in state elections but who may still be called for military service by a foreign nation.[23] The *Times Democrat* contended that since Oregon and Michigan had since repealed provisions that allowed unnaturalized "aliens" the right to vote, Louisiana was the only state to still "support a law which is one of the greatest insults that could be given to American citizenship."[24] While exaggerating the reality of Louisiana's status as the last remaining state to allow declarant aliens the right to vote, the *Times* did rightly observe a nationwide trend in the contraction of immigrant voting rights. Although many states around the nation had previously allowed declarant aliens to vote, all states with this special provision terminated their allowance by 1926.[25]

In addition to the deliberation to revise the "declarant alien" provision, the recommended ballot reform suggested a literacy test and a poll tax.[26] Republicans challenged the proposed literacy test, contending that such a test would place the government in the hands of "an autocratic few, because of their wealth and priority of advantage."[27] Regular Democrats likewise renounced the suffrage amendment, since the proposed revision would effectively limit their immigrant, working-class electorate; they "pledge[d] themselves to use their every endeavor to carry the parish against it and if possible defeat it."[28] Various other Democratic and Republican wards and precincts spoke out against the amendment, citing it as "class legislation . . . contrary to the principles of true Democracy."[29] Demonstrating the factionalism within the Democratic party, the Citizens' League emerged as the champions of the amendment in their politicized "reform" efforts to eliminate the foreign vote.

During these debates, Italian immigrants publicly and candidly joined the fray in proclaiming their opposition to disenfranchisement. Italian participation in Louisiana politics was neither new nor newly visible in New Orleans.[30] In the early 1870s, an Italian Club, one hundred members strong, participated in a torchlight parade with other Reform Democrats.[31] In 1876, the Italian Legion, in white caps and blue capes and accompanied by musical bands and officer-laden carriages, joined thousands marching through central New Orleans; they processed with the "wildest enthusiasm" in opposition to the "frauds committed by the Radical Administration."[32] During the 1870s and 1880s, Italians organized throughout the city, from the Second, Third, Fifth, Sixth, and Tenth Wards, to promote naturalization and voter registration.[33]

Continuing in this tradition, in March of 1896, 1,500 to 2,000 Italians held a mass meeting, conducted entirely in Italian, in Old Fellows Hall on Camp Street (between Poydras Street and Lafayette Street) in New Orleans.[34] The site, known for hosting the Continental Guards clad in American Revolutionary soldier uniforms, offered a symbolic location for the Italian Club to elect their officers and for community leaders to deliver speeches. Among the speakers was Santo Oteri, an astoundingly wealthy and influential businessman who had realized community influence after taking over his Sicilian-born father's Central American fruit import business. Oteri encouraged participants to vote the Democratic Party line since, he explained, the Democrats had "always looked to [our] interest."[35] Oteri went on to exploit the rhetoric and imagery of Italian nationalism: "As [we] remember the glorious deeds of Victor Emmanuel, Garibaldi and other distinguished patriots of [our] native land and revere them, [we] should fire [our] patriotism and stand united in a solid phalanx and vote for the regular Democratic ticket at the next election."[36] So too, Joseph di Carlo, the elected president of the proceedings, invoked the imagery of Italian nationalism when he described the impending "hot" campaign and encouraged participants to "see to it that the result was different from the Italian campaign in Africa."[37] With both Sicilians and other Italians present at the meeting, this calling on the figures of the Italian Risorgimento and reminder for the audience of the nationally embarrassing, failed invasion of Ethiopia (of 1895–1896), reflected the "Italianizing" of Sicilian immigrants and emerging *Italianità* within New Orleans's Italian immigrant community.

Not only had certain Italian emigrants already adopted a sense of *Italianitá* as early as the 1890s and begun to conceptualize themselves in terms of a unified Italy, but community leaders capitalized upon this *Italianitá* to advocate for a united Italian voting bloc. Extending beyond regional differences in his appeal to participants at the Italian Club meeting, Oteri called upon all participants, whether Sicilian, Genovese, or Piedmontese, to unite as "Italian voters." Further indicating the steady erasure of transnationally imported regional factionalism, the infamous and well-known Charles Matranga, one of the defendants in the Hennessy murder, a survivor of the 1891 lynching in New Orleans, and a Sicilian by birth, was not only present but was elected the grand marshal of the proceedings. In times of crisis, whether lynching or disenfranchisement, Sicilians and other Italians in Louisiana began to look beyond their regional differences transported from Italy to forge a more universally Italian American identity; moreover, political organizing in the name of Louisiana politics accelerated these reconfigurations of identity.

The Italian Club concluded the meeting by passing a series of resolutions, including one committing and pledging themselves in support of the Democratic candidate Murphy Foster for governor.[38] Despite the fact that Foster was responsible for sponsoring the suffrage amendment, his disenfranchisement efforts were directed at African Americans and not immigrants, so the Italian voting bloc remained committed to helping "the party which helps the Italians."[39] With the conclusion of the speeches, the Italian Club meeting adjourned, though their demonstrating continued as the gathering moved into the streets and culminated in a "festive" parade.

Subsequently dubbed the "Dago Parade," at least fifty Italians on heavy draft horses made their way through the streets of New Orleans (see map 5); the "thundering of the hoofs on the pavements sounded like the march of two or three regiments of cavalry."[40] Marchers "promiscuously" shot off fireworks and carried lanterns, sticks, and banners, one of which even had a live rooster perched upon it. They carried additional roosters, a longtime symbol of the Democratic Party in Louisiana, in birdcages and "perched on staffs," while at least a dozen goats accompanied the procession, "some of them being led along and others carried in a wagon, and allowed to feed on flowers."[41] Parading beneath an Italian flag, participants carried banners which read, in English, "Death to Dr. Bruns' pet, the suffrage amend-

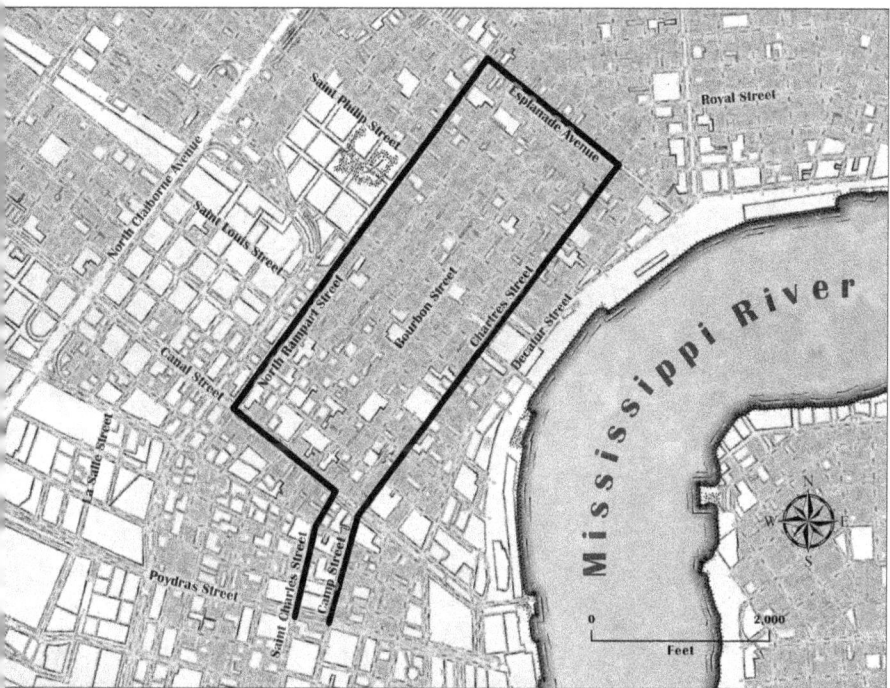

MAP 5. Route of the "Dago Parade," March 22, 1896. Marching in opposition to Louisiana's proposed disenfranchisement efforts, Italians publicly demonstrated across New Orleans's French Quarter. Map by Joshua Reyling. Sources: "Italian Regulars," *Daily Picayune*, March 23, 1896; USGS; US Census Bureau; City of New Orleans.

ment," "Knownothing Bruns," "Down with the suffrage amendment," "We are Democrats and not grasshoppers," and "We demand that the mechanic, the clerk and the laborer, white and black, have the same privilege to cast his ballot on election day as the millionaire."[42]

New Orleans newspapers did not report favorably on the Italian meeting and the "Dago Parade." Both the *Times* and the *Picayune* disparaged the meeting at length, in part because of assumptions about the behavior of the Italian attendees. Estimating that "one-half of them did not know what they were there for," the *Picayune* characterized the participants at the meeting as too "enthusiastic" and acting "with the impetuosity of the Latin races."[43] Noting the use of "profane language," the press described the events as an uncivilized display of "rowdyism" and a "disgraceful spectacle." The marchers were ignorant and not worthy of being voting citizens. The amassed, which included the ward heelers, were "the sorriest looking set of citizens that anybody would care to rest their eye on" and a "a disgrace to a civilized community."[44] The *Times Democrat* qualified its admonishment of the gathering by denying the existence of "Know-Nothing" feelings in Louisiana:

> Foreigners are welcomed here and treated well in every respect; indeed our Constitution is more liberal toward them than that of any other State in the Union, and actually grants them the electoral franchise before they have become naturalized. . . . There is no prejudice here against the Italians. Whatever feeling against them may have been aroused by the tragic events of six years ago has passed away, and when they prove themselves good citizens they are treated with exactly the same consideration as the people of any other nationality.[45]

Notably, the "tragic event" was Chief Hennessy's 1890 assassination, not the New Orleans lynching. Drawing on the nativism that rationalized the 1891 lynching, both the *Times Democrat* and the *Daily Picayune* excused their criticisms on the grounds that the marchers were "uncivilized" and unfit for self-government; they critically appraised the meeting and the parade in the name of self-defense.

Despite certain protestations to the contrary, the employment of ethnic stereotypes explicitly noted the "foreignness" of the meeting. The *Picayune* explained that the act of parading beneath the Italian flag offered evidence to support amending the state's suffrage and naturalization laws: "How long do you suppose they would remain here, if they manage to accumulate a few dollars? Why, they will go back to Italy, and there live in comparative luxury for the rest of their days."[46] Emphasizing the fact that "No English was Spoken" notably marked the meeting as dangerous and uncivilized, since only someone with "some knowledge of the English language" could "raise . . . above the level of a four-footed animal."[47] In contrast to rhetoric from the 1870s and 1880s, supporters of disenfranchisement in 1890s Louisiana invoked the long-standing (northern) stereotypes and perception of the Italian immigrant as a temporary sojourner, a "bird of passage," as fodder for suffrage constraints. Local politician Capt. William C. Dufour, capitalizing on existing xenophobic tropes, asserted that participants at the meeting were "ignorant, brutal and alien [and] did not even know or understand why they were called together for speech and for parade."[48] Just as anti-Italian discourse emerged locally in the postlynching era to justify the violence, the disenfranchisement debates similarly adopted anti-Italian language common in the national press to delegitimize the Italian meeting and substantiate voter restriction.

Citizenship and allegiance dominated the critiques of the meeting. Witnesses considered the demonstration an "interfer[ence] into American politics" since the naturalized Italian was expected to have "abandon[ed] the tricolor for the Stars and Stripes." Not only was this a question of loyalty, but the *Times* observed the audacity of the group marching beneath a "foreign flag" in "dictat[ing] to us what our Constitution and our laws should be."[49] The "Italian Parade" was an "interference by a foreign body in the political affairs of an American city," which made the parade "obnoxious," "distasteful," and "un-American and offensive in the highest degree.[50] As the *Times* explained, Italian citizens had the "right to express their views as Democrats or Republicans, as supporters of the Regular Democrats or the Citizens' League, but when, as Italians, organized on the basis of nationality, they march beneath the Italian flag, and when they interfere in American politics, and tell us what kind of a Constitution, what systems of law and what suffrage is acceptable to them as Italians, they must arouse a very strong feeling against themselves."[51]

The rhetoric of "interference" and "un-American-ness," hearkening back to the interference of Reconstruction carpetbaggers, marked the Italian meeting as distinctly outside of Louisiana politics. Such an invocation of the participants as "ignorant foreigners," in opposition to "purer politics and higher civilization," appropriated existing xenophobic and anti-Italian rhetoric and challenged the legitimacy of the Italian meeting and parade.[52] Just as Sicilian importers were rising in the city's economic ranks, establishing global trading ties, and no longer commercially bound to native-born elites, the Italian Parade's show of force symbolized the Italian community's ability to displace the white, native-born order. Such sentiment echoed the recurring fear that contributed to the lynchings of Italians. The magnitude of the Italians' demonstration—with its participants organized as Italians and speaking Italian under an Italian flag within the political context of a splintered Democratic Party—evidenced the growing political and economic threat posed by New Orleans's Italian population.

Beyond the specter of Italians organizing as Italians, opponents asserted that local bosses were responsible for manipulating the Italian voters.[53] Particularly objectionable was the role of the Regulars "who control the Italian vote" and the claim that the Italians had "adopt[ed] a set of resolutions of which nine-tenths of them had not the slightest understanding."[54] The press questioned the imprudence of such a public spectacle, since "corralling a lot of dagoes and making such a display" was an "insult" and a "positive disgrace to every American." Italians acting and organizing as Italians remained a dangerous precedent in defiance of Louisiana politics. Although newspapers blamed Italian immigrants for their willingness to participate in the parade, they additionally focused on the fact that the Regulars had manipulated them.[55] In the shadow of the imagined Italian conspiracy responsible for Hennessy's assassination, which fueled a very real anxiety concerning the Italian-ness of the "Dago Parade," anti-Regular sentiment, local politics, and divisions within the Democratic Party propelled this anti-Italian rhetoric.

While the "Dago Parade" may have garnered further criticism because of a perception that Italians marched in solidarity with black New Orleanians against disenfranchisement, Italians did not politically align themselves alongside black voters.[56] Rather, the Italian Club justified their opposition to the suffrage amendment on the grounds of their long-standing allegiance to the Democratic Party. Italian immigrants, they claimed, deserved the right to vote not only because of their party loyalty, but because they had "contributed to that success which assured home government to Louisiana."[57] Constructing itself in opposition to black voters, the Italian Club declared how instrumental it had been in wresting control away from Republicans and carpetbaggers and in helping to reinstitute (white, Democratic) home rule in Louisiana. By appealing to the Democratic Party on the basis of their contribution to native-born anti-Reconstruction politics, the Italian Club thus aligned itself with the white majority in Louisiana and positioned itself as disenfranchisers, rather than the disenfranchised. This manner of fashioning themselves as native-born, white "southerners," as well as emphasizing their economic and political contributions to the state, may have simply been political pandering on the part of Italians working to place themselves in the most politically advantageous position possible.[58] Therefore, while the Italian meeting does not suggest evidence of genuine Italian-as-southerner identity, it does show Italians deliberately articulating themselves in opposition to black Louisianans and overtly representing themselves as members of the white majority; Italians marched to defend their own voting interests. Still, even if no interracial coalition actually existed, Italian opposition to the suffrage amendment may have been read by contemporaries as an alliance with black voters, which would have certainly fostered fears and anxieties concerning Italian voting.

Ultimately, criticism levied against the "Dago Parade" exploited questions of loyalty and citizenship and invoked existing xenophobic tropes in order to legitimize a political critique of bossism and the Regular Democrats. Amidst these political controversies, Louisiana lawmakers deferred comprehensive action regarding suffrage in 1896, though they did pass a temporary voter registration law to limit suffrage. Legislators additionally called for a constitutional convention to develop an official voting policy to make the restriction permanent.[59]

Louisiana convened its 1898 Constitutional Convention in January. No black legislators, four foreign-born, 120 southerners, and ten transplanted northerners represented the state.[60] Ernest B. Kruttschnitt, the preeminent lawyer and New Orleans–born son of the former German consul, presided over the convention.[61] Explicitly characterizing the work of the convention and the Suffrage Committee as necessary to maintain white supremacy, the *Daily Picayune* reported, "The white people of Louisiana are at this moment engaged in the work of saving their State from the black flood of ignorance, shiftlessness and moral and mental unfitness for the exercise of political power that was poured out upon it in the form of negro suffrage."[62] In initial discussions, legislators offered general consensus for the establishment of an Australian or secret ballot (which would replace party ballots with government-funded ballots), a biennial registration requirement, and voting supervision by commissioners.[63] The "declarant alien" reemerged as a prominent feature of discord. Legislators contended that unnaturalized and unassimilated foreign citizens were freely voting in Louisiana state elections making ballot reform necessary to "take the power to vote out of the hands of foreigners" and to "secure white supremacy for all time in Louisiana."[64] Unlike the disenfranchisement debates of the same era that took place in Mississippi and South Carolina, the voting rights of immigrants and "foreigners" remained in the foreground of considerations in Louisiana.[65]

Under the chairmanship of General T. F. Bell, a lawyer from Shreveport, the Suffrage Committee developed and submitted the draft of its voting amendment. The main premise of the committee's proposed voting ordinance was an educational qualification or literacy test (in one's native language). However, for those who were unable to meet the educational qualification, the committee included a series of additional entitlements for the franchise: if a voter did not meet the educational qualification, they were still eligible to vote if they owned $300 in property, if their wife owned property, if their child owned property, if they were registered to vote in 1868, if they were not registered to vote in 1868 but would have qualified to register, if their father or grandfather were either registered in 1868 or could have been, or if they were foreign-born but naturalized before the Constitution was adopted.[66]

Upon its announcement, the suffrage proposal met with mixed responses. The *Daily Picayune* favored the policy of "enfranchising all who were voters" before 1868 and advocated on behalf of the constitutionality of the exclusions in the proposal since they were not based on race.[67] According to the *Picayune,* an "accident of circumstances," rather than a violation of the Fourteenth Amendment, would lead to the desired disenfranchisement results.[68] While the *Times Democrat* supported the educational and property requirements, they dubbed the ordinance as a whole a "Monstrous Suffrage Plan" and railed against the plan's numerous exemptions. Deliberately designed to ridicule "undeserving" voters and to characterize them as "other", the *Times* labeled the clauses granting voting rights to someone if their wife owned property or if their child owned property as the "Squaw Voter" and the "Papoose Voter," respectively. The *Times* used derisive terms with unmistakable references to native culture and language to signal the provisions as both farcical and dangerous.[69] As the *Times* explained, the "Squaw Voter" clause allowed an "unspeakable thing in breeches" to vote simply because his wife owned property, while the "Papoose Voter," a member of the otherwise "prohibited classes," was a "degenerate" who was only able to vote because his child owned property.[70]

In addition to the "Squaw Voter" and "Papoose Voter" exemptions, the *Times* also objected to Section 5 of the proposed suffrage ordinance, which included the "Hereditary [or 1868] Voter" exemption. The stated intention behind the "1868 voter" provision was to preserve the franchise for Civil War (primarily Confederate) veterans. Because the clause granted suffrage to all those *eligible* to vote in 1868, whether or not they had actually registered or exercised their voting entitlement, the *Times* mocked the ordinance for enfranchising "the Could have Been Voter—the fellow who might have voted in 1868 but did not think it worthwhile."[71] Additionally controversial was the fact that the exception granted the right to vote to those who were descendants of someone who voted or who was entitled to vote in 1868, thus enfranchising by "right of descent." The *Times* admonished the convention for granting "degenerates" the right to "vote on inheritance," and for creating a "monstrosity and absurdity" who is unfit to vote "but enjoys the franchise because some ancestor of his was a voter . . . or might have been a voter . . . if he had thought it worth his while to get registered."[72]

Beyond the "Hereditary Voter" or grandfather clause, Section 5 also contained the following provision: "No male person of foreign birth, who shall have been naturalized prior to the adoption of this constitution, shall ever be denied the right to register and vote in this state by reason of his failure to possess the educational or property qualifications prescribed by this constitution."[73] Dubbing the provision the "Privileged Dago" Clause, the *Times Democrat* exploded with indignation and denounced the exemption as "distinctly unamerican [sic]," which "gives persons born abroad privileges denied [to] natives of Louisiana."[74] Calling it an "insult," an "injustice," a "scandal," the *Times* maintained that the provision was a "glaring show of partiality in favor of the illiterate and naturalized foreigner as against the illiterate of native birth."[75] Certain delegates at the convention concurred with this critical assessment and reportedly considered the exemption as "not only wrong in principle, injurious in effect, but distinctly and emphatically unconstitutional."[76] According to the *Times*, the convention's exemptions had created a series of "electoral freaks and monstrosities."[77]

Evidence of the polarizing political divide between the Regulars and the Reformers, debate erupted over Section 5's "Privileged Dago" Clause and the question of whether foreign-born individuals should have the right to vote in Louisiana. The *Times Democrat*, unrepentant in its critique, argued that Section 5 had been passed by partisan interests and factional support and made "permanent citizens of every naturalized Italian of this city, whether fit for the suffrage or not, whether literate or illiterate, whether owning property or a pauper."[78] Vociferating against the "foreign vote," they proclaimed that anyone who was not an American citizen (native-born or otherwise) should not be permitted to vote, and that Section 5 provided illiterate foreigners and "tramps" with special privileges and "greater rights than natives."[79] The *Times* cited language, culture, and education as further barriers making Italians unfit and undeserving of the franchise: "One's gorge so rises at the attempt to force 5000 or 6000 ignorant voters upon this city simply because they are foreigners to the exclusion of native-born illiterates, who have forgotten more about the institutions and the genius of republican government than these ignorant foreign-born voters, who can neither read American literature nor comprehend American speakers, can ever acquire."[80] According to the *Times*, the foreign-born allowance extended the franchise privilege above and beyond those rights offered to native-born and at the expense of the rights of native-born. Similarly, parishes across Louisiana voiced their discontent with the ordinance through mass meetings and protests: Acadia Parish denounced Section 5 as "un-American" and proclaimed it an "insult and slap in the face to every native-born citizen."[81] Avoyelles Parish protested the suffrage ordinance as an "insult" and a "nefarious and iniquitous measure, full of contamination and bossism."[82] As in 1896, critics of foreign-born voting capitalized on existing xenophobic tropes and nativist fears in order to attack that which gave their political opponents an electoral advantage.

Despite the *Times*'s contention, "opposition" to the suffrage amendment was not monolithic and varied across the state. The *Daily Picayune*, relatively unconcerned with the foreign-born exemption, pointed out that few foreigners had naturalized and therefore the exception would allow only a few foreign-born to vote. As Chairman Bell explained and the Suffrage Committee reasoned, the foreign-born allowance was a means to enfranchise a naturalized foreigner who would otherwise not fall under the 1868 provision, thus putting him "on the same plane as the native-born citizen."[83] Depicted in map 6, demonstrations raged across Louisiana during the first two weeks of March 1898, both in favor of and opposed to the suffrage amendment.[84] Colfax, Shreveport, and New Orleans hosted demonstrations in favor of the suffrage proposal, while demonstrations in Acadia

Parish, Avoyelles Parish, East Feliciana Parish, Shreveport, Jackson Parish, Caddo Parish, Mansfield, and De Soto Parish protested either Section 5 or the entire amendment. Neither support nor opposition for the suffrage amendment was geographically or geospatially confined. Support for the amendment and the foreign-born voting exception was strongest in and around New Orleans, with the largest contingency of Italian immigrant constituents; opposition to the "Dago Clause" spanned both black belt parishes and sugar parishes where planters worried that disenfranchisement would eliminate the manipulable black vote, and the backland cotton parishes and mixed soil parishes where white subsistence farmers resented the foreign-born voting exception.

Just days after its initial announcement, the Suffrage Committee released a "vastly improved" proposal, which amended Section 5 so that only foreigners who naturalized as of January 1, 1898, would be granted the right to vote outside the educational and property requirement.[85] Convention delegate John St. Paul, a young Orleans attorney, reported that since 1879, a mere 1,189 immigrants had actually naturalized as citizens in Louisiana. but ten times that number had been voting "without discarding allegiance to foreign kings, princes and potentates."[86] Based on St. Paul's estimate, the revised Section 5 served to remedy this flagrant abuse, since it "cut off the thousands of ignorant incomers of the lowest class from the purlieus of Europe, who, although not making any claim to be citizens, have been for years marched to the polls as so many dumb cattle and voted at the command of the bosses."[87] St. Paul reasoned, the clause would enfranchise a relatively small number of foreigners and only those who did not herald from the "lowest class from the purlieus of Europe" would be eligible "white" voters. With revisions, the *Daily Picayune* abandoned its criticism of Section 5.

In spite of the modifications, the *Times* continued to fulminate and accused the Suffrage Committee of carelessness; it admitted that Section 5 was less offensive since it had dropped the "Squaw Voter" and "Papoose Voter" provisions, but it "retained most of the worst features of the original ordinance."[88] As the *Times* proclaimed, even in its amended form, "It does not cure its inherent and insuperable defect—the fact that it grants foreigners privileges which it denies to native . . . It gives the electoral franchise to illiterate persons if born in Italy while it denies it to those born in the

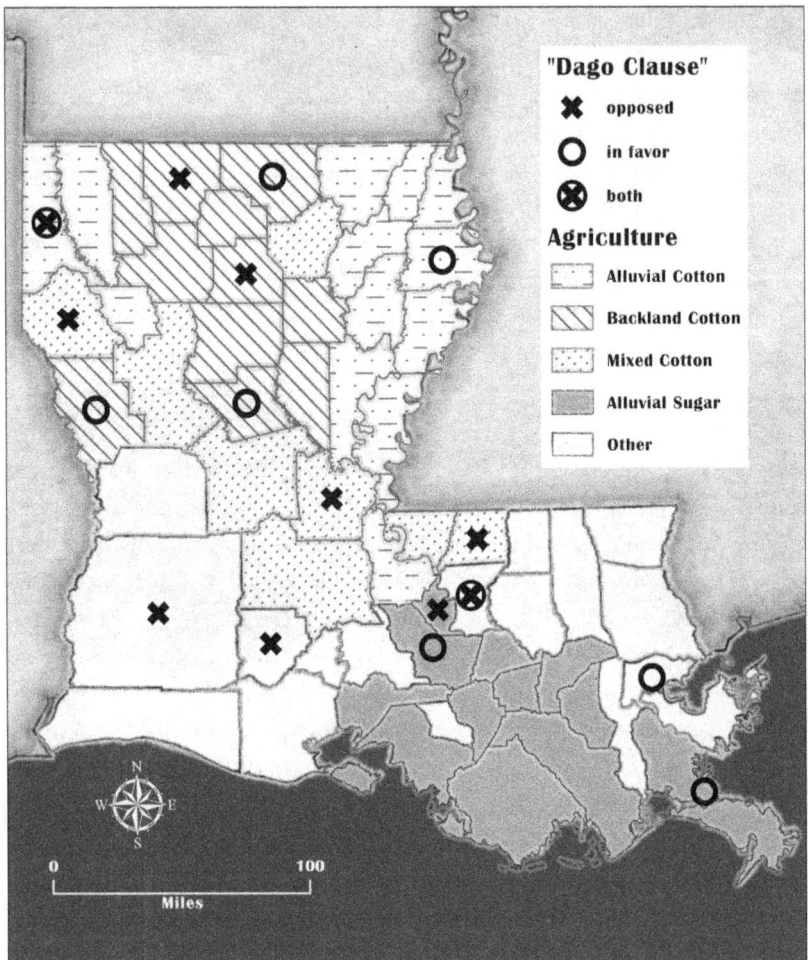

MAP 6. Reactions to the "Dago Clause" according to agriculturally disparate regions. Map by Joshua Reyling. Sources: Barnes, *The Louisiana Populist Movement, 1881–1900*, 34–35; "The Suffrage," *Times Democrat*, March 11, 1898; various articles, *Daily Picayune*, March 1898.

United States."[89] Opinions across the state corroborated the assessment of the *Times* and questioned the legitimacy of Section 5 and the "Privileged Dago" Clause. The *Shreveport Caucasian* reported that Section 5 enfranchised a "series of misfits" and resulted in a "satire, a travesty on honest and fair suffrage qualification, an unintentional affront to every intelligent citizen of the State."[90] The *Shreveport Times* noted that the "most objection-able" section of the ordinance was the enfranchisement of foreigners who lacked an understanding of the "government or its blessings," especially in the face of disenfranchising "white native born who have been deprived of educational facilities."[91] The *Baton Rouge Bulletin* advocated on behalf of the poll tax, which it felt would "relegate to the rear a mass of undesirable, corrupt voters—principally negroes [and] Dagoes."[92] With varying degrees of acerbity, the regional press opposed privileging "dagoes" and preserving an exception for foreign-born voting.

At its core, the underlying and vigorous debate over Section 5 and the "Privileged Dago" Clause remained a political dispute between the Ring/Regulars and members of the Citizens' League/Reformers. Evincing both a political censure of bossism and a veiled resistance to disenfranchising the manipulable black voter, Reformers appropriated an existing and ra-cializing parlance against Italians, only sporadically employed in Louisiana before 1896. Characterizing Italians as racially suspect and suggesting that Italians lacked the proper credentials for citizenship, these two often en-tangled positions articulated opposition to the "Privileged Dago" voter on the grounds that Italians were a suspect, dangerous, and transient voting population.

Despite a legal reality that Italians were "white on arrival," Reformers suggested that the suffrage amendment was "simply and solely a petty fog-ging trick intended to permit a lot of illiterates and riffraffs, whose skin happens to be white, to vote, whether they know what a ballot is or not."[93] By censuring the "Privileged Dago" Clause for enfranchising "a lot of igno-rant Dagoes and shut[ting] out a great many whites," opponents challenged the very place of Italians within a "white man's" government.[94] Dismissing the legal consideration of Italian whiteness, critics noted, "When we speak of a white man's government, [Italians] are as black as the blackest Negro in existence."[95] Some Reformers even suggested that black voters were pref-erable to Italian voters. Such opinions criticized the suffrage amendment, because it desired to make citizens of the "Dagoes . . . and disfranchise the Negro, and God knows if there is any difference between them it is largely in the darkies favor."[96] Ground in an understanding of the black vote as more easily controlled, such palpably racist language designated the foreign vote as considerably more dangerous than the black vote and disregarded the legal whiteness of Italians. This explicit denial of Italian whiteness wherein the racial questionability of Italians overshadowed their skin that "happen[ed] to be white," like the very act of lynching, collapsed Italians' race and color and constructed "Dagoes" in opposition to or outside whiteness.[97]

In addition to questioning Italian whiteness, Reformers and their allies doubted the ability of Italians to properly exercise their rights of the citizenship. Critics reasoned, since Italians were categorically illiterate, propertyless, and "grossly ignorant of America and its institutions," they were too ignorant to exercise the franchise and lacked the skills and interest in the requirements of citizenship.[98] If the rights of the citizenry were finite, offering Italians the right to vote was inherently an "insult" to native-born and a deprivation of their own rights. Just as native-born white Louisianans exploited a racialized vernacular to validate the lynchings of Italians in the early 1890s, Reformers and Citizens' League advocates adopted similar language to cast doubt upon the racial and civic fitness of Italians in 1898. Opposing suffrage in terms of citizenship, xenophobia, and racial questionability offered a popularly compelling and convincing argument against Italian suffrage. Critics capitalized on these existing prejudices against Italians to secure popular support for their larger objective: the elimination of "bossism."

According to Reformers and allies of the Citizens' League, the problem with bossism was that it allowed ward leaders of precincts with a high number of Italian voters the means to secure elections through political maneuvering and pandering. By this unconcealed critique, that permitting Italians to vote enabled ward bosses to maintain their control of Louisiana electioneering, the *Times* marked the "Privileged Dago" Clause as an "outrageous concession to the ward bosses and potential factor of corruption."[99] Even after the revisions that limited foreign-born access to the franchise to those who had already naturalized, the *Times* questioned: "Why should [the convention] cling to the Privileged Dago . . . unless it is due to the subtle but potent influence of the bosses, who have maintained their political strength and carried primaries and elections through the use of these voters."[100] Reports from Claiborne Parish, a northern backland parish along the Arkansas border, opposed the "anxious" efforts of the "corrupt ward bosses of New Orleans . . . to save the hoodlum voters."[101] Even sugar planters in West Baton Rouge reaffirmed this accusation of bossism:

"There are too many Farrells and Fitzpatricks in that convention for Louisiana's good. . . . John Brewster's 5000 Dagoes and Fitzpatrick's and Farrell's ignorant hoodlums and heelers must be allowed to vote in order to maintain the prestige of the bosses. Their influence is responsible for that unspeakably infamous and damnable section of the bill which accords the right of suffrage to foreign-born illiterates and denies to native illiterates the same privilege."[102]

Less evidence of widespread anti-Irish sentiment, the reference about "too many Farrells and Fitzpatricks" posed a critical commentary of John Fitzpatrick, the former mayor of New Orleans, active president of the Choctaw Club, and famed ward boss of Orleans.[103] The Citizens' League (and Choctaw Club rivals) employed the rhetoric of nativism in their reproach of Fitzpatrick and his control of the urban political machine in New Orleans. With Fitzpatrick and bossism controlling the foreign vote, the Citizens' League condemned Italian voting as a coded critique of their disadvantage as the political minority.

Countering the claims of the Reformers and Citizens' League, a vocal contingent of legislators, made up of members of the Ring/Choctaw Club and even some Bourbon Democrats, supported the right of the foreign-born to vote. Subsuming Italians under the category of entitled "white" voters, supporters expressed approbation for the suffrage plan because it would "disfranchise very few white men . . . [and the] Negro [would be] eliminated from politics . . . Nine-tenths of the Negroes will be disfranchised."[104] Mr. Montgomery of Madison Parish, a planter and Confederate veteran who resided in a black belt parish in northeastern Louisiana where Italians made up more than three-quarters of the foreign-born white population, identified Section 5 as a means of self-preservation in the name of the "Caucasian enterprise."[105] He went on to elaborate that illiterate whites made better voters than the "average negro," because "the former is, by hereditary traits, a representative of the conquering and civilizing race, and the latter the representative of a race that has so far utterly failed to accomplish a civilization in any land or clime. I would rather trust the instincts of the Caucasian voter, associated with the intelligence of his community, unlettered though he may be, to the slightly educated negro linked to his race habits and traditions."[106] By equivocating "Caucasian" with an inherited civility and intelligence, Montgomery reasoned that race vested certain individuals with an instinctual sense of voting. In his discerning between the "average negro" and the "Caucasian voter," and by not distinguishing the foreign-vote from the "white vote," Montgomery incorporated Italians as members of the "civilizing . . . Caucasian" race.

As an effort toward ballot reform compromise, support for the "Dago Clause" eventually spanned the regionally disparate geographies, demographies, and economies of the state. A letter to the editor from New Orleans justified the exemption based on the fact that the naturalized foreigner had chosen their citizenship, thus making them more vested in the franchise than native-born citizens.[107] Even delegates from backland parishes that mainly comprised poor, illiterate white farmers supported the "Dago Clause." Amos Ponder, a "strong" Democratic lawyer representing Sabine Parish, defended the exception by explaining, "We are native-born by accident; they are citizens by choice and preference. When a man chooses the proud American flag, he has as much right and privileges as the men who were born under its colors."[108] R. B. Dawkins, a lawyer from Union Parish in northern Louisiana on the Arkansas border, explained that the "naturalized voters had no equals. They made the best citizens. Of twenty-four foreign voters in [my] parish all but two would come in under the educational or property qualification."[109] Because of their limited proximity to (and competition with) Italians—less than a quarter of foreign-born whites in Sabine Parish (along the Texas border) were Italian, while no Italians resided in Union—backland residents challenged their historic association with "knownothing-ism" and supported the proposed ballot reform.[110] According to certain supporters of Section 5, not only would the clause enfranchise few, but those few had earned the rights of citizenship through their choice of naturalization.

Beyond those claims favoring the Italians' right to citizenship, many convention-goers and advocates of the "Privileged Dago" Clause additionally recognized the provision as a means of expanding the power of the Democratic Party. As a delegate for Orleans Parish, former mayor Fitzpatrick explained that the voting rights of the "dagoes" should be protected because "those people who they termed foreigners had pledged their lives to the Democratic Party in assisting it to maintain white supremacy, and many of them had been carried home corpses."[111] This was significant not only because he highlighted the participation of Italians in the Civil War and as members of the Democratic Party; Fitzpatrick also considered them a necessary component for maintaining "white supremacy." Similarly, John Dymond, a sugar planter in Plaquemines just south of New Orleans and self-defined "tiller of the soil," explained, "He knew the difficulties of maintaining white supremacy. . . . They needed the '68 voter, the squaw voter, the papoose voter, the naturalized voter and every white man they could get into the electorate."[112] Again marking the Italian as racially transient, these considerations of the Italian as politically useful for securing "white supremacy" reinforced the extent to which at least some Louisianans and certain convention legislators either considered Italians "white" or were willing to accept them within the "white" majority as a means of wresting political control from black voters. Aligning Italians within the white mainstream served to bifurcate Louisiana's racial discourse and articulate Louisiana legal categories more readily in terms of racial binaries.

In addition to considering Italian voters as favorable to both the Democratic Party and "white" supremacy, an active and outspoken coalition at the convention substantiated their support of Section 5 in historical terms, linking Italian immigrants to the history of "civilized" European immigration. In his plea for the convention to be fair and just, Dymond noted his personal role in having recruited many of the foreign-born who currently resided in Louisiana; he rationalized, "They nearly all voted the Democratic ticket, and were good citizens. They came from Sicily, which had been the battleground of liberty for thousands of years. The Englishman and the Dutchman and others had at various times been looked down upon, just as the Italians were now looked down upon, in fifteen or twenty years they would prove their good citizenship."[113] Distinguishing the immigrant community in Louisiana as largely Sicilian, rather than flattening their identity as simply Italians, Dymond recognized the particularities and dimensionality of the state's Italian population. In acclaiming their participation in a historical tradition of fighting for democracy and the rights of self-government and acknowledging their unique contribution to Louisiana, Dymond argued that Sicilians would make "good Democrats." Based on their history as a conquered people fighting for "liberty," they would prove themselves useful citizens.

Likewise, Thomas Kernan, a second-generation native-born Louisianan, Democratic lawyer of East Baton Rouge, and "one of the most prominent and popular statesmen of Louisiana," challenged the cyclicality of nativism.[114] In his eloquent defense of the "Dago voter," he orated:

> And now they say that we should exclude from the electorate the men whose assistance we invited in the dark days of reconstruction, whom they are pleased to designate by the contemptuous epithet of the privileged Dago voter . . . Now, who are these men of foreign birth who have cast their lot among us and given in [sic] their allegiance to this government? They are not Dagoes, privileged or otherwise. Who are we, I may ask, but foreigners, one or two degrees removed. And, gentlemen of the convention, when I give my consent to do an injustice to a man of foreign birth, I hope I may cease to honor my living Irish father and forget the memory of my dead French-English mother. We called them when we needed them, and they came to our assistance. They must have been faithful allies from '68–'79 or the Democratic majority in the convention of 1879 would have never have granted [sic] the extreme courtesy and privilege which they held out to them as an inducement, that they should be permitted to vote upon a mere declaration of intention. And who are these that they call "privileged Dagoes?" Why, gentlemen of the convention, they are the men of civilized Europe. They are the noble Briton, the sturdy German, the chivalrous Spaniard, the gallant Frenchman and the hardy Russian and the genial Irishman. These are they whom the committee has admitted to the franchise, and these are they who have been contemptuously ycleped—privileged Dagoes![115]

While advocating for the "Privileged Dago" Clause, Kernan persuasively contested the equivalence of Italians and "dagoes." In direct contrast with the use of the term "dago" in the 1880s and early 1890s, by 1898, "dago" possessed a more pejorative connotation. This etymological shift required Kernan to distinguish between the "Dago" and the Italian and encourage Louisianans to understand Italians and "Dagoes" as fundamentally different types of immigrants. By reminding his audience that they were only "one or two degrees removed" from being foreigners themselves, Kernan, the grandson of Irish-born grandparents, constructed a historical link and political alliance between Italians and the "native-born." Differentiating the foreigner from the "Dago," Italians were both their evolutionary descendants and allies. By considering Italians members of "civilized Europe," in opposition to black southerners, Kernan diminished the racial undesirability of Italians. Kernan's contentions gave Italians not just a legal color status as "white," but distinguished them as racially and anthropologically "white" as well. Appealing in part to his constituents where more than half of the foreign-born white population were Italian in East Baton Rouge, Kernan also advocated on behalf of the "Privileged Dago" as a means of expanding the "white electorate." Thus, members of the Ring and other Regular allies placed Italian immigrants steadily within the confines of "whiteness" (just as Italians had attempted when they marched in defense of their voting rights in 1896), which served to further collapse Italian race and color and progressively align Italians (as distinct from "Dagoes") as "white southerners."

After weeks of debate, convention legislators ultimately passed the suffrage amendment, upon which this chapter began, which included a residency requirement, a literacy provision, a property requirement (ownership of at least $300), and a poll tax. The residency clause required prospective voters to have lived in Louisiana for at least two years (one year in the parish and six months in the precinct), which effectively eliminated transient sharecroppers from the voting rolls.[116] Illiterate whites were "grandfathered" in so long as they could prove that they themselves, their father, or their grandfather had registered to vote (or had been eligible to do so) before January 1, 1867, the last year before military Reconstruction began.[117] The final version of the amendment accomplished its intended disenfranchising goals: from 130,000 in 1897, black voter registration dwindled to only 5,320 in 1900 (less than 5 percent of the 1897 registrants) and to 1,342 in 1904 (just over 1 percent of the 1897 registrants). General voter registration also declined, but at a less extreme rate: from 164,000 in 1897 to 125,000 in 1900 to 92,000 in 1904.[118]

Despite the at-times hostile anti-Italian remarks during the 1890s debates and a certain sentiment that cautioned against trusting "white" foreigners to vote, the Louisiana convention passed the "Privileged Dago" Clause. The final iteration of the controversial and hotly debated Section

5 specifically granted "male person[s] of foreign birth" the right to register and vote in the state of Louisiana. As long as a foreign-born man had naturalized before January 1, 1898, he was eligible to vote even if he did not meet the literacy and property requirements.[119] The preservation of Italian voting functioned as a product of legislators recognizing Italians as useful constituents and voters. Because "Sicilians nearly all voted the Democratic ticket and were good citizens," legislators, led by Ring Democrats, protected foreign and Italian voting rights over the voting rights of black southerners.[120] Regardless of opinions that problematized the racial position of Italians, Italians remained enfranchised, collapsing their race and color in the name of "home rule."

Notwithstanding the convention's conclusions, these disenfranchisement debates reveal that Italians in Louisiana were available pawns within local politicking. Reformers who contested the "Privileged Dago" Clause articulated their opposition in terms of rightful citizenship, loyalty, xenophobia, and racial questionability, all of which garnered publicly consumable support to eliminate the political machine and to defeat the Regulars. Those who favored the "Privileged Dago" Clause did so because of the professed political functionality of Italians; the efficacy of Italians compelled Regulars to protect the Italian voting bloc and their constituent base. Italians retained their right to vote in Louisiana not because of their racial acceptability or elevated status but because of their value in serving the (Regular) Democratic machine.

In the midst of these contestations over voting rights, Italians themselves made calculated choices. Rather than allying themselves in these debates alongside black Louisianans, Italians strategically attempted to align themselves on the side of the disenfranchisers, as native, white "southerners." Representing themselves as "white Redeemers" limited the effectiveness of their opponents' xenophobic attacks. Not only did this identity maneuvering divide the opposition and facilitate the steady disenfranchisement of black voters, but it also contributed to the progressive categorization of a statewide discourse more explicitly in terms of "black" and "white," rather than the more fluid racial structure that historically characterized Louisiana. Sicilians and other Italians organizing as "Italian voters" steadily worked to expand *Italianità* and erase regional differences transported from Italy. In this sense, Louisiana's disenfranchisement debates served as a moment of identity reconfiguration: Sicilians and other Italians as "Italians," Italians as "white southerners," the disenfranchiseable as "black," and the Regulars, including the Ring and the Choctaw Club, as the redeemers of "home rule" in Louisiana.

4

Segregating Italians, Sicilians, and Schools in Turn-of-the-Century Mississippi

Can it be possible that Mississippians hold that Italians, like the negro,
are of a different race from our own, or do they place different
nationality on the same plane with different race?

—*The Outlook,* 1907

We ain't got no desks for Dagoes!

—schoolgirl in Blocton, Alabama, 1929

A s the 1907 school year began in Sumrall, Mississippi, Joseph and Josephine Frier, two Italian children, applied for admission to the public
white school.[1] What followed was a complex back-and-forth school segregation story that predated *Brown v. Board of Education.* Interpreting the Friers' enrollment as "forcing" their way in, parents of the native-born white
students "objected to the presence" of the Italians and "demanded that
they be excluded."[2] The local community began to take measures to expel
the "suspect" children from the "white" school. When the Italian children
arrived on the first day of school, Principal Harbert suspended the Friers
"pending a decision" from the state superintendent of education.[3] To protest the expulsion, a group of Italian laborers led by Sicilian shoemaker
Frank Scaglioni appealed to the state authorities and to the Italian consulate in New Orleans.[4] When the state superintendent ruled in favor of the
Italian children's right to attend the "white" school, the Friers returned to
classes for the remainder of the week. Yet with tensions so heightened, the
"usually quiet place [of Sumrall] was . . . in the throes of a racial revolution
that [could] shake the entire State of Mississippi."[5]

In the darkness of Friday night, a mass of local "white citizens" kid-
napped Scaglioni from his home. Hurling insults as they bound him with
rope, they hauled him to the woods beyond the outskirts of town; there, the

mob viciously beat and whipped him. Left bleeding in the woods, "more dead than alive, [Scaglioni] later dragged himself home."[6] On Monday, the Italian schoolchildren did not return to classes, but instead packed their belongings with their families and fled Sumrall.

While vivid and violent, school segregation cases involving Sicilians and other Italians in the South were rare. The two most reported endeavors to exclude Sicilians and other Italians from white schools both took place in rural Mississippi: the Frier incident in Sumrall, Lamar County, in 1907, and an earlier incident in 1906 Shelby, Bolivar County.[7] The rarity of these episodes prompts several key questions. What motivated local communities' efforts to expel Italian children? What do these incidents, and accompanying violent hostility, reveal about the racial, religious, and economic location of Sicilians and other Italians in turn-of-the-century Mississippi? Furthermore, what do these moments (and lack of other similar incidents outside of Mississippi) reveal about the larger patterns and racial placement of Sicilians and other Italians in the Gulf South?

Beginning with an overview of the racial and political context, including public school policy, in Mississippi and the Gulf South, this chapter applies the Shelby and Sumrall events as case studies to highlight the paradoxical predicament that Sicilian and other Italian children found themselves in: they were allowed to attend native-born white schools elsewhere in the Gulf South, but they were, at times, violently segregated in Mississippi. The exclusionary efforts of rural school boards and communities in these unusual episodes demonstrate the racially mobile position of Italian racial identity. The shifting nature of Italian racialization meant that viewers could read and interpret the racial identity of Sicilians and other Italians at their own convenience; anti-Italian prejudice could be utilitarian. In the cases of Shelby and Sumrall, the native-born white community justified their efforts to exclude Italian children from local schools by accessing an existing anti-Italian script that defended separation in racial terms. More than just ethnic prejudice, native-born whites employed this racialized discourse to segregate, so that they might validate the near-lynching of Scaglioni, and ultimately remove what they perceived to be economically threatening Italians from their community. A symptom of larger issues, these twenty-five Italian schoolchildren in Sumrall became caught up in a bias and prejudice intended to pressure their parents into labor conformity.

The segregation efforts, and especially the conflict in Sumrall, expose the socioeconomic motivation behind anti-Italian prejudice and the existing class conflict within southern industry and agriculture. While (native-born white) employers in the Gulf South encouraged and advocated in favor of Sicilian and other Italian immigrant workers, poor, working-class whites remained more directly in conflict with this influx of cheap immigrant labor. Economic competition fueled the campaign against Sicilians and other Italian children and factored into the ensuing violence in Sumrall. These moments of crisis, like the 1898 disenfranchisement efforts in Louisiana and the campaign against Italian schoolchildren in 1906 and 1907 rural Mississippi, reveal the efforts of Sicilians and other Italians to prescribe their own identity and to position themselves as "white" within the racial landscape of the Jim Crow Gulf South.

Before 1870, there was no public education system in Mississippi. The state's 1868 Reconstruction-era constitutional convention defeated contradictory proposals: to institute a statewide integrated school system and to require that schools be segregated. Short on details, the convention ordered state legislators to develop a statewide education system.[8] By 1875, Democrats had reclaimed control over the state and imposed a new constitution that disenfranchised the state's African American population by imposing a literacy requirement for voting, along with complicating the guidelines for residency and voter registration.[9] Consequently, in 1878, legislators rewrote the state's education law in order to codify segregation into Mississippi's public school system: "The schools in each county shall be so arranged as to offer ample free school facilities to all educable youths in that county but white and colored children shall not be taught in the same school-house, but in separate school-houses."[10] The new law imposed geographic parameters requiring black and white schools to be established at least two and a half miles apart and additionally gave the county superintendent the sole power to certify teachers.[11] Revising their 1868 constitution into the version that still remains in place today, Mississippi legislators in 1890 crafted the new education law into the state's constitution and formalized a constitutional mandate for a segregated public education system: "Separate schools shall be maintained for children of the white and colored races."[12]

But how and where did Mississippians racially locate "inbetween" groups within a hegemonic system of segregation articulated in terms of black and white? For instance, about 1,200 Chinese immigrants had settled in the Mississippi Delta by 1870.[13] According to white Mississippians, these immigrants were neither white nor black; instead, white Mississippians considered the Chinese to possess a "roughly Negro" or "near-Negro" status.[14] Though not exactly a "third race," Chinese coolies challenged the dualism of the South, as Jim Crow laws made no provisions for the "partly colored" or the "almost white."[15] In 1924 Rosedale, Mississippi, for instance, the local white school excluded Martha Lum, a nine-year-old Chinese American, from attending.[16] While the Mississippi Circuit Court initially ruled in favor of Lum, the Mississippi Supreme Court reversed the decision, claiming that the Chinese were "not white . . . they must fall under the heading 'colored races.'"[17] Upon appeal, the US Supreme Court sustained the state's ruling in *Gong Lum v. Rice* (1927). Since Lum was a member of the "Mongolian or yellow race" and Mississippi's policy was intended to "preserve the white schools for members of the Caucasian race," Lum was "not entitled to attend the white public school."[18] The court did invite Lum to attend the local "colored" school—meaning that a student who was not "white" could be "colored" by default—and established the precedent that barring Chinese children from attending white schools did not violate the Fourteenth Amendment.[19] While convention placed the Delta Chinese within a "tri-part" racial structure—neither white nor necessarily "Negro"—because segregation did not make space for gradations, Jim Crow legislation relegated the Chinese in the South to the legal status of nonwhite.[20] Of course, the Chinese and Italians in Mississippi occupied distinct racial trajectories—southerners would ultimately categorize Chinese in the South as nonwhite, whereas groups like Italians eventually gained access to white identification. Still, since Jim Crow segregation was officially codified without in-between spaces within the binary caste system of segregation law, such racial ambiguity confused boundaries, redefined both whiteness and blackness, and ultimately meant that those constructed as nonwhite *could* be consigned to the status of "colored."

Partly responsible for overseeing Mississippi's implementation of a binary school segregation law was Governor Longino (1900–1904). Longino was of Italian descent and remains one of only two Italian Americans to

serve as governor of a southern state.[21] Longino, whose ancestors had emigrated from Northern Italy to Virginia in 1752, was born and raised in
Mississippi, where he attended public school, university, and law school.
An active Democrat of the Baptist faith, Longino was a native-born, white
Mississippian by both birthright and practice; while he possessed Italian
ancestry, he did not actually represent himself as Italian, nor did Mississippians see him as an ethnic figure.[22] In addition to these attributes, Longino
held relatively moderate political positions. Considering extralegal violence
as an obstruction to economic investment and progress in the state, Longino vowed to enhance existing state laws to prevent lynchings and went
on to propose legislation making the county in which a lynching took place
financially responsible for supporting the family of the victim.[23] Despite
his more progressive antilynching stance, Longino remained a product of
the southern racial order and displayed racial attitudes consistent with a
"white" native-born agenda. Holding a paternalistic view of public-school
funding, he reasoned that it was the duty of white Mississippians to provide a public education for a member of the "weaker race" that would "help
to make him a better man, a better citizen, and a better Christian."[24] Longino's gubernatorial successor, James Vardaman (1904–1908), felt differently; known as the "Great White Chief," he espoused a particular brand
of white supremacy. With the federal sanction of the 1899 Supreme Court
case *Cumming v. Richmond County Board of Education*, which gave states
control over determining the parameters of "separate but equal education,"
Vardaman continued the charge to defund black schools in Mississippi.[25]
Vardaman told the Mississippi legislature in 1906 that he wanted to stop
funding black schools because black education would result in "rapes and
murders, which precipitated the unpleasantries of hangings and burnings
. . . [and] ultimately undermined one of the primary reasons for preserving
racial segregation: to prevent social equality and miscegenation."[26]

In the political climate of turn-of-the-century Mississippi, Longino and
Vardaman represented the growing dissension between paternalistic mod-
eration and flagrant white supremacy. Vardaman's election in 1904 signaled a move away from tempered restraint and an intensification of the
class divisions between the elite patrician planters and the increasingly dis-
contented poor, laboring whites.[27] The Vardaman brand of populist white

supremacy represented the interests of the latter, which viewed the nationwide influx of immigrants and the exponential growth of the Catholic Church as job competition and as a threat to the American way of life. In response, they advocated "100 percent Americanism" and practiced violent vigilante justice.[28]

Patrician planters, many of whom had participated in the recruitment of Italian laborers to Mississippi, took a more tempered approach to white supremacy owing to their concerns about regional labor shortages.[29] Planters who critiqued Vardaman as a "vain demagogue . . . whose inability to reason was contagious" reflected sentiments that fueled the political divisions that would develop between pro-Klan and anti-Klan forces in Mississippi by the early 1920s.[30] As part of their patriotic (re)conceptualization, the Delta Klan identified "bootleggers, gamblers, and all other law-breakers" in their targeted efforts to reconfigure America as a "Christian" nation.[31] Opponents of the Klan did not contest white supremacy in principle, but cited the vigilantes' reactionary practices of fear, intimidation, secrecy, violence, and lawlessness as a threat to labor stability and the planter class's cultural and economic authority.[32] In addition to political discord, anti-Catholicism—concerned with questions of immorality, disloyalty, sexual impropriety, and liquor consumption—exploded onto the southern stage by 1910, manifesting itself in public opposition to the organized institutions of the Catholic Church and open hostility to Catholics, especially Catholic immigrants.[33] All of this served as a backdrop to the debates involving the place of Roman Catholic Italian immigrants in Mississippi and its schools.[34]

Amidst the state's growing animosity toward Catholics and increasingly binary legal structure, Sicilians and other Italians in Mississippi represented a population that defied easy categorization. In 1900, 845 Italian-born immigrants lived in Mississippi, a population that nearly tripled to 2,137 by 1910.[35] These increasing numbers still represented only a small minority across the state—Italians made up 10 percent of the foreign-born white population in 1900 and 22 percent in 1910.[36] And yet, Mississippi's school disputes both took place in counties with an uncharacteristically and disproportionately large number of Italians: Italians comprised 72 percent of foreign-born whites in Bolivar County and 46 percent in Lamar County.[37] Within Mississippi's racial landscape, where did "inbetween" Sicilians and other Italians reside? More specifically, with the implementation of a binary educational system, where did they attend school?

Generally, in the Gulf South, including elsewhere in Mississippi, Italian children went to public schools with "white" children without issue. Besides local, white schools, they attended privately funded industrial schools for immigrants, orphans' schools, or schools developed for the Italian children of a particular laboring community. Such schools may have accommodated an Italian majority, but were not restricted to Italian schoolchildren.[38] Most commonly, Italian children, especially those in Louisiana, attended schools under the patronage of the Catholic Church run by Italian or French-Catholic nuns.[39] The Orleans Parish School Board even warmly received a 1908 proposal from the city's League of Italian Societies to offer Italian language classes, the "language of Dante," for Italian children and "American citizens" in Orleans public schools.[40] In an exceptional 1908 moment, the *Daily Picayune* reported that two Italian children had enrolled in the "same school as Negroes" in Monroe, Louisiana. The black schoolteacher, Mary Cook, explained that the "children's parents had consented" and that "she did not know that she was doing anything wrong" by allowing the Italian children to attend school alongside black classmates.[41] Although the press unambiguously identified the Italian schoolchildren as "white," the public upheaval in Monroe was short-lived.[42] A schoolgirl in Blocton, Alabama, in 1929 reportedly shouted at an acquantaince, "We ain't got no desks for Dagoes!" which remains more revealing of social convention than of legal precedent or of a protracted effort to remove "dagoes" from the local, white schools.[43] Ultimately, southerners only engaged in two sustained efforts to remove Sicilians and other Italians from white schools, both in rural Mississippi: in 1907 in Lamar County, upon which this chapter began, and in 1906 in Bolivar County.

In the fall of 1906, just after the school year had begun, the parents of native-born, white children in Shelby, Mississippi—deep in the northwest Delta region of the state along the Arkansas border—submitted a complaint to the Bolivar County School Board: "Are Italian children entitled to admission to the white public schools?"[44] The request for removing Italian children from the white school and establishing separate schools for the

"Caucasian race" and the "Italian race" offered several rationales. First, there were enough Italian children in the community to warrant a separate school, and the "clannishness" of the Italian community would welcome the division. Next, Italian children were "not on the same footing as those of Anglo-Saxon birth, according to the laws of ethuology [sic] as well as public education." Along those same lines, the request stated that the children of "pauper" Italians were "not desirable companions" and were "unfit" to associate with Shelby's white children.[45] Furthermore, the Italians in the community "do not make good citizens but are almost without exception criminals" and "content to live in dives and hovels and find associates among the negroes of the lowest class."[46] Citing Italian impoverishment and their predisposition to criminal delinquency, the native-born white community located Italians outside the "Caucasian race" and in opposition to "Anglo-Saxon-ness."

Despite his sympathy for the native-born complainants, Bolivar County superintendent Thos Owens explained that there was no legal means by which to establish a separate school for the Italian children. Section 3995 of Mississippi's 1892 school code authorized "separate districts for . . . the white and colored races," but there was no provision to divide "the schools of the white race."[47] The law of separation, one Mississippi daily reported, "does not apply to race but to color."[48] Because of their "color"—even if they possessed physically darker skin—Italians were still legally "white." And, according to Owens, the law did not permit exclusions based on "race," and Italians could not be expelled for being Italian. No matter the protestations across the state and concerns that "mixing the races in schools means the mixing of the races in marriage which will bring forth a hybred [sic] of the sorriest type," the state school board upheld the superintendent's ruling: Italian children were entitled to attend Mississippi's white schools.[49] According to one suggestion, the best way to settle the school question moving forward was to restrict Italian immigration, which would reduce the number of Italian children and thus mitigate the need to provide them with formal schooling. While state law was clear, unresolved objections and an unsatisfactory response to the influx of Italian immigration meant that, as predicted, Italians were set to "become as troublesome to progress as cocoa grass is to the cultivation of the fertile bottom land plantations."[50]

* * *

Sumrall, Mississippi, in Lamar County, in the midst of the state's pine belt located two hundred miles south of Shelby and eighty miles north of Gulfport and Biloxi, developed as a timber and lumber town. After the J. J. Newman Lumber Company set up operations in neighboring Hattiesburg in 1894, it purchased Sumrall's mill and gin and opened a large sawmill.[51] Throughout the first quarter of the new century, timber and lumber quickly became the region's main industry and Newman the main employer for both native and migrant laborers. Incorporated in 1903 with a population of 525, Sumrall soon expanded to a bustling town of 3,000 as workers flocked to the area for employment at the mill. With the town's rapid expansion, the cultural landscape broadened as well; the first church in Sumrall, West Sumrall Baptist Church, opened its doors in 1904, soon followed by a second Baptist church, a Methodist church, and, very significantly, a Catholic church.[52] On the whole, Lamar County developed with a native-born white majority; less than one-third of the county was nonwhite and only about two hundred of the over 8,000 white inhabitants were foreign-born or had foreign-born parents.[53] A small but proportionately significant population, Italians made up nearly half of the white foreign-born residents. Within a town built with migrant labor and with a small Italian minority, considerable enough to warrant opening a Catholic church, Mississippi's unequivocal mandate that schools be racially segregated was bound to create incertitude.

In October of 1907, "a race question with unusual features" surfaced in Sumrall, and "it is feared that there will be serious consequences."[54] The "ugly manifestation of race prejudice" that had emerged, upon which this chapter began, involved ten Italian families—with twenty-five children of school age among them—employed at the Newman Lumber Company.[55] When the children of Charlie Frier, Joseph and Josephine, enrolled in Sumrall's local, white school, the town's native-born residents fumed in response to the Italian "insiste[nce on] attending the public white schools."[56]

Local commentary mirrored the prior year's deliberations regarding where Italian children should attend school in Shelby and employed a fervent anti-Italian rhetoric comparable with Governor Vardaman's antiblack claims that black education would lead to "rapes and murders." According to the *Hattiesburg Daily News*, the Italians working in the Sumrall sawmills were "lower than the negroes—that they tried to associate with the negroes and were snubbed. . . . The [Italian] children were not . . . fit to sit in school with the white children."[57] The native-born white community in Sumrall, recent migrants to the region themselves, defined themselves as the rightful "native" residents and identified the Italian families in question as visiting interlopers and outsiders. The press referred to the dispute between the white community and the Italians as "racial," which, resembling the case in Shelby, indicated that the Italians fell outside the category of whiteness. In response to the uproar, Principal Harbert removed the Italian schoolchildren from their classes, suspended them indefinitely, and dispatched them to their homes.

One can only imagine Charlie's bewilderment upon returning home from the sawmill to find Joseph and Josephine waiting for their father on their front stoop; how would they explain that they had been sent home from school, not for misbehaving but for being Italian? The town's Italian families swiftly mobilized. With the help of Sicilian community leader Frank Scaglioni, they conveyed their grievances regarding the removal of their children from the "white" school to the Italian consulate in New Orleans; the consul, in turn, brought their challenge to the Mississippi state superintendent of education. Italian parents were determined that their children attend the "white" school, and they were willing to fight for that right. In so doing, Italians endeavored to prescribe their own racial identity, rather than allowing the larger community to impose a "nonwhite" identity upon them. Reminiscent of the Italians who marched in protest of the 1898 disenfranchisement efforts in Louisiana, the Italian community in Sumrall positioned themselves as white and with the right to attend the white school.

The local and northern presses were pointedly aware of the transregional connection between Sumrall and national anti-immigration conversations. Referring to the contemporaneous attempted segregation of Japanese students in San Francisco public schools, the *Hattiesburg Daily News* explained that the "race issue" in Sumrall was similar to "the recent disturbance on the Pacific coast."[58] In an action precipitated by the April 1906 earthquake, the San Francisco Board of Education had issued an October order instructing all Chinese, Japanese, and Korean students to attend the city's "Oriental School."[59] The vast majority of Japanese parents refused. Interpreting the segregation order as a humiliating insult, they instead kept their children at home and engaged their local officials. The swift involvement of the Japanese consul in San Francisco, who argued the order was a violation of existing treaty rights between the United States and Japan, followed by a public protest by San Francisco's Japanese community, led to a diplomatic and judicial standoff. Ultimately, in order to resolve the impasse, federal forces intervened by negotiating the "Gentleman's Agreement": the Japanese government would agree not to issue passports to (unskilled) Japanese laborers who might immigrate to the United States, in return for the US State Department pressuring San Francisco to withdraw the segregation order.[60] When delegates rescinded the segregation policy in February of 1907, anti-Japanese riots erupted in San Francisco.[61] Explicitly reading the Sumrall confrontation as "identical" to the "case of the Japanese at San Francisco," local conversations in rural Mississippi anxiously predicted a similar (federal) reprisal. Meanwhile, the *Washington Post* pontificated that events in Mississippi would unfold differently from those in California: "We did not come out of the San Francisco misunderstanding with plumage unruffled . . . California had eaten something like a leek . . . In our opinion [Lamar County], Miss. is made of sterner stuff than that which represented San Francisco . . . last winter. If [Lamar County] will not go to school with an alien, she won't, and that is the end of it."[62]

Considering the "international" impact conceivably posed by the Sumrall segregation efforts, national papers from Detroit to Chicago to Washington, DC, to New York picked up the story.[63] Weighing in with its outsider's perspective, New York's *The Outlook* cautioned the Sumrall community: "By excluding the children of these immigrants from the limited social equality and privileges of the schools, Mississippians will not only retard the desired assimilation of a class of laborers they and the South in general need so badly, but they will also by that act contribute another cause for National embarrassment and international ill feeling."[64] *The Outlook* acknowledged the immigrant children as "alien," but warned that preventing them from accessing local public education would exacerbate their ability to assimilate. The report also noted that immigrant labor was desperately needed in the South and cautioned the citizens in Sumrall against inciting a diplomatic crisis on par with the postlynching indemnity crises. Critical of the segregation actions, the *Chicago Daily Tribune* attributed the "outcry" to Mississippi's white community made up of "ignorant and poverty stricken" families.[65]

Initially, the Lamar County episode transpired identically to the events in Bolivar County the previous year. State Superintendent Powers forwarded the issue to state attorney general R. V. Fletcher, who explained that while he "sympathized" with the parents and community, "the law was plain and there was no way to exclude [the Italian schoolchildren] from the benefits of public education."[66] According to the attorney general, the only legal solution was the establishment of a separate school for Italians, since there was no way to keep a "white child out of the white schools."[67] Fletcher personally regretted that the Italian children must be permitted to attend the same school with "white" children, but warned the local school trustees that if they denied Italian children the "privileges of attending white schools," they risked interference from the federal government and the Italian ambassador.[68] Disregarding the potential international implications, the *Hattiesburg Daily News* articulated the localized racial precept: "There is no objection to the decent Italian, nor to the foreigner from any other shore, but the line is drawn on the Dago."[69] Even if the Italian schoolchildren were technically white, they were still "dagoes." This discernment, occasioned by mapping a class status onto Italian families or differentiating between and hierarchically ordering Italians above Sicilians—merely a discursive means to justifiably exclude some—reminded the community that "dagoes" and Italians were not the same brand of immigrant. Notwithstanding the distinction, Fletcher did not suggest that the Italian students should attend the region's black school. Marking the Italians in Sumrall as racially "other" did not mean that native-born, white Mississippians regarded Italians as a third race, and, unlike the Chinese in Mississippi, Italians were not "other" enough to be dispatched into the "colored" or black community. Instead, following the attorney general's ruling, the Italian children returned to school, where they were given "instructions along with the white pupils" through the end of the school week.[70]

As night fell on Friday, the "racial revolution" feared by the local press manifested itself. Local Italian community leader Frank Scaglioni, who ran a small shoe shop in town, heard a sharp rap on his door; with the support of a crutch, the single amputee skillfully maneuvered to respond.[71] A message awaited alerting him of a communication from the Italian consul in New Orleans; not realizing the message was a decoy, Scaglioni stepped out onto his dimly lit porch. Almost immediately, a horde of thirty men descended from the darkness; surrounding the cobbler, they seized his arms from behind and threatened him with death as he struggled. Throwing a heavy rope around the Italian's neck, they dragged him for nearly a mile into the woods beyond the town limits. In a clearing, with thick log rope, clubs, and rods, Scaglioni's captors "unmercifully" whipped and beat him, "whacking him repeatedly on the stump of his amputated leg."[72] According to later explanations for the thrashing, Scaglioni had been "too active in his leadership" and had "perniciously . . . [tried] to force the children into the school"; the whipping was an admonishment to desist in his efforts.[73] Leaving his "half dead" body—bruised, cut, and bleeding—in the woods, one of the mob leaders warned Scaglioni that the "same punishment would be measured out to every other Italian who sent his child to the public school."[74]

The following Monday, the citizens of Sumrall "spoke in whispers" awaiting the arrival of the Italian children at school; the children never arrived.[75] Charlie Frier and his children, along with most other Italian families in Sumrall, were hastily packing their belongings and preparing to leave town.[76] Upon the urgent request of the Italian laborers, the Newman Lumber Company reassigned all but two of the Italian families to nearby Hattiesburg.[77] Meanwhile, local, white native-born citizens, fearful of a violent retribution for the attack on Scaglioni, implored the sheriff to investigate and to "swear in a posse to preserve the peace."[78] In a clear revelation of allegiances, the Newman Lumber Company offered to deputize a hundred men to protect the local "native" community from Italians attempting to "wreak their vengeance."[79] As was the case in Shelby, press reports warned that relocating the Italian families to Hattiesburg could have international ramifications, on par with the postlynching indemnity crises.[80] But even with the possibility of diplomatic retribution and "international questions," the mill facilitated the transfer of Frier and the majority of the Italian families out of Sumrall.

With immediate tensions dissipating, subsequent reports revealed that Scaglioni's "unspeakably brutal treatment" was "even more outrageous" than originally reported.[81] According to the investigation undertaken by Count Gerolamo Moroni of the Italian consulate in New Orleans, not only was Scaglioni whipped, but "other outrages were perpetrated upon him as well."[82] So ruthless was the treatment of the shoemaker that multiple newspapers invoked turn-of-the-century anti-indigenous rhetoric, characterizing the ferocity as "savage" and "somewhat of the nature of Indian brutality."[83] Other reports, even in the historical era of yellow journalism and salacious reporting, remarked that Scaglioni's flogging had been so vicious they could not print the exact details.[84] As the *Times Democrat* explained, the violence was beyond "barbaraoies [*sic*]" and "no appeal to race prejudice can justify the atrocity committed at Sumrall."[85]

While disavowing Scaglioni's vicious attack, contemporary interpretations soon divulged that the motive for the violence was not in fact a "serious scholastic question."[86] Scaglioni's whipping may have been triggered by the school issue, but the exceptional cruelty arose from a question of labor: "It now develops that the whipping was not the result of an attempt to place Italian children in the public schools at all, but . . . fear that the Italians employed in Sumrall would accept the ten per cent cut in wages."[87] Provoked by the concern that Italians would consent to a wage reduction, "which other white laborers would not accept," and in an effort to "drive both the Italian and the negro laborers from the sawmill field," "malcontents" among Sumrall's unskilled white laborers unleashed an unrestrained response.[88] Count Moroni's investigation as well as multiple news sources made the same assertion: the fierce reprisal was incited, not by the school incident, but by a labor conflict.[89]

The readjusted wage scale of the sawmills of southern Mississippi had, in fact, led to a temporary depression in the state's yellow pine lumber industry.[90] As moments of economic depression often bore witness to increases in labor rioting and violent labor conflicts, the economic depression of 1907 was no exception. Other incidents in the region, like the events that transpired in December of that same year in the neighboring lumber town of Chathamville, Louisiana, reinforced the notion that native-born white workers resented nonwhite laborers.[91] Local residents, who "resented" the fact that the Tremont Lumber Company had imported Italian workers, organized in opposition; arming themselves, they fired upon the "newcomers."[92] At least two Italians were killed in the "lumber riot."[93] Whether or not the lumber company had introduced the Italian workers as strikebreakers, "native" laborers felt threatened and displaced.[94] The anti-Italian attack at Chathamville exposed labor unrest as an inciting factor for nativist violence, a pattern that was repeated in the case of Sumrall.

Chathamville, Shelby, and Sumrall unmask the contradictory factions that interpreted Italians differently—planters and industrialists in favor of recruiting a cheap, foreign workforce, and white, southern (unskilled) laborers hostile to immigrant competition.[95] Employers seeking cheap labor defended the presence of Italians and their racial status as "white" laborers. Unskilled, native-born white laborers—competing with Italians for jobs and wages—validated the Sumrall segregation efforts and Scaglioni's beating, and questioned Italians' whiteness and their very presence in the region.[96] Sumrall reveals how violently a community of white, unskilled laborers could respond—violence on par in motive and practice with the lynchings of Italians—when their job security felt diminished or threatened. If economics motivated Scaglioni's vicious whipping, the Sumrall mob rationalized their violent reprisal for the wage dispute in explicitly racial terms.

Responding to the crisis, the Newman Lumber Company transferred fifteen "negro laborers" to Sumrall to replace the Italian workers.[97] Up to this point, industrialists could interpret immigrant Italian laborers as "white"; now the pendulum would begin to swing in reverse. The class conflict and unrest made clear the failed immigrant experiment and showed that black workers represented a more controllable form of labor (to both the employers and white laborers). Italians could be dispatched, on racial terms, in order to assuage the unrest among the mill's native-born, white Mississippian labor force.

Meanwhile, press accounts feature a clear disconnect between the on-the-ground mob actions and the motivation and assessment of their violence. Local papers offered contrasting estimations of the mob: the *Columbus Dispatch* commended the party responsible for the violence as "a few cool heads," while the *Daily States* more critically hypothesized, based on the "character of the outrages," that "the mob was composed of people of the lower class."[98] Yet, even as the violence mirrored that of the lynchings of Italians of the 1890s, most press reports now repudiated the violence. More similar to accounts of the 1901 lynching in Erwin, Mississippi, which described the lynch mob as murderers, 1907 press rhetoric claimed the violence against Scaglioni as other and foreign and on par with "Indian brutality." Press reports that attributed the conflict to a "race question" and an "ugly manifestation of race prejudice" placed the events in Sumrall squarely within the narrative of racialized lynching violence.[99]

After all, planters had recruited and encouraged Italians to settle in Mississippi when labor was scarce; the Italian still offered the best solution to meet the South's great demand for labor, since he was "best fitted to the conditions of soil and climate" and was "industrious, acquisitive, ready to learn, and quick to adopt higher standards of living and culture as soon as he is financially able to avail himself of them."[100] Weighing in on the Sumrall case, Colonel F. L. Maxwell of North Louisiana explained that he was "entirely satisfied with Italian labor," as his Italian laborer "gives him 33.3% better satisfaction than any other kind."[101] As the *Times* argued, the attacks against the Italians in Sumrall were entirely unjustified since Italians had not been brought in as strikebreakers "nor to hammer down the price of wages."[102] In contrast to suppositions of Italian criminality, the *Times* maintained that the Italians in Sumrall had "aroused no race feeling by the commission of any crimes, for it is conceded that they have conducted themselves as peaceable and law-abiding citizens." Departing from the anti-Italian rhetoric that the *Times* itself had propagated throughout the 1890s and despite having justified mob action in 1891 New Orleans, the *Times* in 1907 criticized anti-Italian mob rule: "It is clearly the duty of the Mississippi authorities to run down the monsters who partitipated [*sic*] in the outrage and to punish them with the severity which their crime demands." Admonishing the actions undertaken by the "cowardly . . . monsters" who had unjustifiably persecuted the Italian laborers and run them out of town, the *Times* now deemed the Italian laborers the wronged party in need of protection from the mob's "lawless intimidation and barbarity."[103] At least according to southern planters, employers, and patrician elites, what marked Italians as "best fitted" was their cultural and racial proximity to whiteness. Portending their racial transiency and their ultimate arc toward whiteness, Italians could be defensibly segregated as "dagoes" but were deemed racially "white" enough to solve the South's labor crisis.

In the months following the Sumrall episode, Governor Vardaman, under pressure from the Italian government, ordered an official investigation.[104] Vardaman concluded that the alleged "outrages" against Italians were "groundless."[105] Vardaman, who had made anti-Italian sentiment one of his chief campaign platforms in his gubernatorial run and had even gone on record asserting that "Italian children are undesirable aliens," dismissed any anti-Italian allegations as "absolutely unfounded and ridiculous."[106] The mayor of Sumrall concurred with Vardaman as he explained that the "so-called outrage" was more of a "tempest in a teapot."[107]

Yet new allegations soon surfaced that not only had Sumrall excluded Italian children from its public school, but the state of Mississippi had barred Italians from entering the state entirely. Affidavits collected by state agents as part of the official investigation concluded that the Italian children were of "cleanly habits, free from disease," and had attended public schools in New Orleans; they were native-born citizens and "therefore free to travel as they will within the limits of the United States."[108] Governor Vardaman denied any personal knowledge or wrongdoing related to the claim that Italian children had been excluded from the state: "It is the first that I have heard of anything of the kind, and it seems so absolutely unfounded and ridiculous that it seems unnecessary to make any statement. . . . I am inclined to believe that there must be some mistake somewhere, unless some local official has exceeded his authority, or else has some valid reason for action."[109] Even while Vardaman dismissed the veracity of the charges, he steadfastly upheld the right of state officials to theoretically refuse entry to "undesirable immigrants."[110] Undeniably hostile, Vardaman concluded that "Normal, healthy Italian children, altho [sic] citizens of the United States and residents of New Orleans, are 'undesirable aliens' so far as the state of Mississippi is concerned."[111] Vardaman's declarations, while not indicative of public opinion in Mississippi at large, advanced a calculated pitch of his populist white supremacy to poor, native-born white workers. Contemporary opponents noted that it was impossible to determine whether Vardaman's "reactionary racial doctrine" was a form of "idealism" or simply "demagoguery."[112] Representative of the historical moment, Vardaman fell in line with other Populist politicians of the era who invoked a racialized doctrine in order to rally his working-class white constituents. Even while patrician planters read Italians as a benign, "white" labor force, Vardaman's fear-mongering—directed at the more extreme xenophobic factions in rural Mississippi—worked to usher in a new wave of white supremacy that challenged Italian access to whiteness.

Following the pattern of lynching violence, local law enforcement never arrested or held accountable the members of the violent mob who attacked

Scaglioni. All but two Italian families in Sumrall relocated to nearby Hattiesburg.[113] In response to the Sumrall "commotion" and the sudden influx of Italian families, the school board trustees of Hattiesburg ordered the establishment of a "separate school for the children of all 'dagoes,' Italians, Assyrians and Russian Jews."[114] Evidence of the transiency of the Italians (and contrasting their experience with the Delta Chinese), the trustees did not suggest that Italians should attend Hattiesburg's black school alongside black classmates. Rather, distinguishing "dagoes" as a distinct group from "Italians" and revealing their class-based nativism, the Hattiesburg school board moved to separate Italians from native-born whites.

In response, local newspapers commented on the hypocrisy of the policymakers' antipathy. The *Columbus Dispatch* observed that Hattiesburg's school trustees must be motivated by a "dislike of all foreign blood" since "Italian and Greek bloods are equally as pure white as that of those who people many other European countries." The *Dispatch* pointed out that "many of the citizens in Mississippi are only one or two generations removed from the newly arriving immigrants."[115] Likewise, the *Meridian Star* questioned the logic of xenophobic bigotry, considering the "impoverished pure white blood" of some of the natives of the South:

> Would the Hattiesburg school trustees hold that the children of these men are not fit by birth and breeding to enter the public schools of that place on an equality with native sons and daughters? . . . There are many thousands of useful, educated and cultured men and women citizens of this country who are not more than a generation removed from the peasantry of Italy or Greece, a peasantry which for centuries has peacefully submitted to the oppressive head of a system of government that has dwarfed and starved their intellectual and physical development. That these people have been able to produce children which under the American school system have demonstrated their fitness for every high calling in life comes from the germ of the unconquerable white blood that centuries of misrule have not destroyed.[116]

While commenting on the "stunted intellectual and moral vigor" of native southerners, the *Star* observed that many immigrants, even Italian or Greek peasants, are "useful, educated and cultured." Additionally noting the environmental causes that led to the racial "backwardness" of the Italian peasantry, the *Star* explained that oppressive governments, not biological factors, stunted immigrant development. By declaring that Italians possessed "unconquerable white blood," which reaffirmed their "whiteness," the Mississippi press challenged the trustees' rationale for establishing a separate and third school for Italian schoolchildren.

As in Shelby and Sumrall, Hattiesburg trustees did inquire with the state attorney general about whether or not they could legally deny Italian children the "privileges of attending white schools."[117] Mr. Fletcher advised against the move, unless they wanted to encourage the interference of the federal government and Italian ambassador in local affairs. In response to Fletcher's warning, the trustees did not ultimately move forward with their efforts. Given the school board's reversal—and lacking evidence to suggest that Italians ever attended the city's black school—the Italian schoolchildren chased out of Sumrall presumably went on to attend the local white school in Hattiesburg.

Sumrall, Shelby, and Hattiesburg marked turning points in the Gulf South's reception of immigrants. While southern states had previously promoted the arrival of immigrants and their labor, heightened class tensions compelled employers to dispense with Italians in order to appease the white, native-born Mississippian labor force. Responding to what they now read as the "harmful effect" of "promot[ing] Italian immigration as a substitute for negro farm labor," rural Mississippians endeavored to establish separate schools for Italian schoolchildren.[118] Racializing the failed experiment of immigrant labor—using racial and xenophobic discourse to make a class-based argument—explained immigrants who had turned into economic competition through the justifiable lens of racial difference. In the context of a long-standing tension between planters and industrialists demanding cheap labor and native-born white laborers competing for jobs, Sumrall signaled a rise in nativism even among those who had previously recruited and encouraged immigration. The very act of the Newman Lumber Company's transferring its Italian employees from Sumrall to Hattiesburg showed that certain employers in the South were becoming increasingly hostile to their immigrant labor or at least responding to pressure from their native-born white workers.

"Whiteness" meant something different depending on the particular class lens through which it was viewed. The class-based racial hierarchy that operated in rural Mississippi communities meant that patrician elites, in the name of retaining a cheap labor force, were willing to look past Italian suspectability and consider Italian laborers as members of a "white" labor force. Alternatively, "lower-class" Vardaman-like advocates of white supremacy employed race-based nativism to challenge Italian access to whiteness and to defend and explain their fear of Italians as economic competition.[119] In both rural Bolivar County and Lamar County, local native-born, white community members attempted to exclude Italian children from local schools on the racial premise that Italian schoolchildren were not "white" enough. While the segregation endeavor was perhaps a covert means of forcing the removal of Italian families, the distinctive violence that erupted in Sumrall demonstrated the brutalizing effect of race compounded by class. This contributes to revising the narrative of the South as a transnational space (rather than a provincial space of isolationism), as Sumrall forces a reconsideration of the intersectional and relational nature of this kind of racial formation.

Present here in Sumrall, Mississippi, in 1907 is evidence of both the fungibility of race and the self-interest of prejudicial discourse. To some, Italian laborerers in Mississippi were undeniably "pure white," whereas others continued to read them as racially problematic. Such racial transiency enabled an existing and expanding nativism to justify efforts to exclude twenty-five Italian children from the local white school, even as a Sicilian community leader attempted to position Italian families within the white mainstream and as others reaffirmed Italian whiteness and attested to their "pure blood." Ultimately, this friction, magnified by class conflict and an increasingly threatened native-born white working class, exploded in the ruthless beating and whipping of Scaglioni. Such an explosive response signals the underlying socioeconomic fears that could be masked by nativist xenophobia. Italians may have been "white," but in their position as labor and wage competitors in rural Mississippi, they were expendable.

5

Legislating Miscegenation, Marriages, Whiteness, and Italians in Louisiana and Alabama

> The evil tendency of the crime of living in adultery or fornication is greater
> when it is committed between persons of the two races, than between persons of
> the same race. Its result may be the amalgamation of the two races, producing a
> mongrel population and a degraded civilization.
>
> —*Pace & Cox v. the State*, Supreme Court of Alabama, 1881

Italian-born Pietro Albanese and Mary Bossier, a black woman, secured a license to marry in Orleans Parish in 1890.[1] Six years later in New Orleans, an Italian fruit peddler named Paul Rogudo would be taken into custody and charged with miscegenation owing to his "interracial" relationship with a "negro girl" named Agnes Thompson.[2] Based on this precedent, in 1921, Jim Rollins, a black man, was accused and convicted of violating Alabama's miscegenation statute since he and Edith Labue, "a white person . . . did intermarry or live in adultery or fornication with each other, against the peace and dignity of the State of Alabama."[3] The following year, however, Rollins's conviction was overturned on appeal, because, according to the judge, there was "no material evidence" to prove that Labue, an Italian, was in fact a "white woman."[4]

What does the inconsistent application of miscegenation laws as they pertained to Italians in Louisiana and Alabama reveal about the transient racial assessment of Sicilians and other Italians? To what extent and where were Sicilians and other Italians "white," making their marriages to African Americans illegal and prohibited? If marriages between Italians and African Americans were permissible, what did this mean for the racial placement of Italians in the Gulf South? Considering questions of whether Italian legal whiteness necessarily translated into "marriage whiteness," the above episodes already reveal that certain intimate unions were permitted and others criminalized. As marriage licensing bureaucrats, law enforcement officers, and southern courtrooms offered Sicilians and other Italians varying access to "marriage whiteness," a process further complicated by the variable operations of gender and class, Italians under Jim Crow miscegenation statutes defied easy racial categorization.

This chapter explores the extent and regularity of Italians' intermarriages with both African Americans and native-born whites in Louisiana and Alabama. This inquiry advances with a particular focus on Alabama and Louisiana since, by the turn of the century, both states bore significant populations of Italian immigrants. Sicilians and other Italians, about one-third of whom came specifically from Bisacquino, Sicily, flocked to Birmingham to pursue wage work in the industrial factories and iron and steel industries.[5] By 1910, more than one-quarter of the foreign-born white population in both Birmingham and New Orleans was Italian.[6] Additionally, both states remained particular legislative and judicial battlegrounds for miscegenation cases.[7]

This chapter draws on a legislative history of miscegenation cases in the Gulf South, a review of public press accounts of miscegenation cases involving Italians in Louisiana and Alabama, and a genealogical investigation of late nineteenth-century and early twentieth-century Orleans Parish marriage records.[8] Regardless of existing legal mandates, Italians and African Americans did engage in intimate relationships and were in fact permitted marriage licenses. Concurrently, while state officials granted some of these interracial relationships legal and bureaucratic sanction, in other instances, law enforcement found such liaisons in violation of the state's miscegenation statute. Legislative and criminal case histories suggest that interracial relationships between Italians and persons of color remained generally consistent with postbellum gender patterns—the involvement of a man of color, rather than an Italian man, was more likely to render an interracial relationship visible; additionally, law enforcement officers were more likely to charge (or charge more severely) a man of color, rather than a woman of color, an Italian man, or an Italian woman.[9] Marriage documents show that through the regulation of boundaries and the bureaucratizing of movement, miscegenation laws operated as a means of both exclusion and inclusion. Such marginalization and incorporation rendered Sicilians and other

Italians in the Gulf South as racially transient and restricted to a liminal racial status, even as marriage assessments progressively included Italians within the category of "white."

This liminal racial status was nowhere more apparent than in the 1922 State of Alabama case *Rollins v. State*. This chapter concludes with an extended discussion of Jim Rollins's successful appeal of his 1921 miscegenation conviction for his alleged relationship with an Italian woman, Edith Labue. In contrast to dominant readings that Jim Rollins's acquittal implied that Labue's "whiteness" was inconclusive, the *Rollins* litigation does not provide tangible evidence to challenge or dispute Italian "whiteness." Instead, this case actually serves to reaffirm Italian "whiteness," while also providing insight into the hierarchically different racial assessments of Italians as contrasted with Sicilians. The *Rollins* suit offers insight into broader patterns regarding miscegenation statutes, namely that these laws were intended to regulate against visible and long-standing interracial relationships; more importantly, however, the *Rollins* case exposes the operations of unofficial citizenship that were in line with other miscegenation cases in the 1920s Gulf South.

The complicated language I interrogate in this chapter requires certain discursive choices. While these marriage bans were technically "antimiscegenation" laws, I use the common nomenclature "miscegenation"—meaning the mixing or amalgamation of (racial) blood—to identify laws that prohibited exogamous relationships.[10] Noting throughout this discussion the ambiguous designation of Italians within these considerations even while problematizing the unequivocal categorizing of Italians as "white," I employ "interracial" or "mixed-race" to refer to relationships that miscegenation laws attempted to legislate against: those marriages and relationships between "whites" and "nonwhites" (including blacks, Latinos, Asians, and indigenous persons).[11] Despite this more expansive categorical definition, miscegenation laws in the Gulf South—especially within the era of the "one drop rule" whereby any traceable black ancestry marked someone as black—specifically legislated against blurring the black/white color line. As a category of law, miscegenation and marriage bans regulated an "intimacy color line" not a "sexual color line."[12] Less about controlling interracial sex, mixed-race procreation, or racial amalgamation, edicts on miscegenation policed intimacy, monitored long-term and public relationships, and ultimately regulated the social and political hierarchies of the Reconstruction and post-Reconstruction Gulf South. Miscegenation decrees, in addition to reflecting both a social reality and a utopian ideal, operated as a "legal factory" for manufacturing racial categories.[13] Marriage laws were a critical factor in the state-making project of defining certain populations as residing outside official citizenship. More than simply reflecting social attitudes, these processes of naming and classifying contributed to a system of bureaucratic decision making that informed and produced social categories and attitudes.[14] Whether as a means of regulating the intimacy color line or as a means of governance and social control, marriage laws promoted the larger project of white supremacy by delegitimizing racial mixing.[15]

After the United States' acquisition of Louisiana, the Civil Digest of 1808 explained that "free persons and slaves" and "free white persons and free people of color" were "incapable of contracting marriage together."[16] The Louisiana legislature revised its civil code in 1825 to outlaw the legitimization of biracial children by white fathers.[17] Still, like their colonial antecedents, much of the antebellum legislation against interracial marriages existed more in name than in practice.[18] While the concept of legislating against interracial marriages was not a nineteenth-century phenomenon, the vocabulary was in fact a new invention, as the term "miscegenation" was the product of an 1863 anti-Lincoln campaign pamphlet.[19] Despite the fact that southerners largely tolerated relationships across the color line in the antebellum period, naming a concern over racial mixing in the midst of the Civil War spoke to a growing anxiety over the "natural" order of society.

Within the transformed post–Civil War landscape, southern tolerance for interracial relationships steadily dissipated, and efforts to legislate against racial mixing—and to protect what was "natural"—increased.[20] For example, Alabama legislators passed an initial interracial marriage ban in 1852, a lenient statute that only made it a misdemeanor to officiate an interracial marriage.[21] By 1866, Alabama's Penal Code drastically revised its early tolerance and charged "any white person and any negro" who did "intermarry, or live in adultery or fornication with each other" with a felony conviction bearing two to seven years of hard labor; the prohibition against *living* in "adultery or fornication" policed a long-term commitment to interracial sex.[22] Other southern states followed suit and implemented more severe marriage bans in the aftermath of the Civil War than those previously passed in the antebellum era. However, under military oversight of the civil rights legislation passed during radical Reconstruction, southern states removed such prohibitions: Louisiana repealed its ban in 1868 and Alabama courts declared their prohibition unconstitutional in 1869.[23] Not simply the result of federal enforcement of civil rights legislation, the temporary legalization of interracial marriage across the South was based in part on an effort to protect "white male privilege" and the perception that interracial marriage bans infringed on white male access to black female bodies.[24]

However, this loosening of laws regarding cross-racial mingling was short-lived. During the post-Reconstruction era, exogamous marriages resurfaced as a site to monitor and legislate the social order. Five of the former Confederate states that had repealed their marriage bans during Reconstruction (Louisiana, Mississippi, South Carolina, Arkansas, and Florida), reinstated them between 1879 and 1894.[25] Alabama went even further by including an interracial marriage ban in their amended constitution; the 1901 revision banned the legislature from *ever* passing "any law to authorize or legalize any marriage between any white person and a negro, or descendant of a negro."[26] Not only was this part of the legislative program of white supremacy, but antimiscegenation discourse operated as a form of rhetorical terror that constructed black Americans, especially black men, as socially, sexually, and politically dangerous. Such discourse conflated political power with interracial sex, which meant that miscegenation laws were a means of protesting against black freedmen as "legitimate patriarchs."[27] Even black legislators participated in the recodification of marriage bans in the post-Reconstruction era, but as a means of protest against the history of sexual violence that black women had suffered at the hands of white men and a way to protect and claim black women from white men.[28] Accordingly, miscegenation regulations were not exactly rooted in a fear of "physical amalgamation" or mixing of blood but were embedded in a contest over citizenship claims and the rights of manhood.

With the end of the Civil War, and as early as the 1870s, miscegenation laws had already begun to make a steady resurgence throughout the South owing to constitutional validation by a series of local and federal court rulings.[29] In *Pace & Cox v. the State* (Alabama, 1881), Tony Pace, a black man, appealed his miscegenation conviction on the grounds that his punishment violated the Fourteenth Amendment since he was sentenced to a longer term than those convicted of same-race adultery. The Appeals Court upheld his conviction and further affirmed that the state's interracial marriage ban did not in fact violate the equal protection clause of the Fourteenth Amendment. Since interracial sex was a specific and "greater" crime than same-race sex because it "produc[ed] a mongrel population and a degraded civilization," the court concluded that it warranted a more extreme punishment.[30] Additionally, because states allegedly punished both "offending part[ies], white and black," in the same way, the court legitimized prohibitions against interracial marriage and validated longer sentences when "defendants were of different races." The US Supreme Court went on to reaffirm the constitutionality of the *Pace v. State* ruling in 1883.[31]

While such legislative rulings served to construct miscegenation as something which was legally definable and knowable, understandings of and abilities to define race remained vague. Considering race to be "knowable," courtrooms in the nineteenth century identified race by using a combination of legal, visible, and performative markers. Did, for instance, an individual behave like a "white person," meaning, did he vote, did he attend white churches and white schools?[32] Even with the growing understanding of ancestry and the increasing popularity of racial science and eugenics, southern courtrooms still relied heavily on appearance, performance, association, and "common sense" to determine race.[33] Thus, race could be prescribed based on community wisdom, or by what the neighbors said, either literally or by the racial makeup of one's neighborhood and associations. Such a reliance on community testimony, rumor, and reputation constructed race locally and regionally and carried legal ramifications. As (white) juries retained the prerogative for evaluating an individual's appearance, the reading of bodies persisted at the center of miscegenation cases in the courtroom.

In 1894, Louisiana legislators prohibited "marriage between white persons and persons of color."[34] Realizing they had not gone far enough, they went on to specify in 1908 that "concubinage [defined as those living together or found in cohabitation] between a person of the Caucasian or white race and a person of the negro or black race is hereby made a felony."[35] Still, Louisiana law did not account for those who were neither "white" nor clearly definable as "negro" or "black." The question of how to categorize those who did not fit into the prescribed legal categories of "white" or "black" remained at the forefront of the landmark decision in *State v. Treadaway*. In 1910, the Parish of Orleans indicted Octave Treadaway for cohabitating with a white woman and violating Louisiana's miscegenation statute. Treadaway's defense argued that, since he was an "octoroon" and not in fact a "person of the Negro or black race," he had not actually violated the aforementioned 1908 concubinage edict; with this argument, Treadaway was acquitted.[36] However, the state appealed the ruling by arguing, "An octoroon was a person of the Negro or black race within the meaning of the statute."[37] As part of this inquiry, the Supreme Court of Louisiana undertook a painstaking evaluation of whether or not an "octoroon" was in fact a "Negro" and whether a "popular" understanding of race was legally and conclusively admissible. The *Treadaway* court ultimately found that "negro" and "colored" were never in fact used interchangeably, and because "negro" and "colored" were not synonyms, they upheld Treadaway's exoneration. As a result, Louisiana revised its miscegenation statute later that year to read: "Concubinage between a person of the Caucasian or white race and a person of the colored or black race is hereby made a felony."[38]

Notwithstanding these landmark decisions, miscegenation cases rarely found their way into the courtroom.[39] Even though Alabama's appellate court and Louisiana's Supreme Court reviewed more miscegenation cases than any other southern courts, these correspond to a numerically small number of cases.[40] The sparsity in the court records reveals the difficulty in proving miscegenation in court, since children were generally the only proof that a crime had been committed. Furthermore, policing interracial marriages relied on a public objection; so long as a relationship remained inconspicuous, interracial adultery, fornication, and illicit sex conducted in private customarily went unpunished. Miscegenation statutes served as a deterrent against the visibility and public legitimating of interracial relationships. By the twentieth century, certain attitudes about race had become so ingrained and so obvious that the enforcement of legal statutes shifted from legislators and judiciaries to bureaucratic marriage-licensing agents.[41] As marriage licensing became the most direct legal means for regulating race, individuals and bureaucrats acquired the prerogative for naming race and disallowing certain couples the right to marry. These individualized decisions denaturalized mixed-race unions and denied priv-ileges of citizenship even without a specific legislative mandate. The very act of prescribing or denying citizenship, legally but without an official directive, worked to produce race and inscribe modes of racial classifica-tions into the law.

What did any of this mean for the Italian immigrants of Alabama and Louisiana, and where did Italians fit into these legal precedents and stat-utes? According to racial taxonomies of the time, Italians were legally white, technically and anthropologically Caucasian, meaning they possessed rel-atively undisputed access to naturalization and citizenship rights. But as members of the Mediterranean subcategory, did Italians' legal whiteness necessarily translate into "marriage whiteness"? According to the *Tread-away* decision, the term "colored" designated "a person of mixed negro and other blood . . . a negro is necessarily a person of color; but not that a person of color is necessarily a negro. There are no negroes who are not persons of color; but there are persons of color who are not negroes."[42] By this logic, an Italian might not possess "negro blood" but could have been defined as a person of color. It was through bureaucratic acts of scrutiniz-ing bodies and naming physical markers that these determinations were made. Both state-sponsored and non-state-affiliated actors governed who would be a legally acceptable marriage partner for an Italian or Sicilian, and thus participated in categorizing Italians' race and constructing their citizenship. In so doing, Gulf South courts and marriage licensing agents rendered those, like Italians, who were "subpar" Caucasians—not "negro" but possibly "colored"—into a liminal racial space. Italians may have been formally white or have been able to access formal citizenship, but their rights of informal citizenship and their whiteness when it came to marriage partners were debated, occasionally denied, and more often than not, un-evenly assessed and applied.

A genealogical analysis of vital records of US census data uncovers those instances wherein marriage licensing agents and census enumera-tors granted legal sanction to Italian and African American couples. Op-erationally, bureaucratic marriage licensing clerks served as racial gate-keepers; through the act of evaluating bodies and making unofficial racial assessments, marriage licensing agents denied certain couples a license to marry while they conferred validity and official sanction upon others.[43]

Similarly relevant remain the racial determinations made by census enumerators, who, until 1960, recorded race not by how a person characterized
herself but instead based on a racial judgment by the census enumerator.[44]
Like marriage licensing bureaucrats, census enumerators made their racial determinations, not as a direct measure of ancestry, but based on assessments of appearance and physicality.[45] Tracing and scrutinizing census
data, vital and marriage license records, and draft and voter registrations
uncovers those cases where Italians intermarried or engaged in intimate
relationships with black southerners, thus affecting their own racial classifications and the racial identification of their offspring.

Joseph Giuseppe Lavizzo, born in 1820 in Milan, Italy, offers an example of an intimate relationship (although perhaps not an official marriage)
between an Italian and a person of color. Lavizzo immigrated to the United
States sometime before the Civil War and fought on behalf of the Con-
federacy as part of the Sixth Regiment European Brigade. As a member
of the Louisiana Militia (Italian Guards Battalion), he earned the rank of
captain, after which point he and his wife Catharine had a "White" daughter named Lucy Lavizzo in 1865 in Louisiana.[46] Yet, two years previously
in 1863, Joseph also had had another child named Joseph Lavizzo with a
woman named Elizabeth Hawkins. Census records variously categorized
Joseph Lavizzo II as "Mulatto" or "Black" and recorded his children as "Mulatto," "Colored," or "Black," even though they were descendants of the
Italian-born, "White" Joseph Lavizzo. While this may appear simply reminiscent of certain relationships between white slave owners and their slave
mistresses, this family tree confirms that Italian men and women of color
did engage in intimate and publicly visible relationships in nineteenth-century New Orleans. Furthermore, that Lavizzo recognized and legitimized
his mixed-race son by passing on his first and last name demonstrates that
such interracial liaisons were not necessarily socially taboo.

By 1870, 1,890 foreign-born Italians lived in Louisiana; at least five were
"Colored": Sary Domingo, a twenty-year-old Italian-born laborer; Francis
Snaer, a sixty-four-year-old naturalized citizen born on the Tuscan island
of Monte Cristo; and forty-year-old Italian-born "keep[er] of house" Celeste Escarpe and her two adolescent children Fortune and Edmond.[47]
Sary Domingo, classified as "Mulatto," lived with his Italian-born, naturalized "White" father Salvador, Salvador's common-law wife Mary Dupera,

a "Black" Louisiana-born native, and Mary's "Mulatto" children Victoria, Alfonse, Alice, and Abertine. Not only did Sary's categorization conflict with his Italian-born father's, but Sary's father maintained an intimate (and publicly acknowledged) interracial relationship with Mary. Francis Snaer, owing to his last name and contested history of his birthplace on Monte Cristo, may not have been ethnically Italian, but he still possessed an ascribed nationality as Italian. He and his wife Anna, both categorized as "White" in 1860, gave birth to as many as ten children, all categorized as "Mulatto" by 1870 and 1880. At least two of their children, Louis and Victoria, were listed as "Colored" on their birth certificates but were "White" by 1880 (and onward). Francis's racial ambiguity contributed to the indeterminate classification of his children. Celeste Escarpe lived with her common-law husband Jean Escarpe, a fifty-year-old "White" Italian-born fisherman; their Italian-born children, bearing the last name Escarpe, were all identified as "Mulatto" in 1870. Celeste and Jean sustained a publicly recognized mixed-race marriage, which complicated the racial classification of their offspring. Ultimately, that Italians could be officially classified as "Colored," at least in 1870, meant that Italians would go on to cross both racial and marriage boundaries. Their Italian-ness influenced a racial indistinctness that categorized them, or at least made them available to be categorized, as both white and non-white.

Such boundary crossing persisted in an era of increasingly stringent miscegenation codes. Bringing the racial appraisals of marriage licensing bureaucrats and census enumerators into correspondence with Orleans Parish Marriage Records between 1890 and 1915 further discloses the complicated racial placement and constrained access to citizenship of Italians in the Jim Crow Gulf South.[48] In 1890, at least 140 of the 2,165 officially sanctioned marriages in Orleans Parish were intra-Italian; Italians also regularly intermarried with other non-Italians, such as Germans, Irish, and French. Besides these more common Italian marriage contracts, Italians and African Americans did engage in both intimate relationships and officially sanctioned marriages.

Take the case of Italian-born Pietro Albanese. In December of 1878, Pietro and Josephine Albanese gave birth to a daughter, Mary Albanese. Census records identified Pietro's birthplace as Italy while categorizing his daughter Mary as "Black."[49] Census enumerators corrected the record of this interracial parentage, as either an enumerator or supervisor converted Pietro's race directly on the 1880 Census schedule from a "W" for "White" to an "M" for "Mulatto." Marriage licensing agents went on to grant Pietro and a "Black" woman named Mary Bossier a license to marry in 1890 in Louisiana. While Pietro's Italian-ness could account for his apparent racial ambiguity, this genealogy offers evidence of both an intimate relationship and an officially sanctioned marriage between an Italian and a woman of color. While this type of legally sanctioned interracial marriage did not follow with any sort of regularity, these kinds of relationships did occur. Relationships like those between Albanese and Bossier were not simply cases of interracial concubinage; they involved official bureaucratic recognition that granted the couple a formal marriage license. Of the credible interracial marriage contracts in 1890 Orleans Parish, the majority involved an Italian/"White" man and a woman of color, since interracial relationships that escaped adjudication in both the antebellum and postbellum South were more common between white men and slave women or white men and black women.

Numerically, Italian immigration to the Gulf South during the 1890s was increasing—the Italian foreign-born population between 1890 and 1900 swelled by nearly 10,000 in Louisiana.[50] Yet by 1900, while a number of Italian/European or Italian/native-born "White" couples secured licenses to marry, there were a decreasing number of intra-Italian marriages. In part, this pattern resulted due to an increase in Italian family reunifications as seasonal laborers began to settle more permanently in Louisiana and transplant their preexisting Italian wives and children from Italy. Additionally, the increasing number of intermarrying second and third generation Italians—native-born Italians had surpassed foreign-born Italians in Louisiana by more than 2,000 in 1910—meant that an equally increasing number of residents were of a more mixed-European background.[51] But even after Louisiana prohibited "marriage between white persons and persons of color" in 1894, certain marriage licensing agents persisted in granting "White" Italians a license to marry "Black" partners.[52] Nicolo Provenzano, born in Italy in 1862, immigrated to the United States in 1870. Despite the fact that the 1900 Census registered him as "White," he secured a license to marry a "Black" Louisiana-born woman of French origin named Marie Angela Meteye in 1896.[53] Not only did the Provenzanos secure official sanction of their interracial marriage, census enumerators confirmed their interracial cohabitation in 1900. Even though enumerators (or Nicolo himself) Americanized his name to Nicholas, Nicolo's Italian-ness blurred his legal whiteness, thereby making him unaffected by the newly passed marriage ban.

The Fascio family offers another peculiar case of the indeterminate racial status of Italians: Amerigo Fascio was born in New Orleans in 1841 to an Italian-born father and a Spanish mother.[54] In 1880 Louisiana, Amerigo Fascio was living with his wife, French-born Louisa Duplessis, and their children, all categorized as "White."[55] Yet by 1900, Amerigo, Louisa, and their children, including their son Albert, were all listed as "Black."[56] Despite being listed as "Black" in 1900, Amerigo and Louisa were categorized as "White" in 1910, while their son Albert was classified as "Mulatto" in 1910, "Black" in 1920, and "White" on his World War I draft registration card. Owing to his Italian ancestry, Albert may have possessed a darker complexion or indistinct phenotypic markers, or, because of his Italian/Latin ancestry, he may have been perceived as having a darker complexion. In any case, Albert's racial ambiguity could have been the result of either (or both) the reading of his physical appearance as inconclusive or the presumed imagining of his physicality based on assumptions about his Italian nativity. Moreover, even though Albert Fascio's brother Emanuel was listed on his World War II draft card as "White" but with a "dark brown complexion," one of Albert's sons and Emanuel's nephew, Albert Amerigo, was categorized as "Black" but noted as having a "light brown complexion." Underscoring the constructed nature of racial classifications, whereby an uncle and his nephew could share the same complexion and pigmentation but be racially classified differently, the forms themselves (not just the bureaucrats who filled them in) possessed the power to racialize; the indeterminacy of Italian-ness contributed to the possibility of this transiency. This complicated genealogical record, whereby the Fascio family moved back and forth across the official color line between 1880 and 1920, reveals the Fascios' racial classification as tangible, transient, and far from a foregone conclusion. Especially in New Orleans, mixed-race people often moved across the color lines in ways that led to contradictory classifications for their children; the fact that a family of Italian origin followed this same pattern speaks to the liminal racial identity that could be mapped onto Italian-ness.

These assessments of Italians' "changing race" may represent the few exceptional cases of Sicilians and other Italians participating in the transgressive phenomenon of racial passing. A social reality from the antebellum era well into the twentieth century, the collaborative act of passing extended racially indeterminate individuals the choice of performance in terms of the side of the color line to which they would be assigned.[57] As individuals grappled with choices, they could pass in both directions; therefore, these contradictory records could be cases of Italians struggling to secure official certification of their whiteness or instances of Italians passing as "nonwhite" in order to marry persons of their choosing. Passing, however, by definition left few clues in the historical record, which suggests that other cases may endure undetected.[58] The fact that Sicilians and other Italians or persons of color with Italian-sounding last names could pass meant that Sicilians and other Italians were not "white on arrival," but white depending on their performance and on who was doing the reading.

In 1908, Louisiana legislators made "concubinage between a person of the Caucasian or white race and a person of the negro or black race" a felony.[59] Italians continued to (inter)marry with other Europeans (especially Germans) as well as with native-born white individuals, but with the increasing specificity of Louisiana's miscegenation statutes, few Italians secured official marriage licenses for their intimate relationships with persons of color. In 1915, even with several cases involving persons of color marrying individuals with plausibly Italian surnames, like the marriage of Leonie Pizero to August Ellsworth and Agnes Reggio to William Smith, none of these unions conclusively reveal themselves as Italians intermarrying with persons of color.[60] While one should be cautious against presuming that legal changes necessarily corresponded to enforcement of those practices, the hardening of Louisiana's miscegenation statutes certainly contributed to the decline in the number of legally sanctioned marriage licenses issued between Italians and persons of color after the turn of the century.

As in 1910, several cases in 1915 reveal instances of Italians "changing" race or passing. For example, Rosalie Sconza married Louis Gabriel in 1915; as of 1920 (and 1930), census enumerators identified both with Italian fathers and classified both as "White." Likewise, while census enumerators in 1900 read Rosalie and her family as "White," in 1910, enumerators classified Rosalie, her siblings, and her son Goodwin Sansorrich as Mulatto.

Even after the turn-of-the-century, bureaucratic agents considered Italian racial identity as tenuous and subjective. Yet the absence of definitive marriages between an Italian and a person of color in 1915 speaks to the fact that Louisiana's antimiscegenation legislation after 1908 served to regulate interracial marriages into invisibility. The racial classifications of Italians in Louisiana by this later moment were less racially transient and less racially subjective as they ultimately moved into a more definitively "white" position within the racial hierarchy of the Jim Crow Gulf South.

Just as local bureaucrats declared certain marriages between Italians and black southerners as legally permissible in Louisiana (at least in the early 1890s), the local press rendered an equal number of interracial unions between Italians and African Americans visible. In 1896 in New Orleans, authorities took an Italian fruit peddler named Paul Rogudo into custody and charged him with abducting a "negro girl" named Agnes Thompson.[61] At least one newspaper article on the incident titled its report "A Miscegenation Mess." The relationship between Rogudo and Thompson, even in 1890s Louisiana, was popularly understood as *inter*racial and violated the state's miscegenation statute: "The Italian stated that he was willing to marry the girl, and she was also willing to accept him as her husband. This request, however, could not be granted, as it would be in violation of the anti-miscegenation law."[62] Significantly, the tone of the press reports remained sympathetic to the couple: "An Italian Fruit Man and a Negro Girl Love Each Other and Were Anxious to Marry—They are Now Separated."[63] As the *Daily States* recounted, "both [were] willing" but the marriage was not allowed due to "the presence on the statute books of the anti-miscegenation law." Even though the press recorded Rogudo as "Italian," never as "white," they went on to explain that "the laws prevent a marriage of the races."[64]

However, Thompson's mother was unwilling to grant her approval for the marriage; her opposition was the only reason that this case made its way into the press record. Thompson had run away from home to be with Rogudo; when her mother found her "living with the Italian," Thompson refused to leave.[65] The *Daily States*, which described Thompson as "comely," "quite good looking," and "attract[ing] attention," invoked language reminiscent of the exoticized consumption and commodification of light-skinned women of color that contributed to the widespread French colonial practices in New Orleans of Octoroon Balls and *plaçage*.[66] Historically, *plaçage* was a special form of concubinage characterized by a long-standing, formal relationship between a free woman of color and a white man of European origins. Because of their sought-after status, "octoroon" women and other light-skinned women of color in New Orleans could make pragmatic choices in their relationships with white European men and secure educational advantages and economic security for themselves and their children.[67] Owing to this history, Thompson's mother may not have considered Rogudo, whether because of his class status or Italian-ness, to be the most economically or socially pragmatic choice for her daughter. In her unwillingness to grant her approval, Thompson's mother criminalized her daughter's interracial relationship and rendered it visible.

In spite of the couple's mutual affection, it was "the law" (and Thompson's mother) that would not sanction the marriage, not popular convention. Press assessments of the liaison contrasted the legal from social estimations of the affair: "The only feature out of the ordinary in the matter is that this is probably the first case on record where the law prevented a marriage under such circumstances. The girl is in love with the Italian and he is also greatly attached to her. She declared that she wanted to live with him whether they were married or not, but her mother would not allow it."[68] What marked this incident as "out of the ordinary" was the state's miscegenation statute, not the relationship itself; the law was "prevent[ing]" the union of a couple otherwise in love. Absent from consideration was a discussion of the relationship posing a challenge to the natural order. Silence regarding the union as "unnaturally interracial" indicates the extent to which a relationship between an Italian and an African American girl could, in fact, be normalized.[69] Social convention deviated from legal edict as unofficial opinion strayed from official mandates.

Another case in 1901 in Alabama further demonstrates this divergence. Henry Johnson, a "negro," and Charlotte Mareno, a "white girl," ran away together from Bessemer; initially believing them to be "eloping," officials found them as they passed through nearby Birmingham.[70] Mareno, the press revealed, was an "Italian girl," though local papers employed the descriptions of "white" and Italian interchangeably. Initially, Johnson and Mareno gave different explanations for their "elopement." Johnson reported that "the girl came after him and begged him to run away with her"; Mareno explained that she came to Birmingham to rendezvous with a "man she expected to marry," but being unable to find him, she entreated Johnson to escort her to Nashville, where she planned to enter a convent.[71] The details, corroborated after the fact, were that Johnson and Mareno were not actually in a relationship, but instead, were simply traveling together. True to Jim Crow operations of race and gender, local law enforcement still arrested Johnson, who was black and male, and charged him with larceny and miscegenation; Mareno, read here as a "white" woman, was not arrested nor charged with miscegenation. In the case against Johnson, the grand jury "fail[ed] to find an indictment."[72] One account reported that the grand jury had ruled that Johnson had not in fact committed a crime.[73] However, a second explained that, "no prosecutors appeared and the negro was allowed to go his way."[74] In the end, Johnson may have been released because the local court did not perceive the infraction severe enough to warrant trial, or Johnson may simply have been released on a technicality.

Johnson and Mareno's case diverged from the circumstances of Thompson and Rogudo's. While a relationship between an Italian and a "negro" was legally defined as miscegenation in both Louisiana and Alabama, social convention in Alabama read the closeness of the relationship between Johnson and Mareno (whether or not it was actually an intimate relationship) as problematic. According to the *Biloxi Daily Herald*, Johnson did not even pause to dress when he found out that he had been released; instead, he talked with a reporter while he dressed outside the jail. Based on his arrest, Johnson was surely aware that locals read his intimate proximity with Mareno, however innocuous, as objectionable; his precarious position left his own safety in jeopardy. As a result, Johnson felt compelled to leave Alabama and head to New Orleans as quickly as possible. Press accounts in both Alabama and Mississippi perceived Mareno, "the pretty Bessemer Italian girl, daughter of M. Mareno, a merchant," as legally and socially "white," which meant that she fell under the category of "white" womanhood whose respectability warranted protection.[75] Additionally, by explaining that the grand jury "failed" to find an indictment and that Johnson was "in luck," the tone of the *Herald* intimated that, under different circumstances, Johnson would have most certainly been charged with violating the state's miscegenation statute or perhaps even been judged by a lynch mob.

In part serving as evidence of the regionally disparate interpretations of interracial relationships in Louisiana and Alabama, these incidents display the gendered variability of miscegenation charges involving Italians. If the party of color was a man, rather than an Italian, social and legal convention was more likely to find the liaison problematic and then legislate it into invisibility. Since an Italian woman could be "white" and in need of protection, convention marked an intimate liaison between a black man and an Italian woman (like Johnson and Mareno) as lacking social acceptability. Alternatively, an Italian *man* (like Rogudo) could be either "nonwhite," whereby his relationship with a woman of color was nonthreatening, or "white," thus granting him entitlement to a woman of color. The contrasting treatment of Rogudo and Mareno's interracial relationships further throws light on the liminal racial status of Italians within Gulf South marriage statutes.

The *Rollins v. State* case from 1921 in Alabama presents the most infamous example of this liminal space and how Sicilians and other Italians complicated Jim Crow miscegenation laws.[76] Edith Labue was married to a Sicilian man named Joe Labue, who worked as a taxicab driver, a mechanic, or a musician, depending on the record consulted.[77] Joe Labue left Birmingham on June 24, 1918, after being drafted into the army during World War I. He returned on January 27, 1919, to find his wife roughly six or seven months pregnant; Edith gave birth, according to her husband, "in April some time, 1919."[78] In the employ of Edith Labue's father-in-law was "a negro or descendant of a negro" by the name of Jim Rollins; the Labues' next door neighbor reported seeing Rollins bringing food to the family from time to time.

On the evening of February 11, 1921, Birmingham City Police arrived at the Labue home; without warning, they "kicked open the door" and "busted" inside. There in the kitchen, toward the back of the house, the detectives' flashlights cut through the darkness; joltingly, their beams halted when they landed on the mildly bewildered, somewhat expectant countenances of Jim Rollins and Edith Labue, standing "face to face." While they were both dressed, detectives reported, "there was no light in the room . . . they were in the room alone . . . and it was dark." Why did the police enter and search the Labue home that evening? Given how the ensuing trial played out, Joe Labue likely reported his suspicions regarding his wife to the police, thus leading them to investigate.

As a result, on March 21, 1921, Rollins was indicted on the charge that he and Edith Labue, "a white person . . . did intermarry or live in adultery or fornication with each other, against the peace and dignity of the State of Alabama." At the ensuing trial, Birmingham City Detective H. H. Sullivan reported that Rollins had confessed while in custody:

> He stated to me that in July or August of 1918 he had had intercourse with this woman Edith Labue; that about three weeks after this she called him to her home and told him there was something wrong, and wanted to know what to do about it, and he said he didn't know what to do, and after the child was born he said she called him over there and showed him the child and asked him what he was going to do about it. . . . He said he had had illicit intercourse with this woman. I talked to him about whether he had had intercourse with this woman on other occasions. He said he had. He said he had been about once a month; he said sometimes he would go every two or three months . . . From July or August, 1918 up until the time that he was arrested and placed in custody.

Despite Sullivan's testimony, Rollins's defense attorney asserted that Sullivan's partner, Detective Hubbard, had prompted the alleged confession by threatening and intimidating Rollins with a pistol. Since Hubbard purportedly drew and brandished his weapon, Rollins's defense disputed the veracity of the confession and the means by which it was elicited.

In addition to the problematic confession, two other key moments in the trial stand out: first, Francis Labue, Edith Labue's youngest child (allegedly fathered by Rollins while Joe Labue was away in the army), was brought into the court for the jury to inspect on three separate occasions. Noting his use as an object of evidence, Francis's name was never mentioned in the actual court proceedings. When asked to describe the "color" of the youngest child, Detective J. McGill testified, "*It* was a dark brown child, with kinky hair."[79] Hubbard confirmed this assessment, explaining that the third Labue child was a "dark brown skin child" who "had curly hair."[80] McGill described the other two Labue children as "white children." Given the timing of his tenure in the army, it is technically possible that Joe Labue was in fact the biological father of Francis Labue; the 1920 Federal Census Records assumed as much, which additionally recorded Francis's color as "white," along with the rest of his family. At least according to the subjective assessment of the census enumerator, the Labue family was "white." Still, Francis was likely darker than his siblings, as the defense objected on each occasion that Francis was brought into the courtroom, claiming that the "exhibition" of the child would "prejudice the minds of the jury against the defendant." The judge overruled each objection as the prosecution asked two detectives and Joe Labue to confirm Francis's identity in open court, thereby displaying the two-year-old for the jury and essentially reading the body of the child as evidence of the violated miscegenation statute.

The question and discussion of Edith Labue's "whiteness" remains a second striking moment of the trial, as the court did engage in an extended evaluation of Edith Labue's racial and ethnic background. Significantly, this testimony, largely given by Joe Labue, served to reaffirm Edith Labue's "whiteness" rather than discredit it. Joe Labue, who notably testified as a witness for the prosecution, bore a pointed self-interest in confirming Edith Labue's whiteness. Were Edith Labue not in fact white, Joe Labue himself could have been in violation of Alabama's miscegenation statute.

Joe began his testimony by explaining that he and Edith had married in Gadsden "about ten or eleven years ago, something like that," but did not remember the exact date. While Joe claimed that he had lived with his wife continuously up until her arrest, the tone of his testimony revealed a marked effort to distance himself from his wife:

> I came to this Country from Sicily. Sicily is in Southern Europe. I came from the Highlands of Sicily. It was not the mainland, but in an island. . . . My wife came from Birmingham, I reckon. The first time I ever saw her was in Birmingham. I couldn't say whether she came from Sicily or not, but she did come from some foreign country. She came from Italy, from middle Italy. I have not studied Geography, but it is not over in Africa, across from Africa. I ain't seen it. I have never been across to Liberia.

Although Joe seemed unsure of his wife's origins, even though both the 1910 and 1920 Federal Census recorded Edith's birthplace as Italy, he did emphasize that his wife came from "middle Italy," while he came from Sicily. The explicit subtext, that Italy was not near Africa, functioned to verify Edith's whiteness and thus reaffirm her (and Rollins's) violation of the miscegenation statute.

Detective McGill corroborated this geographic and racial assessment of Edith Labue:

> Yes, I have seen Edith Labue frequently, and she is a white woman. I do not know where she is from. She is an Italian I think. She is either an Italian or a Greek. I don't know which. I do not know whether she has any African blood in her veins or not, but she is not dark. She is of foreign decent [sic], and is an Italian or a Greek. I don't know whether she is right adjacent to the Mediterranean Sea or whether she is from Liberia or among those colored races down there or not. I am sorry to say I never had an opportunity to study Geography.

In their testimony, both Joe Labue and McGill referred to the significance of geography, reaffirming that race was produced from a multiplicity of factors. In addition to phenotype and physical appearance (McGill testified that Edith's skin was "not dark"), geographic origins also prescribed one's "color." Both witnesses marked Edith Labue as foreign, possibly "Italian or Greek," but specifically not from somewhere "adjacent to the Mediterranean" or "over in Africa."

Joe Labue and McGill's efforts to pointedly distance Italy from Africa functioned to construct Edith Labue as unaffiliated with Africa, thus reasserting her whiteness. In response to his wife's infidelity, Joe Labue's testimony—less of a sustained proclamation of Italian "whiteness" and more of an effort to fulfill a personal vendetta—provided the evidence necessary to convict his wife, and thus, Rollins by default. As an act of self-preservation, Joe Labue needed to render Edith as conclusively "white" in order to protect himself from a charge—legally or socially—of miscegenation.

At the conclusion of the trial, the court charged the jury with evaluating whether Jim Rollins and Edith Labue had "liv[ed] together in a state of adultery or fornication." Significantly, the court reminded them that Rollins "is not charged with being the father of that child that you saw brought in here and alleged to have been the child of this woman, Edith Labue." The court additionally specified: "Just one act of illicit sexual intercourse would not make a state of adultery or fornication unless there was an agreement to continue that relation. Just an occasional sexual intercourse would not make it a state of adultery or fornication." Despite these charges and the defense attorney's claim that Rollins's confession was coerced and involuntary, Rollins was found guilty on April 8, 1921, and sentenced to a minimum of six or maximum of seven years in the state penitentiary. Rollins filed a Notice of Appeal the following September on the grounds that "the evidence in this case [was] wholly circumstantial."[81] Of note, Edith Labue, initially referred to as Rollins's codefendant, was also charged with violating Alabama's miscegenation statute, yet, after filing a severance, Edith Labue and Rollins were tried separately. Edith Labue was convicted of miscegenation at a separate trial and sentenced to a term of two to five years on May 14, 1921. Labue spent the next six months in the Jefferson County Jail, at which point she was paroled "into the custody of Mrs. W. D. Nesbitt" on November 22, 1921, a full two months before Rollins's appeal trial.[82] Given the testimony corroborating her whiteness and her lesser sentence and time served, Edith Labue's case follows the pattern of white women convicted of miscegenation violations.

The following January in 1922, an Alabama Appeals Court reviewed and overturned Rollins's conviction on the grounds that Rollins's confession had been inadmissible. The record demonstrated "without dispute" that Rollins's confession had been "extorted" at gunpoint, concluding that the confession had been coerced "through fear and constraint superinduced by this means and no other."[83] Without the confession, the court explained that the given evidence was "too vague and uncertain" to meet the burden of proof and that "corpus delicti" had not been proven, meaning the prosecution had not actually established that a crime had been committed.[84]

Judge P. J. Bricken, who authored the opinion, explained that the lack of evidence resulted from two main factors: First, "No contention was made that these parties had ever intermarried, and the state relied for a conviction upon the averment that they lived together in adultery or fornication." As the criminal court had originally charged the jury, a single occasion of "illicit sexual intercourse" did not actually violate the state's miscegenation statute. Even if Rollins had in fact fathered the child of "suspicious appearance," such a fact did not actually verify "a state of adultery or fornication."[85] Proving that Edith Labue and Jim Rollins had engaged in more than the "occasional acts of adultery" would have required evidence of "an agreement or understanding to continue" their illicit relationship, something the prosecution had made no effort to contend.[86]

Second, and the cause for the infamy that surrounds this case, Judge Bricken explained that there was "no material evidence" to prove that Edith Labue was in fact white: "There was no competent evidence to show that the woman in question, Edith Labue, was a white woman, or that she did not have negro blood in her veins and was not the descendant of a negro. . . . The mere fact that the testimony showed this woman came from Sicily can in no sense be taken as conclusive that she was therefore a white woman, or that she was not a negro or a descendant of a negro."[87] According to Bricken, just because Edith Labue may have come from Sicily did not preclude her from having "negro blood in her veins." The prosecution had not affirmatively established Edith Labue's "whiteness." On appeal, Bricken reversed and remanded the conviction of Jim Rollins for violating Alabama's miscegenation statute.

Rollins v. State reveals much about the operations of miscegenation law in the Gulf South. To begin with, *Rollins* supports the fact that the intent of miscegenation laws was to delegitimize interracial intimacy, not necessarily to impose a definitive separation of the races.[88] The court's emphasis upon the fact that "occasional acts of adultery" did not constitute the more long-standing and transgressive crime that Rollins was charged with, "living or having lived in a state of adultery or fornication with Edith Labue," meant that the jury had erred in their conviction. Without Rollins's forced confession, the Appeals Court was compelled to overturn the conviction on the grounds of insufficient evidence. Witnesses at the original criminal trial were unable to verify the fact that Rollins and Edith Labue maintained an ongoing physical relationship. In fact, the prosecution's only evidence that they had ever engaged in adultery was Francis Labue, which the court found at the time to be insufficient evidence of an *ongoing* illicit relationship.[89] Given the prosecution's pointed display of Francis Labue for the jury, and the recognition by the defense that this maneuver was meant to prejudice the jury against the defendant, Francis Labue likely displayed certain "non-Italian" physical characteristics. Based on the prosecution's performance, contemporaries seem to have interpreted the alleged relationship between Jim Rollins and Edith Labue as an interracial relationship, one that violated the region's racial standards and norms but that the state of Alabama could not legally legislate given the technicalities of the state's miscegenation law.

In terms of Italian (not to be subsumed with Sicilian) whiteness, this case serves to substantiate Italian whiteness. Joe Labue was oddly unable to comment on his wife's place of origin; maybe she was foreign, but he met her in Birmingham. In his effort to ensure Rollins's (and Edith's) conviction, Joe Labue's imprecision, his ambiguity, and his tone were likely intentional. For Rollins (and Edith) to be convicted of miscegenation, Edith needed to be seen as "white." Joe Labue's testimony did just that—by constructing his wife as from "middle Italy," specifically not Sicilian, and definitely not from or near Africa, he substantiated and attested to his wife's Italian-ness and whiteness.

Additionally, Joe Labue's testimony reveals his awareness of the available anti-Sicilian script in the Gulf South and the existing hierarchical ranking of Italians over Sicilians, whereby Italian and Sicilian whiteness and respectability were socially, if not legally, understood differently. Sicilians were "white" enough to un-problematically marry other "white" Italians but racially ambiguous enough that their relationship with a black individual did not automatically prove miscegenation. Because Sicilian "whiteness" was socially and unofficially suspect, Joe Labue needed to present evidence of his own reliability and legitimacy as a citizen—he explained that he came to the United States when he was twelve, did not "remember anything that happened" there, and was now an American citizen.[90] By noting that he had "never seen the people of Southern Italy or Sicily," an effort meant to distance himself (and by default his wife) from their perceived Sicilian-ness and attendant stereotypes, he constructed himself as a dishonored "white," southern man. Similarly, identifying Edith Labue as Sicilian would have at least raised questions about whether the courts would have interpreted and legislated her relationship with Rollins as miscegenation. Therefore, Joe Labue contested and testified against Edith's proximity to Sicily in order to reassert her whiteness. Joe Labue's testimony engendered his own citizenship—interpreted here as both trustworthiness and masculinity—as well as aiming to prove his wife's whiteness as a means to justify Rollins's conviction. Furthermore, the court's efforts to classify Edith Labue as "middle" Italian or even Greek (as another witness hypothesized), endeavored to remove her racial transiency and mark her as unequivocally and legally "white." By the 1920s, Alabama courts subscribed to the imported dichotomy that hierarchically ranked Northern over Southern Italians and both over Sicilians.

What of Judge Bricken's specific reference to the fact that just because Edith Labue came from Sicily, it was not "conclusive" evidence that she was a "white woman, or that she was not a negro or a descendant of a negro"? Although a provocative and quotable turn of phrase, the judicial rhetoric operated as merely illustrative of the court's conclusion that the state did not actually prove that a crime had been committed. Edith Labue's whiteness was certainly part of the conversation; though later paroled, Edith was apparently "white" enough to have been convicted of miscegenation for her relationship with Jim Rollins on her own accord. Nonetheless, the racial questionability of Sicilian whiteness was not the basis for overturning the *Rollins* verdict. The Alabama Appeals Court overturned Rollins's conviction because of a technicality: the prosecution had not actually proved that Edith Labue and Jim Rollins had broken Alabama's miscegenation statute, which required evidence that the couple had either intermarried or engaged in multiple acts of "illicit intercourse." Despite the "kinky hair" and "dark" skin of two-year-old Francis Labue—whose race was put on trial, unlike his mother's—without Rollins's coerced confession, the prosecution had not provided enough evidence to establish an ongoing intimate relationship. Indeed, this litigation reveals the larger intentionality of miscegenation statutes as well as the unique particularities of official and unofficial racing of Sicilians and other Italians. In the end, Rollins's successful appeal was not not based on a determination of Edith Labue being inconclusively or questionably white—instead, this case reaffirmed that Labue, despite or because of her Italian-ness, was white.

Moreover, the *Rollins* court discussed Edith Labue's race in a manner inconsistent with the way race was commonly evaluated when determining miscegenation violators within judicial disputes in the Gulf South in the 1920s. For example, in *Wilson v. State,* the question before the Court of Appeals of Alabama in 1924 was whether Sarah Wilson, "a negro or a descendant of a negro," and Charles Medicus, "a white person," had in fact "live[d] together in a state of felonious adultery."[91] The Appeals Court was additionally charged with determining, "Was this defendant a negro or a descendent of a negro?" To a large degree, the prosecution's evidence was based on witness testimony that defined Wilson as a "negro" by association. One witness testified that he knew Wilson was "negro" because he had seen her with a "negro woman named Ruby . . . a negro mighty near black," whom Wilson kissed good-bye. The defense counsel asked, "How do you know she has a great amount of negro blood in her?" to which the witness responded, "By her color and associates." Likewise, Mrs. Charles Medicus testified that Wilson "lived in a negro house with negro people." Under cross-examination, Mrs. Medicus explained, "You can tell by her looks she is a negro." The defense counsel went on to ask her, "Do you know whether or not her father or mother have any negro at all in them, of your own knowledge?" Mrs. Medicus responded, "Why certainly, by looking at her. I do not know who they are. I could not swear how that is, by looking at her, I know." In asking whether the witnesses had personal knowledge of Wilson's mother and father, the defense counsel insisted on the witnesses being able to account for Wilson's blood quantum. Yet even without this knowledge, Mrs. Medicus contended that Wilson's race was still knowable by both sense and sight.

As the jilted wife, Mrs. Medicus would have had a vested interest in confirming Wilson's race as "negro" and thus ensuring her conviction, yet other witnesses corroborated her reading and racial determination of Wilson. The first witness admitted that although he did not know Wilson's parentage, he insisted that he could tell Wilson's race by those with whom she associated. As a result, the state sided with the prosecution's witness testimony:

> We think that, if for no other reason, the rule born of necessity should and does permit a witness, if he knows such to be the fact, to testify that a person is a negro, or is a white person, or that he is a man, or that she is a woman; for courts are not supposed to be ignorant of what everybody else is presumed to know, and in this jurisdiction certainly every person possessed of any degree of intelligence knows a negro, and also that the term negro, and colored person, are used interchangeably and mean the same thing.[92]

The court reasoned that anyone with "any degree of intelligence knows a negro."[93] Thus, association, parentage, and "common knowledge" remained the primary means of evaluating one's race.[94] On the contrary, because Edith Labue's whiteness was secure, her associates and associations were never called into question, nor was her blood quantum part of the debate in the *Rollins* case.

Similarly, the same assumption of "whiteness" was present in *Jackson v. State*, an Alabama appeals case from 1930. Sam Jackson, "a negro or a descendant of a negro," and a Greek woman named Alexander Markos, "alleged to be a white person," were both indicted and convicted. Upon appeal, however, their conviction was reversed and remanded. Could this present evidence of the inconclusiveness of Markos's whiteness, that she was only "allegedly" a white person? Upon further reading and as in the *Rollins* ruling, the question of whether Markos was a "white woman" never entered the court's debate. Instead, the court overturned the conviction on the ground that the crime did not meet the burden of proof of miscegenation. The court explained that miscegenation was defined as a "mixture of races in marriage or living together in state of adultery or fornication, by white person and negro, or descendent of negro."[95] The question before the court was not whether or not Markos was definitionally "white"—the court presumed Markos to be "white"—but whether the interaction between Markos and Jackson violated the miscegenation statute. Because both parties testified that their relationship consisted of a "single act of intercourse," the court concluded that such an occurrence did not establish the crime of miscegenation. Markos admitted that she had "sexual intercourse with him one time only . . . I just happened to meet him on the street. When I went up to him I said nothing. . . . I stayed in there about ten minutes. This is the first time I ever had anything to do with him, and when I got through I went my way and he went his, and since that time I have not seen him or spoken to him."[96] This could very easily have been a defense tactic and does not necessarily preclude that Markos and Jackson may have indeed had an ongoing relationship. Yet unlike in Sarah Wilson's case discussed above, the court never evaluated or questioned Markos's associations. Even given her admittance of sexual partners, Markos remained unequivocally white. Very much in line with *Rollins v. State,* Markos's whiteness, like Edith Labue's, was never actually in question, nor was it the reason for the overturned miscegenation verdict. Rather, in both cases the court overturned the miscegenation conviction on the grounds that the interaction in question was an isolated affair, not an ongoing relationship, and thus not in violation of Alabama's miscegenation statute. In the end, Alabama courts conceived of intimate and long-term interracial relationships as more offensive than even mixed-race procreation since the public nature of ongoing interracial affairs categorically threatened the social and political systems in the Gulf South.

As miscegenation debates in the 1920s centered on personal evaluations of race based on associations, observations, and public imagination, these cases taken together also reaffirm the role of informal citizenship. Just as Supreme Court rulings like *Thind v. U.S.* and *Ozawa v. U.S.* demonstrated a growing support for the notion that common or popular evaluations of race (over that of scientific understandings) possessed legal resonance, so too could unofficial actors testify to a common knowledge of race in miscegenation cases.[97] As this collective knowledge entered the legal record, unofficial actors contributed to the fashioning of informal citizenship. These constructions of informal citizenship placed Italians in a liminal racial space owing to the technicalities of the identified racial categories within miscegenation statutes. According to popular understandings, Italians were neither "Negro" nor full-caste "Caucasian." Italians were sometimes criminalized and sometimes not when intimately involved with African Americans in the early twentieth-century Gulf South.

Even though Italians may have been legally white, they were not conclusively white when it came to the regulation of their marriages. Whether or not Italians possessed "marriage whiteness" became a question of regionality and temporality. In particular historical moments, certainly before the turn of the century, Italians occupied a liminal racial place whereby their racial transiency bureaucratically permitted them to marry persons of color as well as native-born whites and other "white" Europeans. While courts and marriage licensing civil servants certainly debated Italian whiteness and their rights of informal citizenship during the late nineteenth and early twentieth centuries, the aforementioned review and analysis of Orleans Parish marriage records demonstrates that over time, Italian whiteness became less transient and less subjective as Italians acquired more definitive access to whiteness.

Rollins v. State demonstrates that by the 1920s, miscegenation cases involving Italians reaffirmed, rather than challenged, their whiteness. Rollins's successful appeal was not based on a determination of Edith Labue as being inconclusively or questionably white. In fact, quite the opposite. The pointed testimony that noted the "kinky hair" and "dark" skin of two-year-old Francis, and declared Edith was from "middle Italy" and definitely not from or "across from" Africa, attested to her Italian-ness and, by the logic of the court, her whiteness. Thus removing her racial transiency, in the particular context of 1920s Alabama, she was marked as legally "white." Taken altogether, these various miscegenation episodes and efforts to police interracial intimacy further reveal the liminal racial status and racial transiency of Italians in the Jim Crow Gulf South.

Epilogue

Italian Citizenship and Immigration Legislation in the Gulf South to 1924 and Beyond

[The Italian] degenerates [were] monsters, capable of any infamy and
[the mob] determined to destroy them root and branch, just as the traveler
places his armed heel upon the head of the viper.

—*Daily States*, July 24, 1899

[The Italians are a] colony of vicious murderers and assassins [to whom] murder
and blood were . . . what roses, moonlight and music are to poets and lovers.

—*Daily States*, July 27, 1899

After the lynching of the eleven Sicilians and other Italians in 1891 in New Orleans, the Gulf South adopted an anti-Italian racial script that replicated the national nativist discourse against Italians.[1] When Italian and Italian American communities around the United States demonstrated in opposition to the lynching, press accounts interpreted the Italian-led anti-lynching protests as providing the nation with a more accurate and illuminating portrait of the Italians' "true colors": "The war-like mouthing of the Italian colonists in their respective cities . . . has opened the eyes of the press of the whole country to the fact that they make poor citizens, and the result is a general demand that legislation shall be enacted at the next session of Congress to restrict if not to exclude altogether immigration from Sicily from which country the Mafia has been transplanted to our soil."[2] Explaining the lynching of Italians as a civil justice against a fundamentally violent people, southerners proposed immigration restrictions specifically targeting Sicilians.[3] In New Orleans, the Committee of Fifty recommended that "immigration from Lower Italy and Sicily should be entirely prohibited."[4] The *Daily Picayune* urged Congress to "exclude absolutely from ingress into the Union all Sicilians and immigrants from Southern Italy . . .

nothing else will cope with this overshadowing evil."[5] By 1897, Italians were no longer "the right sort of immigration," and they had a "demoralizing influence on the general population." In light of the early-1890s lynchings, Louisianans began to consider Italians a problematic and unassimilable immigrant group and declared, "America belongs to Americans and should be ruled by Americans."[6] A reversal from earlier encouragement of Italian immigration in the 1870s and 1880s Gulf South, these late nineteenth-century positions conflated Italian with criminal and classified their delinquent tendencies as inherited characteristics of the Italian people.

Even amid threats and violence, Italian immigration to the Gulf South persisted. Like the seven hundred Sicilians who landed in October of 1901, appearing onshore like a "wildly-excited flock of variegated tropical birds," thousands of Sicilians and other Italians still disembarked through the Port of New Orleans.[7] In response to these turn-of-the-century arrivals, anti-immigrant perspectives in the Gulf South ebbed and flowed. Southern congressmen voted against federal immigration bills (including literacy tests and quota acts), as northern politicians used southern politics (like the 1891 lynching) to advocate for nationwide anti-immigration restrictions. Only after World War I did anti-immigrant conversations and politics in the Gulf South begin to replicate the ongoing national agenda that imposed barriers to immigration.

The effects of such regionalized immigration programs meant that the racial and civic transiency of Italians in the Gulf South continued unabated well into the twentieth century. Italians in the Gulf South eventually made their way into the native-born white mainstream, but context remained critical. Voting and marriage laws expedited the "whitening" of Italians, while violence, lynching, labor conflict, and nativism deferred their access to whiteness. Despite the general course of Italians toward whiteness and inclusion, Gulf South rhetoric during the federal immigration legislative debates of the 1920s still contested Italian access to unqualified citizenship. Leading up to 1924 and beyond, the Italian immigrant experience in the Gulf South remained distinctive.

If the Sicilian and Italian experience of immigration, naturalization, and attendant identity negotiation in the Gulf South was particular to the region, the South was increasingly looked to by advocates for nationwide immigration policies. Henry Cabot Lodge, a Republican senator from Massachusetts and active member of the Immigration Restriction League, referenced the 1891 New Orleans lynching in support of immigration restrictions and literacy tests in the 1890s. His position suggested that the lynchings of Italians resulted from a lack of immigration restrictions, and he further cautioned that these "other races of totally different race origin, with whom the English-speaking people have never hitherto been assimilated or brought in contact . . . [represented] great and perilous change in the very fabric of our race."[8] According to Lodge, groups like Italians were a national peril that endangered "the quality of our race and citizenship through the wholesale infusion of races."[9] Criminality was inherited, and he explained, "If we permit the classes which furnish [criminal elements] for these [Mafia] societies to come freely to this country, we shall have these outrages to deal with, and such scenes as that of the 14 of March will be repeated."[10] The Immigration Restriction League made a similar claim when they advocated for increased immigration restrictions to avoid "dangerous occurrences" like "the Mafia incident in New Orleans," thus holding the Mafia responsible for the 1891 lynching.[11] Federal legislators like Lodge suggested that the 1891 lynching was "unfortunate" but unsurprising. To avoid such violence in the future, Lodge argued that the time had come for an "intelligent restriction."[12]

Extrapolating from the regional to the national, Lodge argued Congress should require immigrants to pass a literacy test, in order to prevent undesirable immigrants—"temporary migrants" of the "pauper and criminal class"—from entering the United States. Such a literacy requirement would avert the conditions that resulted in the lynchings of immigrants, since it was the class of immigrants, not New Orleanians, who were to blame for the violence. In so arguing, politicians began using regional Gulf South politics as support for national anti-immigrant legislative claims.

The Gulf South's regional climate was still more complicated by racial politics, economic needs, and Jim Crow mandates. Certain opinions in the southern press, in line with national discussions favoring immigration limitations, promoted a literacy requirement, since "illiterates" were "incapable of understanding our constitution and free institutions," lowered the nation's moral status, and could not be made into "good Americans."[13] However, despite the shift toward a more vituperative anti-Italian parlance in the press after the 1891 lynching, when the federal literacy bill finally passed Congress in 1897 with only a three-vote majority, both Louisiana senators opposed it.[14] Senator Donelson Caffery acknowledged that Sicilians were "less desirable," but identified those Italians from the "agricultural sections" as "industrious citizens." Likewise, Senator Newton C. Blanchard explained, "[The literacy test] might do in the populous cities, but not in the scantily settled localities of the south and west, where immigration was needed."[15] Not simply a case of anomalous voting in Louisiana, congressional votes on the literacy test throughout the South were rather divided: twelve southern senators voted in favor, five opposed; in the House, forty southerners approved, while twenty-five opposed.[16] Immigrant labor was still in high demand in the Gulf South in the 1890s, and congressional voting patterns represented a clear contradiction between northern and southern regionalized immigration agendas. The literacy requirement—Lodge's and the Immigration Restriction League's focal point—may have been a plausible solution for the overcrowded urban North. Yet in 1897, such a constraint would have impeded the economic needs of southern planters, who still required a great influx of (cheap) immigrant labor. Not only did this southern economic motivation contradict national conversations, but it also paradoxically conflicted with Gulf South politics and efforts to indemnify Jim Crow racial separation.

However, during the following decade, motivated by native-born and immigrant labor conflicts like that which transpired in 1907 in Sumrall, Mississippi, southern congressmen steadily shifted away from their economically motivated support of unrestricted immigration. By 1904, South Carolina's legislature instructed its immigration bureau to only make appeals to "white" immigrants.[17] North Carolina, Alabama, and Kentucky issued similar directives, citing preference for immigrants of "Teutonic, Celtic or Saxon origin" or persons from "English-speaking and Germanic countries"; only in "desperation" should they hire Italians.[18] One labor recruiter from Alabama proclaimed in 1905, "For God's sake, send your Italians to the coal mines of Pennsylvania or some other hot place. We are not in sympathy with the padrone or mafia system."[19] In 1910, Senator Leroy Percy of Mississippi and Representative John L. Burnett of Alabama signed the majority report of the Immigration Commission that recommended the literacy test.[20] Having been defeated by a presidential veto in 1897, when the literacy test came up for debate in Congress again in 1913, the proposal received limited southern opposition; only two southern senators dissented, and the southern representatives in the House voted to support the bill sixty-eight to five.[21]

Contemporaneously, Sicilians and other Italians became ensnared by the nationwide Progressive temperance movement, which would culminate in Prohibition and disproportionally affect Sicilian bar owners and Italian neighborhoods. As early as 1886, Louisiana legislators passed a "Sunday Law," which forbade selling goods, groceries, or alcohol on Sundays; while largely unenforced, the law resulted in a crackdown on immigrant businesses.[22] Moral crusaders in Louisiana successfully lobbied and passed the Gay-Shattuck Law in 1908, adopted the same year as Louisiana's interracial concubinage prohibition.[23] Foremost a segregation law, the new legislation required bars and groceries (not restaurants or hotels) to take out a liquor license that corresponded to the race of their anticipated clientele.[24] The law illegalized interracial customers, barred women from working or being served, outlawed gambling, and required licensees to be of "good moral character." It also discrepantly entangled Italians. During the years 1909–1919, two-thirds of those arrested for Gay-Shattuck infractions were Italians who sold liquor to "whites and negroes" and had violated the segregation mandate.[25] Additionally, implementation of these laws focused primarily on working-class neighborhoods and Sicilian-operated bars, while law enforcement resisted imposing the mandate on upscale establishments. The Louisiana attorney general went on to advise that "only citizens of the State of Louisiana" could obtain liquor licenses under the law, explicitly forbidding "unnaturalized foreigners or a citizen of another State or nation" from acquiring said license.[26] Louisiana judge O'Neill challenged the attorney general's reading and questioned the constitutionality of barring foreigners from selling "intoxicating liquors"; O'Neill argued that that such a charge "had an odor of know-nothingism."[27] With these oscillating interpretations, Sicilians and other Italians became increasingly enmeshed within state-level and national conversations regarding morality, bootlegging, and Prohibition.

Violence toward Italians echoed this statutory back-and-forth. The final instance of Italians being lynched in the Gulf South occurred on September 20, 1910, in the Ybor City neighborhood of Tampa, Florida. In the midst of a labor strike by cigarmakers in West Tampa, J. Frank Esterling, the accountant for the Bustillo Brothers and Diaz Company, attempted to hire scabs to break the walkout when he was fatally shot by two labor activists, Angelo Albano and Castenge Ficarotta.[28] While the Sicilian suspects were in transport to the local jail, a mob of nearly thirty seized the prisoners and lynched them.[29] On Albano's hanged body, they pinned a note that read, "Beware: Others take notice or go the same way. . . . We are watching you. If any more citizens are molested, look out. Justice."[30] The lynching served as an act of antilabor activism to intimidate the striking cigarmakers. The Italian-ness of the victims permitted this utilitarian vigilantism. More explicit but still consistent with previous lynchings of Italians, violent lynch mobs targeted Italians as a way to coerce industry compliance and to compel conduct that was economically advantageous for native-born white southerners.

Yet the same Jim Crow mandates that offered "dagoes" voting rights in 1890s Louisiana increasingly extended Sicilians and other Italians access to southern whiteness and informal citizenship. In contrast to the lynchings of the 1890s, by 1913 lynching was used as a means of protecting the status of Italians within the white mainstream. On a late-summer afternoon in Jennings, Louisiana, a "colored" man by the name of James Comeaux walked past the store of an Italian merchant named A. W. Joseph.[31] Joseph "accidentally" swept dirt on Comeaux's shoes, whereupon, Comeaux attacked Joseph; Comeaux was subsequently arrested for the assault and breach in social convention.[32] Not only did local law enforcement intervene on behalf of an Italian, but a lynch mob took Comeaux from his jail cell in the middle of the night, at which point he was "shot to death and his body left lying at the jail door."[33] The Serios could be "assassinated" in 1901 in Mississippi and Albano and Ficarotta could be lynched in 1910 in Florida as a threat to unionism. But a black southerner in 1913 Jennings, Louisiana, could violate southern norms by striking an Italian merchant and be lynched for the offense. This reasserted the transiency and racial mutability of Italians in the Gulf South.

World War I temporarily changed the terms of the immigration debates and the operations of ascribed nationality in both the Gulf South and at the national level. Wartime revealed a peculiar phenomenon, whereby both native-born US citizens (of foreign ancestry) and naturalized US citizens found they could be compelled to perform military service for their country of origin.[34] The Italian state named and claimed American-born Sicilians and emigrated Southern Italians as Italians. For example, Father Carra, a New Orleans priest and American citizen who came to the United States at the age of eight, was seized during a visit to Palermo and drafted into military service in Italy.[35] According to Italian law, "naturalization of an Italian subject as a citizen of another country does not relieve him from the liability of the performance of military service in Italy." Because the United States did not have a naturalization treaty with Italy, the Italian government maintained that if a citizen left the "fatherland" without having performed military service, he and his male children would still be subject to compulsory military duty.[36] Policies began to shift by 1915, as the Italian government made moves to "disclaim" children born to Italian parents in the United States, but it did not formally end its policy of conscripting emigrated Italians until 1929.[37] As it had been for the American government during the 1890s indemnity debates, the Italian state understood the citizenship status of Sicilians and Southern Italians to be exploitable.

Owing to this ambiguity of citizenship, some southerners began to encourage the naturalization of foreign citizens as a wartime measure.[38] Local organizations published guidebooks and textbooks instructing "aliens" on how to achieve citizenship, and local papers printed daily notices of those foreigners who had taken out naturalization papers.[39] Southern journalist Frederic J. Haskin explained that in wartimes, "when loyalty is an absolute necessity," the "indifference" of foreign immigrants posed a particular "menace [since] they form too fertile a ground for the enemy's propaganda."[40] Haskin noted that "aliens" were not "deliberately disloyal," but that their illiteracy meant that they were "susceptible to bad influences."[41] Accordingly, encouraging immigrants to naturalize was a way to "build up and strengthen the ideals of Americanism" and a means of nurturing "loyalism."[42] In the name of the war effort, certain southerners offered Sicilians and other Italians informal citizenship by urging them to naturalize and to take advantage of their formal citizenship rights.

As confirmation that Italians were subject to civic as well as racial transiency, other southerners worried about conferring citizenship too readily upon "foreigners."[43] The *Daily Picayune* alleged in 1915 that, "The immigrant who puts on American citizenship for convenience merely . . . [is] not yet fit for naturalization."[44] St. Clair Adams, a New Orleanian politician, suggested in 1917 that immigrants should not even be allowed to land if they did not declare their intention to naturalize, and should be deported if they did not learn to read and write in English within five years.[45] Employing nativist stereotypes, Adams decreed, "We do not want immigrants who come here to feed on our fat, bask in our sunshine and live on our wealth until they are sleek and fat, then go back to their native countries and live at ease."[46] To those like Adams, "birds of passage" immigrants such as Italians were no longer valuable contributors to the South's economy but instead opportunistic exploiters.

These increasingly intolerant sentiments bore legislative ramifications at the federal level. In 1917, both houses of Congress passed the literacy test requirement for immigration for a fourth time. Although the bill received a presidential veto for a fourth time, Congress overrode President Wilson's veto, thus passing the "Bill to Regulate the Immigration of Aliens to and the Residence of Aliens in the U.S." into law. Southern support for the legislation was widespread. In overriding the president's veto, all representatives and senators in Alabama, Florida, and Mississippi voted in favor.[47] Louisiana remained somewhat split, with Senator Ransdell Joseph voting "nay" and Senator Robert Broussard abstaining; Joseph was joined by three of Louisiana's eight representatives in registering their opposition against the House Resolution to overturn the president's veto.[48] Of note, the representatives who voted "nay" hailed from the first, second, and third congressional districts, which included the southeastern corner of the state and New Orleans; even in 1917, demands for immigrant labor in certain Louisiana parishes conflicted with statewide and nationwide immigration policy. But by and large, by 1917, southerners emphatically registered their opposition to unrestricted immigration.

With the implementation of the 1920s quota regime through the Emergency Quota Act and National Origins Act—set to disproportionately limit southern and eastern European immigration and virtually halt Asian immigration—southern legislators spoke with one voice and one vote. Unlike in previous deliberations, by 1924, every single voting representative and senator from Alabama, Florida, Louisiana, and Mississippi voted in favor of the "Bill to Limit the Immigration of Aliens into the United States."[49] Signaling a broad shift in southern attitudes that adopted a northern nativist script toward the arrival of new immigrants, legislators in the Gulf South who had previously advocated an open door policy for immigrant labor now sought to limit the arrival of dangerous, unassimilable "aliens." These immigration restrictions, which no longer differentiated between "North Italians" and "South Italians" and constrained all Italian immigration, further codified an ascribed Italian nationality upon Sicilians and Southern Italians.[50]

What of those Sicilians and other Italians already residing in the Gulf South by 1924? Socially, and with evidence of a long-standing denial of informal citizenship, Italians were not allowed to participate alongside native-born whites in Louisiana's Carnival Balls during Mardi Gras through the first half of the twentieth century.[51] Legally, in May of 1924, Joseph Rini and five other Italian Americans were hanged by the State of Louisiana for the alleged murder of a local restaurant owner.[52] Unlike the lynchings of the 1890s, the 1924 hanging was a legal—albeit based on circumstantial evidence and suspect court proceedings—state-led execution, the largest in Louisiana history. This capital execution reveals the residual nativism that still considered Italians and Italian Americans as violently suspect and validated violence against Italians as a means to quash the Mafia.

However, with the passage of time and without the constant influx of new immigrants within the era of the quota regime, second- and third-generation immigrants became further detached from their ancestral labels. As Italians exited ethnic enclaves and developed relationships with non-Italian Americans, neighborhoods in Louisiana and elsewhere in the Gulf South became less ethnically segregated after World War II. According to one assessment, by 1970, Italians were "thoroughly Americanized."[53]

Certainly, Italians steadily made their way into the native-born white mainstream, though the racial transiency of Italians in the Gulf South mitigated a straightforward trajectory. Between the 1870s and 1920s, some moments, like the lynchings in the 1890s, disavowed Italians of their whiteness, while other instances, like *Rollins v. State* in 1921, affirmed Italian whiteness. Violence, labor conflict, and nativism delayed the "whitening" of Italians, just as political debates, voting rights, and marriage laws advanced the "whitening" of Italians in other contexts. This racializing process had civic implications, both privileging and dispossessing Italian access to informal citizenship. These same circumstances compelled the consolidation of *Italianità* and converted Sicilians and Southern Italians into Italians and Italian Americans.

Introducing the transnational construction of Italian-ness into the Jim Crow narrative exposes the fungibility of racial and civic constructions. Italian racialization and citizenship identity were mobile and itinerant—depending on the moment, the location, and the circumstance, Italians in the Gulf South were sometimes white and sometimes not, occasionally offered access to informal citizenship and in other moments denied. Italians could be susceptible to lynching, offered the privilege of voting, and raced after the fact. Because of their racial and civic transiency, Italians helped to both disrupt and consolidate the region's racially binary discourse and profoundly alter the legal and ideological landscape of the Gulf South at the turn of the century. Such transiency meant that in the very act of confounding the black/white paradigm, ethnic immigrants reconfigured conceptions of race and citizenship and contributed to the codification of the South's exclusionary racial practices.

On April 12, 2019, New Orleans mayor LaToya Cantrell issued a formal apology for the lynching of the eleven Italians in New Orleans in 1891. The scene—Italian and American flags in view behind the podium where Cantrell spoke, the performance of both the American and Italian national anthems alongside a memorial wall dedicated to notable Louisiana Italians—bore little resemblance to the decades when Italians were considered a "colony of vicious murderers and assassins" and "degenerate monsters."[54] Likewise, the lynching era—the culture of fear and vigilante violence exerted upon all persons of color—seemed far removed. Cantrell's words were heartfelt and earnest:

> At this late date, we cannot give justice, but we can be intentional and deliberate about what we do going forward . . . I'm here today . . . because I have a responsibility to speak honestly about the challenges we face, those that shape our history and, more importantly, our future. I ask you to continue to stand with me against anti-immigrant violence, against division. . . . And for the idea that we have a responsibility . . . to be the kind of people that our children are not apologizing for 128 years from now.[55]

Cantrell's poignant and cautionary reminder bears witness to the enduring implications of political campaigns waged upon the basis of intolerance, bigotry, and thinly veiled white supremacy. Well into the twenty-first century, current political conditions have facilitated an emboldened resurgence of nativist agendas that replicate the xenophobic strains of purportedly bygone eras—1850s Know-Nothingism, 1880s Chinese Exclusion, the 1920s quota regime. Just as nineteenth-century scripts justified lynching violence and created an environment that validated such enmity, we must reckon with the lasting consequences of ongoing anti-immigrant oratory and policy. Within both historical and contemporary contestations over citizenship, the experience of Sicilians and other Italians in the Jim Crow Gulf South reminds us of the extent to which the language and discourse of race can manipulate—and offers a portent forewarning about our responsibility to our future.

Notes

Introduction

1. "The Immigration Season Started," *Daily Picayune*, October 19, 1901.

2. Justin Nystrom, *Creole Italian: Sicilian Immigrants and the Shaping of New Orleans Food Culture* (Athens: University of Georgia Press, 2018), 60–61; Anthony V. Margavio and Jerome J. Salomone, *Bread and Respect: The Italians of Louisiana* (Gretna, LA: Pelican Publishing, 2002), 37; "Passenger Lists of Vessels Arriving at New Orleans, Louisiana, 1820–1902," Records of the Immigration and Naturalization Service, National Archives, Washington, DC (hereafter NA).

3. Bureau of the Census, *Thirteenth Census of the United States, 1910* (Washington, DC: Government Printing Office, 1910), 3:773; Bureau of the Census, *Fifteenth Census of the United States, 1930* (Washington, DC: Government Printing Office, 1930), 6:27.

4. Bureau of the Census, *Thirteenth Census of the United States, 1910*, 3:41; Bureau of the Census, *Thirteenth Census of the United States, 1910*, 2:1039; Bureau of the Census, *Thirteenth Census of the United States, 1910*, 1:813; Frank Cavaioli, "Andrew Houston Longino," *Italian Americana* 11, no. 2 (1993): 175. Beyond the scope of my inquiry, Italian immigrants also inhabited the coastal communities of Florida's panhandle and the Gulf Coast of Texas.

5. "Citizens Plead Necessity for White Supremacy," *Times Democrat*, July 25, 1899.

6. Massimo D'Azeglio, *I Miei Ricordi* (Firenze, Italia: G. Barbera, 1867); literally translated: "Italy has been made; the Italians remain to be made." See also Spencer Di Scala, *Italy from Revolution to Republic: 1700 to the Present* (Boulder, CO: Westview Press, 2004); Derek Edward Dawson Beales and Eugenio F. Biagini, *The Risorgimento and the Unification of Italy* (New York: Routledge, 2013).

7. John A. Davis, "Italy, 1796–1870: The Age of the Risorgimento," in *The Oxford Illustrated History of Italy*, ed. by George Holmes (Oxford: Oxford University Press, 1997), 186; Di Scala, *Italy from Revolution to Republic*, 51. For more on the "Southern Question" and the cultural and geographic boundaries of Southern Italy, see Giuseppe Tomasi di Lampedusa, *Il Gattopardo*, 1958, trans. by Archibald Colquhoun as *The Leopard* (New York: Pantheon Books, 2007); Carlo Levi, *Cristo si é fermato a Eboli*, 1945, trans. by Frances Frenaye as *Christ Stopped at Eboli: The Story of a Year* (New York: Noonday Press, 1963); Robert Lumley and Jonathan Morris, eds., *The New History of the Italian South: The Mezzogiorno Revisited* (Exeter: Exeter University Press, 1997); Nelson Moe, *The View from Vesuvius: Italian Culture and*

the Southern Question (Berkeley: University of California Press, 2002); Jane Schneider, ed., *Italy's "Southern Question": Orientalism in One Country* (New York: Berg, 1998).

8. John Santore, *Modern Naples: A Documentary History, 1799–1999* (New York: Italica Press, 2001), 199.

9. Di Scala, *Italy from Revolution to Republic*, 132.

10. Santore, *Modern Naples: A Documentary History, 1799–1999*, 192.

11. Martin Clark, *Modern Italy, 1871 to the Present* (New York: Pearson Longman, 2008). See also Davis, "Italy, 1796–1870," 177–209; Di Scala, *Italy from Revolution to Republic;* Luciano J. Iorizzo and Salvatore Mondello, *The Italian Americans* (Boston: G. K. Hall, 1980), 20.

12. Mark Choate, *Emigrant Nation: The Making of Italy Abroad* (Cambridge, MA: Harvard University Press, 2008), 1.

13. Joseph Lopreato, *Italian Americans* (New York: Random House, 1970), 104; see also Humbert S. Nelli, *Italians in Chicago, 1880–1930: A Study in Ethnic Mobility* (Oxford: Oxford University Press, 1970).

14. Offering linguistic evidence for this more local sense of civic identity, leading migration scholar Donna Gabaccia points out that modern Italians use the same word for village (*paese*) as they do for country and that the modern Italian word for citizenship (*cittadinanza*) comes from their word for city (*città*). See "Is Everyone Nowhere? Nomads, Nations, and the Immigrant Paradigm of United States History," *Journal of American History* 86, no. 3 (December 1999): 1115–37; Donna R. Gabaccia, *Italy's Many Diasporas* (London: UCL Press, 2000), 3. See also Thomas Guglielmo, *White on Arrival: Italians, Race, Color, and Power in Chicago, 1890–1945* (New York: Oxford University Press, 2003); Humbert S. Nelli, *From Immigrants to Ethnics: The Italian Americans* (Oxford: Oxford University Press, 1983); Lopreato, *Italian Americans.*

15. Matthew Frye Jacobson, *Whiteness of a Different Color: European Immigrants and the Alchemy of Race* (Cambridge, MA: Harvard University Press, 1998); William J. Connell and Stanislao G. Pugliese, *The Routledge History of Italian Americans* (New York: Routledge, 2018).

16. For a discussion of the impact of Catholicism upon anti-Italian sentiment in northern, largely Protestant cities, see Salvatore J. LaGumina, *Wop!: A Documentary History of Anti-Italian Discrimination in the United States* (Toronto: Guernica, 1999), chapter 4. For a discussion of Italians' seasonal migration, see Mark Wyman, *Round-trip to America: The Immigrants Return to Europe, 1880–1930* (Ithaca, NY: Cornell University Press, 1993); Mark Choate, "Italian Emigration, Remittances and the Rise of the Made-in-Italy," in *The Routledge History of Italian Americans*, ed. William J. Connell and Stanislao G. Pugliese (New York: Routledge, 2018), 337–48; Thomas Kessner, *The Golden Door: Italian and Jewish Immigrant Mobility in New York City, 1880–1915* (New York, Oxford University Press, 1977). For a discussion of the association between Italians and criminality, see Salvatore J. LaGumina, "Discrimination, Prejudice and Italian American History," in *The Routledge History of Italian Americans*, ed. William J. Connell and Stanislao G. Pugliese (New York: Routledge, 2018), 223–38; Michael Topp, "The Sacco and Vanzetti Case and the Psychology of Political Violence," in *The Routledge History of Italian Americans*, ed. William J. Connell and Stanislao G. Pugliese (New York: Routledge, 2018), 286–304.

17. Peter D'Agostino, "Craniums, Criminals, and the 'Cursed Race': Italian Anthropology in American Racial Thought, 1861–1924," *Comparative Studies in Society and History* 44, no. 2 (April 2002): 319–43.

18. Jennifer Guglielmo, *Living the Revolution: Italian Women's Resistance and Radicalism in New York City, 1880–1945* (Chapel Hill: University of North Carolina Press, 2010), 83–89; Cesare Lombroso, *Criminal Man,* trans. Mary Gibson and Nicole Hahn Rafer (Durham, NC: Duke University Press, 2006), 115–18.

19. Margavio and Salomone, *Bread and Respect,* 188.

20. Guglielmo, *Living the Revolution,* 89.

21. Guglielmo, *White on Arrival,* 23; William Paul Dillingham and US Immigration Commission 1907–10, *Reports of the Immigration Commission: Dictionary of Races or Peoples* (Washington, DC: Government Printing Office, 1911), 81–85. See also William Paul Dillingham and US Immigration Commission 1907–10, "Character of Italian Immigration" in *Reports of the Immigration Commission: Emigration Conditions in Europe* (Washington, DC: Government Printing Office, 1911), 177–184; Joel Perlman, *America Classifies the Immigrants: From Ellis Island to the 2020 Census* (Cambridge, MA: Harvard University Press, 2018), chapter 1.

22. Dillingham and US Immigration Commission 1907–10, *Reports of the Immigration Commission: Dictionary of Races or Peoples,* 82. See also Guglielmo, *White on Arrival,* note 36, 183–84.

23. Dillingham and US Immigration Commission 1907–10, *Reports of the Immigration Commission: Dictionary of Races or Peoples,* 82. See also D'Agostino, "Craniums, Criminals, and the 'Cursed Race,'" 331–35.

24. Edward Alsworth Ross, "Italians in America," *Century Magazine,* July 1914, 439–45. See also, Thomas Guglielmo, "No Color Barrier: Italians, Race, and Power in the United States," in *Are Italians White? How Race Is Made in America,* ed. Jennifer Guglielmo and Salvatore Salerno (New York: Routledge, 2003), 34.

25. The estimated 1850 population of Italians in Louisiana was 924 (Paolo Giordano, "Italian Immigration in the State of Louisiana: Its Causes, Effects, and Results," *Italian Americana* 5, no. 2 (1979): 164); Margavio and Salomone, *Bread and Respect,* 44.

26. Giordano, "Italian Immigration in the State of Louisiana," 164.

27. Margavio and Salomone, *Bread and Respect,* 36; Nystrom, *Creole Italian,* 33.

28. Margavio and Salomone, *Bread and Respect,* 44.

29. For foundational examples of the regional case study, see Donna R. Gabaccia, *From Sicily to Elizabeth Street: Housing and Social Change among Italian Immigrants, 1880–1930* (Albany: State University of New York Press, 1984); Virginia Yans-McLaughlin, *Family and Community: Italian Immigrants in Buffalo, 1880–1930* (Ithaca, NY: Cornell University Press, 1977); Rudolph John Vecoli, "Contadini in Chicago: A Critique of *The Uprooted,*" *Journal of American History* 51, no. 3 (December 1964): 404–17; Nelli, *Italians in Chicago, 1880–1930.* Even while offering nuanced interpretations, much of the recent scholarship on Italian immigrants has continued to focus on the experience of Italian immigrants in northern, urban US areas. See, for instance, Guglielmo, *White on Arrival;* Guglielmo, *Living the Revolution;* Teresa Fava Thomas, *The Reluctant Migrants: Migration from the Veneto to Central Massachusetts 1880–1920* (Amherst, NY: Teneo Press, 2015); Vellon, *A Great Conspiracy against Our Race.*

30. Those works I have found particularly helpful include the following: John V. Baia-monte, *Spirit of Vengeance: Nativism and Louisiana Justice, 1921–1924* (Baton Rouge: Lou-isiana State University Press, 1986); Margavio and Salomone, *Bread and Respect;* Justin Nystrom, *Creole Italian;* Vincenza Scarpaci, *Italian Immigrants in Louisiana's Sugar Parishes: Recruitment, Labor Conditions, and Community Relations, 1880–1910* (New York: Arno Press, 1980); Vincenza Scarpaci, "Walking the Color Line: Italian Immigrants in Rural Louisiana, 1880–1910," in *Are Italians White? How Race Is Made in America,* ed. Jennifer Guglielmo and Salvatore Salerno, (New York: Routledge, 2003), 60–76. I elaborate on the history and his-toriography of the 1891 New Orleans lynching in chapter 2.

31. For formative contributions to (and revisions of) critical whiteness scholarship, see Eric Arnesen, "Whiteness and the Historians' Imagination," *International Labor and Working-Class History* 60 (2001): 3–32; Barbara Fields, "Whiteness, Racism, and Identity, " *Interna-tional Labor and Working-Class History* 60 (2001): 48–56; Karen Brodkin, *How Jews Became White Folks and What That Says about Race in America* (New Brunswick, NJ: Rutgers Uni-versity Press, 1998); Matthew Guterl, *The Color of Race in America, 1900–1940* (Cambridge, MA: Harvard University Press, 2001); Grace Elizabeth Hale, *Making Whiteness: The Culture of Segregation in the South, 1890–1940* (New York: Vintage Books, 1999); Cheryl I. Harris, "Whiteness as Property," *Harvard Law Review* 106, no. 8 (June 1993): 1707–91; Jacobson, *Whiteness of a Different Color;* Ian Haney Lopez, *White by Law: The Legal Construction of Race* (New York: New York University Press), 1996; David Roediger, *The Wages of Whiteness: Race and the Making of the American Working Class,* rev. ed. (London: Verso, 2007); David Roedi-ger, *Working toward Whiteness: How America's Immigrants Became White, The Strange Journey from Ellis Island to the Suburbs* (New York: Basic Books, 2005).

32. James Barrett and David Roediger, "Inbetween Peoples: Race, Nationality and the 'New Immigrant' Working Class," *Journal of American Ethnic History* 16, no. 3 (Spring 1997): 101–40. The term "in-betweenness" originally appeared in John Higham's *Strangers in the Land* (New York: Antheneum, 1963), 169. See also Peter G. Vellon, "'Between White Men and Negroes': The Perception of Southern Italian Immigrants through the Lens of Italian Lynchings," in *Anti-Italianism: Essays on a Prejudice,* ed. William J. Connell and Fred Gar-daphé (Basingstoke, UK: Palgrave Macmillan, 2010), 27. Throughout, I employ "inbetween" (in quotation marks and without the hyphen) in reference to this scholarship.

33. Guglielmo, *White on Arrival.*

34. Samuel George Morton, *Crania Americana: A Comparative View of the Skulls of Vari-ous Aboriginal Nations of North and South America* (Philadelphia: J. Dobson, 1839); Johann Friedrich Blumenbach, *The Elements of Physiology,* trans. John Elliotson (London: A. & R. Spottiswoode, 1828).

35. William Zebina Ripley, "The Racial Geography of Europe: A Sociological Study," *Pop-ular Science Monthly* 51 (June 1897): 17–33. American eugenicist Madison Grant renamed Ripley's "Teutonic" category with the more familiar "Nordic." See Madison Grant, *The Pass-ing of the Great Race: The Racial Basis of European History* (New York: Charles Scribner's Sons, 1916).

36. For more on the "multiplicity of white races" as applied to Italians, see Louise De-Salvo, "Color White/Complexion Dark," in *Are Italians White? How Race Is Made in America,* ed. Jennifer Guglielmo and Salvatore Salerno (New York: Routledge, 2003), 17–28.

37. Guglielmo, *White on Arrival*, chapter 1. For more on why the legal claim of Italians as "white" was not more contested, see Guglielmo, "No Color Barrier," 40–41; Guglielmo, *White on Arrival*, chapter 3.

38. For other revisions of Guglielmo's "white on arrival" theory, see Stefano Luconi, "Black Dagoes? Italian Immigrants' Racial Status in the United States: An Ecological View," *Journal of Transatlantic Studies* 14, no. 2 (2016): 188–99; Peter G. Vellon, *A Great Conspiracy against Our Race: Italian Immigrant Newspapers and the Construction of Whiteness in the Early Twentieth Century* (New York: NYU Press, 2014).

39. "Citizens Plead Necessity for White Supremacy," *Times Democrat,* July 25, 1899; "Remarkable Race Prejudice," *Columbus Dispatch,* October 17, 1907 (Columbus, MS).

40. "Suffrage Plan To Be Repaired," *Times Democrat,* March 12, 1898; "Suffrage Plan To Be Repaired," *Daily Picayune,* March 12, 1898; *Daily Picayune,* March 16, 1898; *Daily States,* July 24, 1899; *Daily States,* July 27, 1899.

41. "Our Italian Fellow-Citizens," *Daily Picayune,* March 4, 1889; *Weekly Messenger* March 21, 1891 (St. Martinsville, LA); "Italian Immigration," *Daily Picayune,* January 15, 1895.

42. "Citizens Not to Be Trusted," *Daily Picayune,* March 25, 1896; "The March of the Regulars," *Daily Picayune,* April 18, 1896; "Gov. Vardaman Denies the Story," *Biloxi Daily Herald,* December 31, 1907 (Biloxi, MS).

43. Barbara J. Fields, "Slavery, Race and Ideology in the United States," *New Left Review* 181 (May 1, 1990): 111–12.

44. I invoke here Andreas Fahrmeir's, concept of "formal citizenship," the legal relationship between individuals and the state. See *Citizenship: The Rise and Fall of a Modern Concept* (New Haven: Yale University Press, 2007), 2. For the works that I have found most useful in developing my conception of citizenship, see the following: Natalia Molina, *How Race Is Made in America: Immigration, Citizenship, and the Historical Power of Racial Scripts* (Berkeley: University of California Press, 2014); William J. Novak, "The Legal Transformation of Citizenship in Nineteenth-Century America," in *The Democratic Experiment: New Directions in American Political History,* ed. Meg Jacobs, William J. Novak, and Julian E. Zelizer (Princeton, NJ: Princeton University Press, 2003); Kunal Parker, *Making Foreigners: Immigration and Citizenship Law in America, 1600–2000* (Cambridge: Cambridge University Press, 2015); Rogers M. Smith, *Civic Ideals Conflicting Visions of Citizenship in U.S. History* (New Haven: Yale University Press, 1997); Hannah Rosen, *Terror in the Heart of Freedom: Citizenship, Sexual Violence, and the Meaning of Race in the Postemancipation South* (Chapel Hill: University of North Carolina Press, 2009); Barbara Young Welke, *Law and the Borders of Belonging in the Long Nineteenth Century United States* (Cambridge: Cambridge University Press, 2010).

45. Mae Ngai, *Impossible Subjects: Illegal Aliens and the Making of Modern America* (Princeton, NJ: Princeton University Press, 2004), 8; Bridget Anderson, *Us and Them? The Dangerous Politics of Immigration Control* (Oxford: Oxford University Press, 2013).

46. For other examples of extralegal means of policing citizenship, see Ariela Julie Gross, *What Blood Won't Tell: A History of Race on Trial in America* (Cambridge, MA: Harvard University Press, 2008).

47. Molina, *How Race Is Made in America.*

48. *Cefalutana* included those from Cefalù, while *Contessiotti* referred to those from Contessa Entellina, both small villages in Sicily.

49. For those who argue that Louisiana challenged British colonial patterns, see the following: Gwendolyn Midlo Hall, *Africans in Colonial Louisian: The Development of Afro-Creole Culture in the Eighteenth Century* (Baton Rouge: Louisiana State University Press, 1992); Michael Gomez, *Exchanging Our Country Marks: The Transformation of African Identities in the Colonial and Antebellum South* (Chapel Hill: University of North Carolina Press, 1998); Emily Clark, *Masterless Mistresses: The New Orleans Ursulines and the Development of a New World Society, 1727–1834* (Chapel Hill: University of North Carolina Press, 2007).

50. Shannon Lee Dawdy, *Building the Devil's Empire: French Colonial New Orleans* (Chicago: University of Chicago Press, 2008). With regard to the extent that slavery in French Louisiana challenged British models, see Daniel H. Usner, *Indians, Settlers & Slaves in a Frontier Exchange Economy: The Lower Mississippi Valley Before 1783* (Chapel Hill: University of North Carolina Press, 1992); Virginia Meacham Gould, "'A Chaos of Iniquity and Discord': Slave and Free Women of Color in the Spanish Ports of New Orleans, Mobile, and Pensacola," in *The Devil's Lane: Sex and Race in the Early South,* ed. Catherine Clinton and Michele Gillespie (Oxford: Oxford University Press, 1997), 232–46. For more on the fluidity that persisted when the Spanish acquired the region in the latter half of the eighteenth century, see Kimberly S. Hanger, "Coping in a Complex World: Free Black Women in Colonial New Orleans," in *The Devil's Lane: Sex and Race in the Early South,* ed. Catherine Clinton and Michele Gillespie (Oxford: Oxford University Press, 1997), 218–31; Kimberly S. Hanger, "Patronage, Property and Persistence: The Emergence of a Free Black Elite in Spanish New Orleans," *Slavery and Abolition* 17, no. 1 (1996): 44–64; Joan M. Martin, "Plaçage and the Louisiana *Gens de Couleur Libre:* How Race and Sex Defined the Lifestyles of Free Women of Color," in *Creole: The History and Legacy of Louisiana's Free People of Color,* ed. Sybil Kein (Baton Rouge: Louisiana State University Press, 2000), 57–70. For more on how slavery continued to operate differently in the region from elsewhere in the American South, see Adam Rothman, *Slave Country: American Expansion and the Origins of the Deep South* (Cambridge, MA: Harvard University Press, 2005.

51. Dawdy's *Building the Devil's Empire: French Colonial New Orleans;* Gould, "'A Chaos of Iniquity and Discord.'"

52. For scholars who contend that southern race relations in general should be reevaluated for atypicality, rather than presuming Louisiana to be the perennial outsider, see Jennifer M. Spear, *Race, Sex, and Social Order in Early New Orleans* (Baltimore: Johns Hopkins University Press, 2009); Long, *The Great Southern Babylon: Sex, Race, and Respectability in New Orleans, 1865–1920.*

53. Spear, *Race, Sex, and Social Order in Early New Orleans.*

54. Department of Commerce and Labor, Bureau of the Census, *Thirteenth Census of the United States Taken in the Year 1910, Vol. 2: Population* (Washington, DC: Government Printing Office, 1913), 46–58; Department of Commerce and Labor, Bureau of the Census, *Thirteenth Census,* 1044–58.

55. For a similar theory on the interconnectedness between the Deep South and other slave-holding regions, see Rothman, *Slave Country: American Expansion and the Origins of the Deep South.*

56. Richard Campanella, *Time and Place in New Orleans: Past Geographies in the Present*

Day (Gretna, LA: Pelican Publishing, 2002), 149; Thomas Ewing Dabney, *One Hundred Great Years: The Story of the Times-Picayune from Its Founding to 1940* (Baton Rouge: Louisiana State University Press, 1944), 313–14. For more on how printed circulation numbers underestimated actual readership, due in part to the prevalent tradition of reading newspapers aloud, see Vellon, *A Great Conspiracy Against our Race: Italian Immigrant Newspapers and the Construction of Whiteness in the Early 20th Century,* 10–11.

57. John S. Kendall, *History of New Orleans* (Chicago: Lewis Publishing, 1922), chapter 31.

58. For more on considerations when analyzing legal statutes, see Peter Winthrop Bardaglio, *Reconstructing the Household: Families, Sex, and the Law in the Nineteenth Century South* (Chapel Hill: University of North Carolina Press, 1995); Nancy F. Cott, *Public Vows: A History of Marriage and the Nation* (Cambridge, MA: Harvard University Press, 2000); Ngai, *Impossible Subjects: Illegal Aliens and the Making of Modern America,* 12; Spear, *Race, Sex, and Social Order in Early New Orleans,* 315; Welke, *Law and the Borders of Belonging in the Long Nineteenth Century United States,* 8; Aristide R. Zolberg, "The Great Wall Against China: Responses to the First Immigration Crisis, 1885–1925," in *How Many Exceptionalisms? Explorations in Comparative Macroanalysis* (Philadelphia: Temple University Press, 2008).

59. Margavio and Salomone, *Bread and Respect,* 44.

60. *Daily Picayune,* April 20, 1898; *Daily Picayune,* July 8, 1898. See also Luconi, "Black Dagoes?," 196.

61. "The Fruit Trade of New Orleans," *Daily Picayune,* July 20, 1872; *Daily Picayune,* April 20, 1898.

62. Giose Rimanelli, "The 1891 New Orleans Lynching: Southern Politics, Mafia, Immigration and the American Press," in *The 1891 New Orleans Lynching and U.S.-Italian Relations: A Look Back,* ed. Marco Rimanelli and Sheryl L. Postman (New York: P. Lang, 1992), 60.

63. I have retained variations in spelling from the original historical source material; as they appear, I use both "dagoes" and "dagos."

1. From "Proper Citizens" to "Alien Electors": Reconsidering the Experience of Sicilians in Louisiana before and after the Lynchings

1. I elaborate at length on the 1891 lynching and other lynchings of Sicilians and other Italians in chapter 2. For more on the historiography of the 1891 lynching, see Richard Gambino, *Vendetta: The True Story of the Largest Lynching in U.S. History* (Garden City, NY: Doubleday, 1977), and Humbert S. Nelli, *The Business of Crime: Italians and Syndicate Crime in the United States* (New York: Oxford University Press, 1976). The spelling of the police chief's surname varies across both historical and scholarly sources. In keeping with the more common spelling found in contemporary reporting, I have adopted the spelling as "Hennessy" but have preserved the alternate spelling of "Hennessey" for quoted material found in previously published works.

2. In contrast to the claim that "anti-Italian racism exploded" in 1891 New Orleans, see Jessica Barbata Jackson, "Before the Lynching: Reconsidering the Experience of Italians and

Sicilians in Louisiana, 1870s–1890s," *Louisiana History* 58, no. 3 (2017): 300–338. For those scholars who read the lynching as an explosion of long-standing anti-Italian sentiment, see Jacobson, *Whiteness of a Different Color*, 56; Gambino, *Vendetta*, 255; Jerre Mangione and Ben Morreale, *La Storia: Five Centuries of the Italian American Experience* (New York: HarperCollins, 1992), 201.

3. In documenting assessments of Sicilians and other Italians found in the national press, I offer a broad reading from the *New York Times, Chicago Daily Tribune, San Francisco Chronicle, Los Angeles Times, Washington Post, Pittsburgh Dispatch, New York Sun, New York Evening World,* and Washington, DC's *National Republican* and *National Tribune.* For the local press, I consulted New Orleans newspapers like the *Daily Picayune* and *Times Democrat*, as well as regional newspapers from around the state of Louisiana and the larger Gulf South (including Alabama and Mississippi).

4. Campbell Gibson and Emily Lennon, "Region and Country or Area of Birth of the Foreign-Born Population, With Geographic Detail Shown in Decennial Census Publications of 1930 or Earlier: 1850 to 1930 and 1960 to 1990," *U.S. Census Bureau, Population Division*, March 9, 1999.

5. "The Poor Italians," *New York Times*, December 15, 1872; "Italian Immigration," *New York Times*, December 17, 1872; "The Italians," *New York Times*, December 11, 1872; "The Homeless Italians," *New York Times*, December 13, 1872; "The Suffering Italians," *New York Times*, December 14, 1872.

6. "The Italians," *New York Times*, December 11, 1872; "The Homeless Italians," *New York Times*, December 13, 1872; "The Suffering Italians," *New York Times*, December 14, 1872; "The Poor Italians," *New York Times*, December 15, 1872; "Italian Immigration," *New York Times*, December 17, 1872; "Our Future Citizens," *New York Times*, March 5, 1882; "Italian Degeneracy," *New York Times*, April 17, 1885.

7. "Compulsory Cleanliness," *New York Times*, July 11, 1880.

8. "Undesirable Immigrants," *New York Times*, December 18, 1880; *New York Tribune*, August 5, 1888.

9. *National Tribune*, August 2, 1888 (Washington, DC); *San Francisco Chronicle*, May 2, 1890. See also "Cut by a Dago," *Daily Inter Ocean*, March 18, 1882 (Chicago); "Stabbed on the Levee," *St. Louis Globe Democrat*, June 20 1882; *Los Angeles Times*, July 10, 1883; "A Dago's Dirk," *Rocky Mountain News*, April 6, 1884 (Denver, CO); "Downed by a Dago," *Washington Post*, July 7, 1888; *Chicago Daily Tribune*, July 8, 1888 and July 23, 1888.

10. *Chicago Daily Tribune*, July 12, 1887; *Chicago Daily Tribune*, July 8, 1888; *Chicago Daily Tribune*, July 23, 1888.

11. *National Tribune*, August 2, 1888 (Washington, DC); *Los Angeles Times*, July 9, 1888.

12. *Chicago Daily Tribune*, July 12, 1887.

13. *National Tribune*, August 2, 1888 (Washington, DC). See also *New York Sun*, November 28, 1887.

14. *Los Angeles Times*, August 10, 1887, reprinted from the *New York Evening Post*.

15. "The Poor Italians," *New York Times*, December 15, 1872; "Italian Immigration," *New York Times*, December 17, 1872; "The Italians," *New York Times*, December 11, 1872; "The Homeless Italians," *New York Times*, December 13, 1872; "The Suffering Italians," *New York Times*, December 14, 1872.

16. *New York Evening World,* August 2, 1888; *San Francisco Chronicle,* August 12, 1888.

17. As explained by the Knights of Labor in the *National Republican,* March 3, 1884 (Washington, DC). For a similar sentiment, see also "The Black Hole," *Daily Inter Ocean,* January 30, 1882 (Chicago); "Double Murder in New Orleans," *Washington Post,* November 6, 1882 (Washington, DC); "A Swindler with a Career," *Washington Post,* March 19, 1886 (Washington, DC); *Chicago Daily Tribune,* July 23, 1888; *New York Sun,* October 28, 1888; "Undesirable Immigrants," *New York Times,* December 18, 1880.

18. "Only Birds of Passage," *New York Times,* July 29, 1888. See also "Birds of Passage," *New York Times,* March 9, 1906; Henry Cabot Lodge, "Lynch Law and Unrestricted Immigration," *North American Review* 152, no. 414 (May 1891): 608–9.

19. Wyman, *Round-Trip to America,* 10; Gabaccia, *Italy's Many Diasporas,* 72; Kessner, *The Golden Door,* 28. As many as 72 percent of Italian immigrations returned to Italy between 1907 and 1911 (Margavio and Salomone, *Bread and Respect,* 31).

20. "Italian Slaves," *New York Times,* January 6, 1871; "White Slavery Traffic in Children," *New York Times,* June 12, 1873; "The Italian Slaves: Arrest of a Padroni," *New York Times,* July 22, 1873.

21. "An Italian Assassinated," *New York Times,* March 14, 1875; "Felonious Assault by Italians," *New York Times,* August 12, 1876; "A Fatal Stabbing Affray: An Italian Killed By his Companion, Result of a Quarrel Over a Game of Cards," *New York Times,* December 5, 1879; "Italian Demonstrations: Proposed Celebration of Italian Unity," *New York Times,* July 30, 1871; "Italian Movements: Meeting of the Italian Benevolent Society," *New York Times,* August 14, 1871; "Italian Festivities," *New York Times,* June 2, 1874; "Eight Hundred Italians Vaccinated," *New York Times,* May 4, 1874; "A Happy Dago," *Washington Post,* October 20, 1899.

22. "Our Italians," *New York Times,* November 12, 1875; "The Homeless Italians," *New York Times,* December 13, 1872; "The Suffering Italians," *New York Times,* December 14, 1872; "The Poor Italians," *New York Times,* December 15, 1872; "Suffering Among the Poor Italians," *New York Times,* December 16, 1873; "Bad State of Affairs: German Criminals and a Low Class of Italians," *Washington Post,* July 29, 1888.

23. "Naples in New York," *New York Times,* January 4, 1873; "Our Italians," *New York Times,* November 12, 1875.

24. Gibson and Lennon, "Region and Country or Area of Birth of the Foreign-Born Population, With Geographic Detail Shown in Decennial Census Publications of 1930 or Earlier: 1850 to 1930 and 1960 to 1990."

25. Press coverage elsewhere in the Gulf South, like Alabama and Mississippi, during the 1870s and 1880s offered a limited discussion of immigrants. While positive mentions of Italians were infrequent, the lack of a pattern of negative commentary concerning Italian immigrants (even with passing mentions of "dagoes") suggests that the larger Gulf South similarly defied the pejorative national stereotypes of Italians. For an example of the occasional encouraging mention found in the Gulf South press outside of Louisiana, see "Sunny South Immigrants," *Weekly Clarion,* December 23, 1880 (Jackson, MS).

26. *Daily Picayune,* January 21, 1890.

27. "The Blood Vengeance," *Daily Picayune,* October 23, 1873; "The Italian-American Citizens Falling into Line," *Daily Picayune,* September 29, 1887; "Our Italian Fellow-Citizens," *Daily Picayune,* March 4, 1889; "Italian Immigration," *Daily Picayune,* January 15, 1895.

28. *Daily Picayune*, November 12, 1890; George E. Cunningham, "The Italian, a Hindrance to White Solidarity in Louisiana, 1890–1898," *Journal of Negro History* 50, no. 1 (January 1965): 24.

29. "The Italian Colony and Celebration," *Daily Picayune*, October 14, 1888.

30. "The Italian Colony and Celebration."

31. *Richland Beacon*, June 25, 1881 (Rayville, LA).

32. *Richland Beacon*, June 25, 1881.

33. *Louisiana Democrat*, September 14, 1881 (Alexandria, LA); *Weekly Messenger*, March 17, 1888; March 24, 1888; August 4, 1888 (St. Martinville, LA).

34. *Weekly Messenger*, March 17, 1888; March 24, 1888; August 4, 1888 (St. Martinville, LA).

35. "Sunny South Immigrants," *Weekly Clarion*, December 23, 1880 (Jackson, MS).

36. *Daily Picayune*, November 4, 1888; "How to Eat an Orange," *Daily Picayune*, February 24, 1890.

37. In my review of Louisiana newspapers in the 1870s and 1880s, besides those articles that referred to the violent tendencies of Italians, I came across only two articles in the 1880s New Orleans press that employed a distinctively pejorative assessment of Italians (*Daily Picayune*, November 4, 1888; *The Mascot*, September 7, 1889).

38. *New York Tribune*, August 5, 1888; *National Tribune*, August 2, 1888 (Washington, DC); *New York Times*, March 16, 1891; *Daily Picayune*, November 4, 1888.

39. For early references to the Mafia in the Gulf South press, see the following: "Brigands; Bitterness," *Daily Commercial*, April 12, 1877 (Vicksburg, MS); "Brigandage in Sicily," *New Orleans Item*, October 2, 1878; "Murder Mystery: Believed to be a Newly Arrived Italian Immigrant, a Victim of the Dread Vendetta," *Daily Picayune*, January, 20, 1889; "News in Brief," *Huntsville Gazette*, April 13, 1889; "The Italian Vendetta," *Daily Advocate*, October 24, 1890 (Baton Rouge); "The Italian Citizens and the Mafia," *Daily Picayune*, March 20, 1891. I elaborate on the (belief in the) Mafia in Louisiana in chapter 2, but for more on the history of the Mafia in Louisiana, see Thomas Hunt and Martha Macheca Sheldon, *Deep Water: Joseph P. Macheca and the Birth of the American Mafia* (New York: iUniverse, Inc., 2007); Michael L. Kurtz, "Organized Crime in Louisiana History: Myth and Reality," *Louisiana History* 24, no. 4 (1983): 355–76; Nelli, *The Business of Crime*, chapters 2–3; Nystrom, *Creole Italian: Sicilian Immigrants and the Shaping of New Orleans Food Culture*, 62–63; Louis Andrew Vyhnanek, *Unorganized Crime: New Orleans in the 1920s* (Lafayette: Center for Louisiana Studies, University of Southwestern Louisiana, 1998).

40. For other examples of the "vendetta" or "blood vengeance," see "The Blood Vengeance: A Sicilian Vendetta," *Daily Picayune*, October 23, 1873; "The Vendetta," *Daily Picayune*, May 23, 1874; "More Murder," *Daily Picayune*, July 14, 1874; "Is It a Vendetta? A Shooting Affray Down Town," *Daily Picayune*, April 20, 1878; "The Vendetta," *Daily Picayune*, July 16, 1881; "Homicide at French Market," *Daily Picayune*, November 1, 1884.

41. "The Vendetta," *Daily Picayune*, May 23, 1874.

42. "Italian Murder," *Daily Picayune*, February 28, 1889; "Our Italian Fellow-Citizens," *Daily Picayune*, March 4, 1889.

43. "The Blood Vengeance: A Sicilian Vendetta," *Daily Picayune*, October 23, 1873.

44. "Assassination as a Lost Art," *Daily Picayune*, December 9, 1884.

45. "Gotham Gossip," *Daily Picayune*, October 27, 1888.

46. "Italian Immigrants," *Daily Picayune*, December 27, 1888.

47. "Italian Immigrants," *Daily Picayune*, October 27, 1890.

48. "From Sunny Italy, Arrival of a Shipload of Immigrants," *Times Democrat*, October 18, 1888.

49. For examples, see the following: "The City," *Daily Picayune*, February 1, 1872; "The Knife," *Daily Picayune*, March 31, 1873; "Homicidal," *Daily Picayune*, June 9, 1874; "Deadly Issues," *Daily Picayune*, July 30, 1875; "Our Picayunes," *Daily Picayune*, August 11, 1884; "Reward for Dago Pete," *Daily Advocate*, September 15, 1884.

50. "Levee Dens," *Daily Picayune*, January 20, 1874.

51. "The Fish Question," *Daily Picayune*, June 16, 1874; *Daily Advocate*, April 16, 1886 (Baton Rouge).

52. Much of the documentation used to claim evidence of widespread anti-Italian sentiment in Louisiana has either been derived from sources outside of Louisiana (Gambino, *Vendetta*, 255; LaGumina, *Wop!*; Jacobson, *Whiteness of a Different Color*, 56–58) or from a misreading of Louisiana newspapers (Mangione and Morreale, *La Storia: Five Centuries of the Italian American Experience*, chapter 13).

53. *American Newspaper Directory*, 19th ed. (New York: Geo. P. Rowell, 1887).

54. *The Mascot*, January 5, 1889.

55. "Result of Encouraging Immigration," *The Mascot*, April 13, 1889.

56. Nystrom, *Creole Italian*, 33.

57. Bureau of the Census, *Eleventh Census of the United States, 1890*, 687 and 691; Bureau of the Census, *Twelfth Census of the United States, 1900*, 815; Bureau of the Census, *Thirteenth Census of the United States, 1910*, clxxiv and 813. By 1910, foreign-born Italians made up nearly 40 percent of the state's foreign-born white population (Bureau of the Census, *Thirteenth Census of the United States, 1910*, 773).

58. "A Morning Tour in Little Italy," *Daily Picayune*, July 30, 1899; *Daily Picayune*, December 12, 1900; Richard Campanella, "An Ethnic Geography of New Orleans," *Journal of American History* 94, no. 3 (2007), 708–9.

59. Margavio and Salomone, *Bread and Respect*, 116. For more on the integrated settlement patterns of immigrants within New Orleans, see Julie M. Weise, *Corazon De Dixie: Mexicanos in the U.S. South since 1910* (Chapel Hill: University of North Carolina Press, 2015), chapter 1.

60. Margavio and Salomone, *Bread and Respect*, chapter 3; LaGumina, *Wop!*, chapter 4.

61. For another case where immigration and ethnicity operated differently in "Europeanized" New Orleans (than elsewhere in the United States), see Weise, *Corazon De Dixie*, chapter 1.

62. Campanella, "An Ethnic Geography of New Orleans," 705–8.

63. Irish immigrants founded a benevolent society in New Orleans as early as 1818. They settled primarily among and developed alliances with the English-speaking, Anglo-American population in the Faubourg St. Marie district. By 1850, the Irish were the largest ethnic group in New Orleans and made up 20 percent of the city's population. For more on

the Irish in New Orleans, see Laura D. Kelley, *The Irish in New Orleans* (Lafayette: University of Louisiana at Lafayette Press, 2014).

64. Vincenza Scarpaci, "Walking the Color Line: Italian Immigrants in Rural Louisiana, 1880–1910," in *Are Italians White? How Race Is Made in America*, ed. Jennifer Guglielmo and Salvatore Salerno (New York: Routledge, 2003), 70.

65. Scarpaci, "Walking the Color Line," 71.

66. Edna Bonacich, "A Theory of Middleman Minorities," *American Sociological Review* 38, no. 5 (1973): 583–94.

67. Scarpaci, "Walking the Color Line," 61–63; Higham, *Strangers in the Land,* chapter 7; Cunningham, "The Italian, a Hindrance to White Solidarity in Louisiana, 1890–1898," 24–25.

68. Scarpaci, "Walking the Color Line," 67; Cunningham, "The Italian"; Fava to U.S. Secretary of State John Hay, 15 January 1900, Notes from the Italian Legation in the U.S. to the Department of State, #1739, Immigration History Research Center Archives, University of Minnesota; G. C. Vinci to U.S. Secretary of State John Hay, 25 July 1899, Notes from the Italian Legation in the U.S. to the Department of State, #1739, Immigration History Research Center Archives, University of Minnesota.

69. Scarpaci, "Walking the Color Line," 63; Guglielmo, *Living the Revolution,* 11; Jacobson, *Whiteness of a Different Color,* 57.

70. "Passenger Lists of Vessels Arriving at New Orleans, Louisiana, 1820–1902," Records of the Immigration and Naturalization Service, NA.

71. Ambassador Baron Fava to U.S. Secretary of State Richard Olney, January 10, 1897, Notes from the Italian Legation in the U.S. to the Department of State, #1729, Immigration History Research Center Archives, University of Minnesota; "The Italian Lynching in St. Charles Parish," *Daily Picayune,* April 14, 1897.

72. Ronald M. Labbe, "That the Reign of Robbery May Never Return to Louisiana: The Constitution of 1879," in *In Search of Fundamental Law: Louisiana's Constitutions, 1812–1974,* ed. Warren M. Billings and Edward F. Haas (Lafayette: Center for Louisiana Studies, University of Southwestern Louisiana, 1993). See also "International Squabble," April 24, 1891. This clause remained at the forefront of the controversial disenfranchisement debates in 1898; for an extended discussion, see chapter 3.

73. *Papers Relating to the Foreign Relations of the United States, 1891* (Washington, DC: Government Printing Office, 1891), Documents 602–62. See also Margavio and Salomone, *Bread and Respect;* Anne Chieko Moore and Hester Anne Hale, *Benjamin Harrison: Centennial President* (New York: Nova Publishers, 2009); Marco Rimanelli and Sheryl L. Postman, *The 1891 New Orleans Lynching and U.S.–Italian Relations: A Look Back* (New York: P. Lang, 1992); Tom Smith, *The Crescent City Lynchings: The Murder of Chief Hennessy, the New Orleans "Mafia" Trials, and the Parish Prison Mob.* (Guilford, CT: Lyons Press, 2007).

74. "International Squabble," *Daily Picayune,* April 24, 1891.

75. "International Squabble," *Daily Picayune,* April 24, 1891; Ambassador Baron Fava to U.S. Secretary of State Richard Olney, December 31, 1896, Notes from the Italian Legation in the U.S. to the Department of State, #1729, Immigration History Research Center Archives, University of Minnesota.

76. Marco Rimanelli, "The New Orleans Lynching and US–Italian Relations from Har-

mony to War-Scare: Immigration, Mafia, Diplomacy," in *The 1891 New Orleans Lynching and U.S.–Italian Relations,* 155–56.

77. *Papers Relating to the Foreign Relations of the United States, 1891,* Document 662; Marco Rimanelli, "The 1891–92 U.S.–Italian Crisis and War-Scare: Foreign and Domestic Policies of the Harrison and Di Rudini Governments," in *The 1891 New Orleans Lynching and U.S.– Italian Relations,* 255–56.

78. For an extended discussion of the Hahnville lynching, see chapter 2.

79. Fava to Olney, December 31, 1896. By "state" in this context, the U.S. State Department meant the State of Louisiana.

80. Fava to Olney, December 31, 1896.

81. Of note, the US State Department, especially in the 1890s, does not appear to have made a similar argument on behalf of the citizenship status of black Americans.

82. Fava to Olney, December 31, 1896; Fava to Olney, August 19, 1896.

83. Fava to Olney, December 31, 1896.

84. Ambassador Baron Fava to U.S. Secretary of State Thomas Bayard, January 27, 1897, Notes from the Italian Legation in the U.S. to the Department of State, #1729, Immigration History Research Center Archives, University of Minnesota.

85. Fava to Bayard, January 27, 1897.

86. Fava to Olney, December 31, 1896.

87. Fava to Olney, December 31, 1896.

88. Fava to Olney, January 10, 1897; Fava to Olney, September 6, 1896.

89. Ambassador Baron Fava to U.S. Secretary of State John Sherman, March 13, 1897.

90. G. P. Vinci to U.S. Secretary of State John Sherman, July 31, 1897.

91. The *Lafayette Gazette* pointed out the significance of these comparatively large indemnity payments for Italians when a jury in Abilene, Kansas awarded the family of a black lynching victim the grand sum of two dollars (January 27, 1894).

92. "The Lynched Italians," *Daily Picayune,* April 20, 1897; "The Italians and the Mafia," *New York Times,* March 25, 1891.

93. Benevolent Society Papers, American Italian Research Library, East Bank Regional Library, Metairie, Louisiana.

94. "The Union of Italy," *Daily Picayune,* June 2, 1884.

95. "The Italian Colony," *Daily Picayune,* November 2, 1890.

96. "Father Manoritta's Response," *Daily Picayune,* November 16, 1890, emphasis mine.

97. See March 1891 issues of *Il Progresso* and *Cristoforo Colombo,* New York City; see also "The Hennessy Case Abroad," *Daily Picayune,* December 3, 1890; "Italians Ask Protection," *New York Times,* July 23, 1899.

98. *Papers Relating to the Foreign Relations of the United States, 1891,* Documents 626; Smith, *The Crescent City Murders,* 232; "What is Said in New York: Italian Journalists Though Still Indignant are Calmer Now," *New York Times,* March 17, 1891.

99. "St. Salvador's Day Celebrated by the Societa Italiana di M. B. Cefalutana," *Daily Picayune,* August 9, 1897; "St. Bartholomew's Day," *Daily Picayune,* August 24, 1899; "Contessa Entellina: The Italian Society Celebrates its Seventeenth Anniversary," *Daily Picayune,* September 9, 1903.

100. "Discovery of America Celebrated by Italians: Societa Italiana di Mutua Honors

the 412th Anniversary with Ceremonies and a Banquet. Mayor Capdevielle Being a Special Guest," *Daily Picayune*, November 13, 1904.

101. "Garibaldi Statue Unveiled in Metairie Cemetery," *Daily Picayune*, September 24, 1906.

2. The Lynchings of Italians in Louisiana and Mississippi (1880s–1910)

1. *Papers Relating to the Foreign Relations of the United States, 1891*, Documents 602–62. The spelling of these names varies across documents; for example, Girolamo Caruso and Vincenzo Traina went by their Americanized names, respectively, James and Charles; Antonio Bagnetto, indicted as such, was identified by his Italianized surname, Abbagnato, within Italian documentation. I have preserved consistency based on the most commonly occurring spellings.

2. Smith, *The Crescent City Lynchings*, 217; Margavio and Salomone, *Bread and Respect*, 212.

3. *Daily States*, March 14, 1891.

4. *Papers Relating to the Foreign Relations of the United States, 1891*, Document 626.

5. *Papers Relating to the Foreign Relations of the United States, 1891*, Document 647. Of the eleven victims, Macheca was born in New Orleans but of Sicilian origins; Bagnetto, James Caruso, Rocco Geraci, Marchesi, Monasterio, Polizzi, and Charles Traina were all natives of Sicily; Antonio Scaffidi was born in Messina and Loreto Comitis near Rome; Frank Romero was an Italian-born American citizen by naturalization (*Papers Relating to the Foreign Relations of the United States, 1891*, Documents 602–62; Nelli, *The Business of Crime: Italians and Syndicate Crime in the United States*, 46).

6. *Times Democrat*, March 15, 1891.

7. *Papers Relating to the Foreign Relations of the United States, 1891*, Document 626.

8. While I am cautious against discounting those deaths that occurred in riots when they might be more accurately identified as lynchings, I have chosen not to include an in-depth analysis of the deaths of Giuseppe Testa and another unknown Italian on May 14, 1906, in Marion, North Carolina, the deaths of two unknown Italians in Chathamville, Louisiana, in 1907, or the deaths of two Sicilians, Angelo Albano and Castenge Ficarotta, in Tampa, Florida, in 1910. The deaths in Marion occurred in the midst of a labor riot at the Spruce Pine Carolina Co., where Italians were employed in railroad construction; likewise, the events in Chathamville occurred under similar circumstances of a labor riot. While these deaths should certainly be considered within narratives of labor and immigrant violence, I do not analyze them as lynchings per se since these men may have died accidentally in the course of the riots rather than having been targeted as individuals. The lynching of Albano and Ficarotta in Tampa falls outside of my geographic focus and has been otherwise well documented. See Stefano Luconi, "Tampa's 1910 Lynching: The Italian-American Perspective and its Implications," *Florida Historical Quarterly* 88, no. 1 (Summer 2009): 30–53. In general, Italians were lynched in parishes and counties where a median number of lynchings

of African Americans occurred relative to the rest of a state; this is to say that Italians were not lynched in parishes and counties particularly known for their penchant for lynching (Equal Justice Initiative, *Supplement: Lynchings By County* [Montgomery, AL: Equal Justice Initiative, 2017], accessed April 14, 2019, https://eji.org/sites/default/files/lynching-in-america-second-edition-supplement-by-county.pdf).

9. Clive Webb, "The Lynching of Sicilian Immigrants in the American South, 1886–1910," in *Lynching Reconsidered: New Perspectives in the Study of Mob Violence*, ed. William D. Carrigan (New York: Routledge, 2008), 175–204. For more on the lynchings of Mexicans and Mexican Americans, see William D. Carrigan and Clive Webb, *Forgotten Dead: Mob Violence against Mexicans in the United States, 1848–1928* (Oxford: Oxford University Press, 2013).

10. Few scholars have considered the lynchings of Sicilians and other Italians or have performed a comprehensive case study of these incidents. For the few broad overviews of the various lynchings of Sicilians/Italians in the South, see Patrizia Salvetti, *Rope and Soap: Lynchings of Italians in the United States*, trans. Fabio Girelli-Carasi (New York: Bordighera Press, John D. Calandra Italian-American Institute, 2017), originally published as *Corda e Sapone: Storie dei Linciaggi di Italiani negli USA* (Rome: Donzelli, 2012); Patrizia Famá Stahle, *The Italian Emigration of Modern Times: Relations between Italy and the United States concerning Emigration Policy, Diplomacy and Anti-Immigrant Sentiment, 1870–1927* (Newcastle, UK: Cambridge Scholars Publishing, 2016); Webb, "The Lynching of Sicilian Immigrants in the American South, 1886–1910." Salvetti, Stahle, and Webb all examine the lynchings in Vicksburg, New Orleans, Hahnville, Tallulah, and Erwin; Webb offers the only secondary recounting of the Shelby or Chathamville lynchings. Edward F. Haas provides one of the most oft-cited scholarly accounts of the Tallulah lynching ("Guns, Goats, and Italians: The Tallulah Lynching of 1899," *North Louisiana Historical Association* 13, no. 2 (1982): 45–58); see also Vellon, "'Between White Men and Negroes.'" For more on the Vicksburg lynching, see Vellon, *A Great Conspiracy against Our Race*, 1–2. For the most widely cited accounts of the 1891 lynching in New Orleans, see Gambino, *Vendetta*; Nelli, *The Business of Crime*.

11. National Association for the Advancement of Colored People (NAACP), quoted in Lisa D. Cook, "Converging to a National Lynching Database: Recent Developments and the Way Forward," *Historical Methods: A Journal of Quantitative and Interdisciplinary History* 45, no. 2 (2012): 56. *Project HAL: Historical American Lynching Data Collection* (University of North Carolina, Wilmington) also uses this as its official definition and means of evaluating what sorts of instances count as a lynching.

12. Hannah Rosen, *Terror in the Heart of Freedom: Citizenship, Sexual Violence, and the Meaning of Race in the Postemancipation South* (Chapel Hill: University of North Carolina Press, 2009), 8.

13. Amy Kate Bailey and Stewart Emory Tolnay, *Lynched: The Victims of Southern Mob Violence* (Chapel Hill: University of North Carolina Press, 2015), 183. The historiography of lynching and violence against African Americans in the American South is vast; for some of the foundational, oft-cited, and latest scholarship, see the following: W. Fitzhugh Brundage, *Lynching in the New South: Georgia and Virginia, 1880–1930* (Urbana: University of Illinois Press, 1993); W. Fitzhugh Brundage, ed., *Under Sentence of Death: Lynching in the South*

(Chapel Hill: University of North Carolina Press, 1997); Equal Justice Initiative, *Lynching in America: Confronting the Legacy of Racial Terror*, 3rd ed. (Montgomery, AL: Equal Justice Initiative, 2017), accessed April 14, 2019, https://lynchinginamerica.eji.org/report/; Crystal N. Feimster, *Southern Horrors: Women and the Politics of Rape and Lynching* (Cambridge, MA: Harvard University Press, 2009); Stewart Emory Tolnay and E. M. Beck, *A Festival of Violence: An Analysis of Southern Lynchings, 1882–1930* (Urbana: University of Illinois Press, 1995); Ida B. Wells-Barnett, *On Lynchings: Southern Horrors; A Red Record; Mob Rule in New Orleans* (1892; repr., New York: Arno Press, 1969); Amy Louise Wood, *Lynching and Spectacle: Witnessing Racial Violence in America, 1890–1940* (Chapel Hill: University of North Carolina Press, 2009).

14. Cook, "Converging to a National Lynching Database," 58. Because of the political focus of the data collectors, rightfully interested in revealing the dangerous realities of life for black Americans at the turn of the century, these data inventories miss entirely the Reconstruction era as well as those lynchings that occurred in the West or Midwest. The number of lynching victims found in these inventories may be both under- and overreported. Lynchings that were not considered "newsworthy," or were only reported in regional papers, may have been easily missed in the data compilation, just as the NAACP may have systematically overcounted victims in their compilation of statistics because of their vested political interest in securing federal antilynching legislation.

15. *Chicago Tribune* (1882–1918); Tuskegee Institute (1892–1968); NAACP, *Thirty Years of Lynching in the United States* (1889–1918); Tolnay and Beck, *A Festival of Violence*; Project HAL: Historical American Lynching Data Collection Project (an open-source, web-based lynching inventory based on NAACP lynching data and supplemented by user-generated recordings); Cook, "Converging to a National Lynching Database, 59."

16. Lynching scholarship has since expanded to provide a more geographically and racially comprehensive assessment of lynchings in the United States. For other scholars who have worked to move lynching studies outside the South and beyond the black/white binary, see the following: Lisa Arellano, *Vigilantes and Lynch Mobs: Narratives of Community and Nation* (Philadelphia: Temple University Press, 2012); William D. Carrigan, *The Making of a Lynching Culture: Violence and Vigilantism in Central Texas, 1836–1916* (Urbana: University of Illinois Press, 2004); William D. Carrigan, ed., *Lynching Reconsidered: New Perspectives in the Study of Mob Violence* (New York: Routledge, 2008); Carrigan and Webb, *Forgotten Dead*; Stephen J. Leonard, *Lynching in Colorado, 1859–1919* (Boulder: University Press of Colorado, 2002); Michael J. Pfeifer, *Rough Justice: Lynching and American Society, 1874–1947* (Urbana: University of Illinois Press, 2004); Michael J. Pfeifer, *The Roots of Rough Justice: Origins of American Lynching* (Urbana: University of Illinois Press, 2011); Ashraf H. A. Rushdy, *The End of American Lynching* (New Brunswick, NJ: Rutgers University Press, 2012); Christopher Waldrep, *The Many Faces of Judge Lynch: Extralegal Violence and Punishment in America* (New York: Palgrave Macmillan, 2002). The scholarship on the lynchings of nonblack or "white" victims remains extremely limited. See Bailey and Tolnay, *Lynched: The Victims of Southern Mob Violence*, chapter 7; Nancy McClean, "Gender, Sexuality, and the Politics of Lynching: The Leo Frank Case Revisited," in *Under Sentence of Death: Lynching in the South*, ed. W. Fitzhugh Brundage (Chapel Hill: University of North Carolina Press, 1997).

17. I compiled these statistics from my own analysis of the raw lynching data from *Project HAL: Historical American Lynching Data Collection*. The data available through *Project HAL* includes date, location, victim's name, race, sex, race of the lynch mob, and alleged offense of the victim. Focusing my analysis on those incidents reported in Louisiana and Mississippi, I recorded all lynching victims reported as "white" and categorized their alleged offenses based on the Bailey and Tolnay typology (*Lynched: The Victims of Southern Mob Violence*, 192). The typology of alleged offenses includes the following: violent action or threat of violence, sexual overtone, attacked because of a connection to someone (either related to or trying to protect an alleged offender), property offenses (burglary, etc.), character violation, "challenger" offenses meaning someone "def[ied] the prevailing racial and economic hierarchies," rebellious actions (arson, etc.), and unknown or those that "defied easy classification."

18. This compares with black lynching victims, of whom about half in both Louisiana and Mississippi were lynched for the (alleged) crime of murder or attempted murder.

19. As Ida B. Wells-Barnett famously demonstrated, despite claims that African Americans were lynched as a means of protecting white women and white women's bodies, in fact, less than one-third of lynchings actually involved a rape charge. Wells-Barnett thus exposed that rape accusations were only a guise to excuse and justify the real motives behind lynching: an effort to quash black economic progress (Wells-Barnett, *On Lynchings: Southern Horrors; A Red Record; Mob Rule in New Orleans*).

20. The victims lynched for "being foreign workers" were the two previously mentioned Sicilians who were killed in Chathamville, Louisiana, in 1907.

21. Bailey and Tolnay, *Lynched*, 196.

22. Bailey and Tolnay, *Lynched*, 184.

23. Bailey and Tolnay, *Lynched*, chapter 7. The risk of a "mulatto" being lynched was only reduced if they unexceptionally lived in an area with a high number of mixed-race persons; agricultural workers were only more likely to be lynched if they were the exception and lived in an area with few black agricultural workers.

24. Department of Commerce and Labor, Bureau of the Census, *Thirteenth Census of the United States Taken in the Year 1910, Volume 2: Population*, 778–88 and 1044–58.

25. Nelli, *The Business of Crime*, chapter 3; Smith, *The Crescent City Lynchings*, 40.

26. "The Hennessy Murder and the Italians," *Daily Picayune*, November 9, 1890. If Italians were responsible for Hennessy's murder, it remains unlikely that it was the same Italians who were arrested and lynched for the crime. For more on the various theories on who actually killed Hennessy and "who killa de chief," a contemporaneous reference in mock-Italian dialect that assumed Italians guilty of Chief Hennessy's murder and which subsequently led to their lynching in 1891, see the following: John V. Baiamonte, "'Who Killa de Chief' Revisited: The Hennessey Assassination and Its Aftermath, 1890–1991," *Louisiana History* 33, no. 2 (1992): 140; John E. Coxe, "The New Orleans Mafia Incident," *Louisiana Historical Quarterly* 20 (1937) 1067–1110; Barbara Botein, "The Hennessy Case: An Episode in Anti-Italian Nativism," *Louisiana History* 20, no. 3 (Summer 1979): 261–79; Gambino, *Vendetta;* Alan G. Gauthreaux, "An Inhospitable Land: Anti-Italian Sentiment and Violence in Louisiana, 1891–1924," *Louisiana History* 51, no. 1 (2010): 41–68; Daniela G. Jäger, "The

Worst 'White Lynching' in American History: Elites vs. Italians in New Orleans, 1891," *AAA: Arbeiten Aus Anglistik Und Amerikanistik* 27, no. 2 (2002): 161–79; John S. Kendall, "Who Killa de Chief?," *Louisiana Historical Quarterly* 22, no. 2 (1939): 492–530; Margavio and Salomone, *Bread and Respect*; Nelli, *The Business of Crime*; Rimanelli and Postman, *The 1891 New Orleans Lynching and U.S.–Italian Relations*; Lyle Saxon, *Gumbo Ya-Ya* (Boston: Houghton Mifflin, 1945); Smith, *The Crescent City Lynchings*.

27. Kurtz, "Organized Crime in Louisiana History," 362.

28. Jäger, "The Worst 'White Lynching' in American History," 168; Nystrom, *New Orleans After the Civil War*, 221; Smith, The Crescent City Lynchings, 44–45.

29. *Papers Relating to the Foreign Relations of the United States, 1891*, Documents 602–62; Criminal District Court Docket Numbers 14220, 14221, 14231, 14414, 14230, 14415 (1890) *David Hennessy Murder Trial Documents*, New Orleans Public Library; Smith, *The Crescent City Lynchings*, 123.

30. The indictments also named the escaped criminal from Aquila, Loreto Comitis, stevedores Rocco Geraci and Salvatore Sinceri, the petty thief Bastian Incardona, the "fool" Emanuele Polizzi from San Cipirello, the naturalized Matranga ally Frank Romero, and the Palermitano laborer Charles Traina (Gambino, *Vendetta*, chapter 3).

31. See March 1891 issues of the *Daily Picayune*.

32. "The Italian Government and The Assassins" and "The Mafia and its Friends," *Daily States*, March 16, 1891.

33. "What Do the Italians Want?," *New York Times*, March 16, 1891; "The Lynching Justifiable," *New York Times*, March 17, 1891.

34. John Dickie, *Cosa Nostra*, 60–63.

35. Kurtz, "Organized Crime in Louisiana History," 359.

36. For more on the belief in the existence of the Mafia in Louisiana, see Thomas Hunt and Martha Macheca Sheldon, *Deep Water: Joseph P. Macheca and the Birth of the American Mafia* (New York: iUniverse, 2007); Kurtz, "Organized Crime in Louisiana History," 355–76; Nelli, *The Business of Crime*, chapters 2–3; Nystrom, *Creole Italian*, 62–63; Louis Andrew Vyhnanek, *Unorganized Crime: New Orleans in the 1920s* (Lafayette: University of Southwestern Louisiana, 1998).

37. "A Shameful Demonstration. Insulting the Stars and Stripes," *New Orleans Item*, March 15, 1891.

38. *Daily Picayune, Times Democrat*, and *New Delta*, March 14, 1891.

39. *Times Democrat*, March 15, 1891; the *New York Times* offered a similar description of the interracial lynch mob. The *New Delta*, a rather unreliable New Orleans daily, later reported that three black mob participants dragged Bagnetto's body through the streets of New Orleans. For more on the rarity of interracial lynch mobs and the paucity of lynching endorsements within the black press, see Brundage, *Lynching in the New South: Georgia and Virginia, 1880–1930*, 45–47. Whether black New Orleanians were present or participated in the lynching of Italians, the varied response to the lynching of Italians in the black press— sympathy, commiseration, bitterness, hostility, and indifference—signaled that Italians were not statically categorized as "white" within the black community ("Editorial," *Freeman's Lance*, April 3, 1891 [Peru, KS)]; "New Orleans," *Plaindealer*, June 26, 1891 [Detroit]).

40. *Daily Picayune*, March 14, 1891.

41. *Times Democrat*, March 15, 1891.

42. All the victims were Sicilian or Sicilian-born, save for Scaffidi, Comitis, and Romero (*Papers Relating to the Foreign Relations of the United States, 1891*, Documents 602–62).

43. *Papers Relating to the Foreign Relations of the United States, 1891*, Document 634 and Document 647.

44. "A Human Fiend," *Weekly Commercial Herald*, April 2, 1886 (Vicksburg, MS).

45. "A Human Fiend"; *Macon Beacon*, April 3, 1886 (Noxubee County, MS).

46. "A Human Fiend"; *Macon Beacon*, April 3, 1886 (Noxubee County, MS).

47. "A Fearful Crime," *Daily Telegraph*, March 29, 1886 (Monroe, LA); "A Human Fiend."

48. *Macon Beacon*, April 3, 1886 (Macon, MS); "A Fearful Crime," *Daily Telegraph*, March 29, 1886 (Monroe, LA).

49. Ambassador Baron Fava to U.S. Secretary of State Thomas Bayard, April 29, 1886, Notes from the Italian Legation in the U.S. to the Department of State, #1725, Immigration History Research Center Archives, University of Minnesota; Ambassador Baron Fava to U.S. Secretary of State Thomas Bayard, May 9, 1886, Notes from the Italian Legation in the U.S. to the Department of State, #1725.

50. This category comes from Bailey and Tolnay's previously cited typology (*Lynched: The Victims of Southern Mob Violence*).

51. *Greenville Times*, May 28, 1887 (Washington County, MS); *Daily Advocate*, June 15, 1887 (Baton Rouge, LA).

52. "A Murderer Captured," *Memphis Daily Appeal*, June 7, 1887. See also *Daily Advocate*, June 15, 1887 (Baton Rouge, LA).

53. *Greenville Times*, June 4, June 11, 1887 (Washington County, MS).

54. "Greenville," *Daily Picayune*, June 14, 1887.

55. Shelby (or Shelby Depot) has only been included in one other study of Sicilian lynchings in the South (Webb, "The Lynching of Sicilian Immigrants in the American South, 1886–1910).

56. "Lynched by a Mob," *New York Times*, June 14, 1887; Webb, "The Lynching of Sicilian Immigrants in the American South, 1886–1910," 176–77. Notwithstanding efforts to further track Joe's background, with only his first name and date of death, "Dago Joe's" background remains untraceable within census records and genealogical data.

57. "Greenville," *Daily Picayune*, June 14, 1887; *Daily Advocate*, June 15, 1887 (Baton Rouge); *Huntsville Gazette*, June 18, 1887 (Huntsville, AL).

58. "A Murderer Captured," *Memphis Daily Appeal*, June 7, 1887.

59. "A Murderer Captured."

60. *Daily Picayune* July 8, 1887.

61. The following articles categorized Joe as either a "colored man" or a "half-breed": *Memphis Daily Appeal*, June 9, 1887; "A Mississippi Lynching," *Fort Worth Daily Gazette*, June 14, 1887; "Lynching a Boy's Murderer," *New York Sun*, June 14, 1887; *Milan Exchange*, June 18, 1887 (Milan, TN). Additionally, and unlike other lynchings of Italians, no diplomatic correspondence between representatives of the Italian state and the U.S. State Department

discussed "Dago Joe's" lynching or requested indemnity payments for his death. This further suggests Joe's non-Italian background.

62. *Papers Relating to the Foreign Relations of the United States, 1896* (Washington: Government Printing Office, 1896), Documents 332.

63. "St. Charles Decides Against a Lynching," *Daily Picayune*, August 7, 1896.

64. *Papers Relating to the Foreign Relations of the United States, 1896*, Documents 332; "The Triple Lynching in St. Charles Parish," *Daily Picayune*, August 10, 1896; "The Italian Lynching," *Daily Picayune*, April 14, 1897; Ambassador Baron Fava to U.S. Secretary of State Richard Olney, August 19, 1896, Notes from the Italian Legation in the U.S. to the Department of State, #1729, Immigration History Research Center Archives, University of Minnesota. See also Margavio and Salomone, *Bread and Respect*; Scarpaci, "Walking the Color Line," 67; Cunningham, "The Italian, a Hindrance to White Solidarity in Louisiana, 1890–1898."

65. "St. Charles Decides Against a Lynching," *Daily Picayune*, August 7, 1896; *Papers Relating to the Foreign Relations of the United States, 1896*, Documents 328.

66. *Colfax Chronicle*, August 22, 1896 (Grant Parish, LA); "The Italians and the Mafia," *Daily Picayune*, August 28, 1897.

67. "The Triple Lynching in St. Charles Parish," *Daily Picayune*, August 10, 1896; "The Italian Lynching," *Daily Picayune*, August 12, 1896.

68. *Daily Picayune*, August 9, 1896, as quoted in Webb, "The Lynching of Sicilian Immigrants in the American South, 1886–1910," 183.

69. *Papers Relating to the Foreign Relations of the United States, 1891*, Documents 647.

70. "The Italians and the Mafia," *Daily Picayune*, August 28, 1897.

71. According to diplomatic correspondence, the local press originally misidentified the victims as Decino Sorcoro and Angelo Marcuso (Ambassador Baron Fava to U.S. Secretary of State Richard Olney, August 19, 1896, Notes from the Italian Legation in the U.S. to the Department of State, #1729).

72. *Papers Relating to the Foreign Relations of the United States, 1896*, Documents 333.

73. *Papers Relating to the Foreign Relations of the United States, 1899* (Washington: Government Printing Office, 1899), Document 445.

74. Report by the Secretary of the Royal Embassy at Washington Camillo Romano, August 1, 1899, Notes from the Italian Legation in the U.S. to the Department of State, #1739; *Papers Relating to the Foreign Relations of the United States, 1899*, Documents 445.

75. *Times Democrat*, July 21, 1899.

76. "Hung Five," *Arkansas Gazette*, July 23, 1899.

77. *Papers Relating to the Foreign Relations of the United States, 1899*, Documents 445.

78. *Weekly Messenger*, July 29, 1899 (St. Martinsville, LA). See also Haas, "Guns, Goats, and Italians."

79. *Weekly Messenger*, July 29, 1899 (St. Martinsville, LA).

80. "Tallulah Lynching. Italians Had Planned a Plot to Murder. Conspiracy Clearly Shown by the Trend of Events. The Dead Men All Had Blackened Records. One of the Remaining Italians Left the Parish Hurriedly," *Times Democrat*, July 22, 1899.

81. "Tallulah Lynching."

82. "Tallulah Lynching." In anticipation of impending international attention, the regional press denied the validity of such claims that Italians were forced out of Tallulah.

83. Fava to U.S. Secretary of State John Hay, January 15, 1900, Notes from the Italian Legation in the U.S. to the Department of State, #1739; G. C. Vinci Letter to U.S. Secretary of State John Hay, July 25, 1899, Notes from the Italian Legation in the U.S. to the Department of State, #1739.

84. Report by the Secretary of the Royal Embassy at Washington Camillo Romano, August 1, 1899, Notes from the Italian Legation in the U.S. to the Department of State, #1739; "The Tallulah Tragedy," *Daily Picayune*, July 24, 1899.

85. Report by the Secretary of the Royal Embassy at Washington Camillo Romano, August 1, 1899, Notes from the Italian Legation in the U.S. to the Department of State, #1739.

86. "Lynching of Sicilians at Tallulah," *Daily Picayune*, July 22, 1899; *Daily States*, July 22, 1899; "Five Italians Lynched," *Times Democrat*, July 22, 1899.

87. Stefano Luconi, "The Lynching of Italian Americans: A Reassessment," ed. Alan J Gravano, Ilaria Serra, and American Italian Historical Association (New York: John D. Calandra Italian-American Institute, 2013), 58; Webb, "The Lynching of Sicilian Immigrants in the American South, 1886–1910," 178 and 187.

88. "Tallulah Lynching," *Times Democrat*, July 22, 1899.

89. "Citizens Plead Necessity For White Supremacy," *Times Democrat*, July 25, 1899.

90. "Our Italian Fellow-Citizens," *Daily Picayune*, October 17, 1890.

91. "Our Italian Fellow-Citizens." See also, "The Italian Colony," *Daily Picayune*, November 2, 1890.

92. "The Hennessy Murder and the Italians," *Daily Picayune*, November 9, 1890.

93. "The Italian Citizen and the Mafia," *Daily Picayune*, March 20, 1891; "Responsible Italians," *Daily States*, March 14, 1891.

94. "Italian Immigrants," *Daily Picayune*, October 17, 1890.

95. *Times Democrat*, October 17, 1890.

96. John Dittmer, *Black Georgia in the Progressive Era, 1900–1920* (Urbana: University of Illinois Press, 1977), 139.

97. For more on the concept of "racial scripts," see Molina, *How Race Is Made in America: Immigration, Citizenship, and the Historical Power of Racial Scripts.*

98. See March 1891 issues of *Il Progresso* and *Cristoforo Colombo*; "The Hennessy Case Abroad," *Daily Picayune*, December 3, 1890; Nelli, *The Business of Crime*, 56.

99. "The Hennessy Assassination," *Daily States*, March 4, 1891.

100. Wilds, *Afternoon Story*, 104.

101. See March 1891 issues of *Daily Picayune* and *Times Democrat*. See also "The Lynchers Justified: Report of the Grand Jury of New Orleans," *Daily Picayune*, May 6, 1891. Similar sentiment may be seen elsewhere in the *New York Times*: "The New Orleans Affair," *New York Times*, March 16, 1891; "The Lynching Justifiable," *New York Times*, March 17, 1891; "Lynch Law and the Mafia," *New York Times*, March 17, 1891; "Sharp Words by Judge Cowing," *New York Times*, March 17, 1891.

102. *Weekly Messenger*, March 21, 1891 (St. Martinsville, LA).

103. *Papers Relating to the Foreign Relations of the United States, 1891,* Document 659.

104. *Papers Relating to the Foreign Relations of the United States, 1901* (Washington: Government Printing Office, 1901), Document 265; Signor Carignani (The Chargé d'Affaires of His Majesty) to Acting U.S. Secretary of State, July 24, 1901, Notes from the Italian Legation in the U.S. to the Department of State, #1726. Although one newspaper called the two Serios "brothers," according to legation documents they were father and son.

105. *Papers Relating to the Foreign Relations of the United States, 1901,* Documents 265.

106. "Italians Killed," *The Caucasian,* July 14, 1901 (Shreveport, LA).

107. "Italians Killed," *The Caucasian,* July 14, 1901. "The Italian Killing," *The Pascagoula Democrat-Star,* July 26, 1901 (Pascagoula, MS).

108. *Greenville Times,* August 17, 1901 (Washington County, MS); *Greenville Times,* July 20, 1901 (Washington County, MS).

109. *Greenville Times,* July 20, 1901 (Washington County, MS).

110. *Greenville Times,* July 20, 1901.

111. "The Italian Killing," *The Pascagoula Democrat-Star,* July 26, 1901 (Pascagoula, MS). *Papers Relating to the Foreign Relations of the United States, 1901,* Documents 266. For an extended discussion of Governor Longino, see chapter 4.

112. Francesco Carignani (The Chargé d'Affaires of His Majesty) to Acting U.S. Secretary of State Alvey Adee, August 30, 1901, Notes from the Italian Legation in the U.S. to the Department of State, #1728.

113. *Greenville Times,* August 17, 1901 (Washington County, MS).

114. "Italy is Indignant," *Le Meschacebe,* July 27, 1901 (Lucy, LA).

115. *Greenville Times,* September 14, 1901 (Washington County, MS).

116. Signor Carignani (The Chargé d'Affaires of His Majesty) to Acting U.S. Secretary of State David Hill, July 22, 1901, Notes from the Italian Legation in the U.S. to the Department of State, #1726.

117. *Greenville Times,* September 14, 1901 (Washington County, MS).

118. *Project HAL: Historical American Lynching Data Collection Project.*

119. Luconi, "The Lynching of Italian Americans: A Reassessment." Amidst labor rioting, and therefore less emblematic of the previously discussed lynchings, Giuseppe Testa and another unknown Italian were killed on May 14, 1906, in Marion, North Carolina, as were two unknown Italians in Chathamville, Louisiana, in 1907.

3. "Electoral Freaks and Monstrosities" in Louisiana's Disenfranchisement Debates (1896–1898)

1. Quoted in "Suffrage Settled," *Daily Picayune* and *Times Democrat,* March 25, 1898; Scarpaci, "Walking the Color Line."

2. Alexander Keyssar, *The Right to Vote: The Contested History of Democracy in the United States* (New York: Basic Books, 2000).

3. Beyond the passing reference to the "Dago Clause" in Louisiana, few immigration and southern scholars have provided sustained attention to this particular historical moment.

For the more in-depth discussions of the impact of Louisiana disenfranchisement upon Italians, see the following: Vincenza Scarpaci, *Italian Immigrants in Louisiana's Sugar Parishes: Recruitment, Labor Conditions, and Community Relations, 1880–1910* (New York: Arno Press, 1980); Scarpaci, "Walking the Color Line," 60–76; Cunningham, "The Italian, a Hindrance to White Solidarity in Louisiana, 1890–1898," 22–36.

4. For more on the political complexities of the time period and the challenges that various people and groups posed to easy categorization, see Justin Nystrom, *New Orleans after the Civil War: Race, Politics, and a New Birth of Freedom* (Baltimore: Johns Hopkins University Press, 2010), and Donna A. Barnes, *The Louisiana Populist Movement, 1881–1900* (Baton Rouge: Louisiana State University Press, 2011). See also Kent B. Germany, *New Orleans after the Promises: Poverty, Citizenship, and the Search for the Great Society* (Athens: University of Georgia Press, 2007); Edward F. Haas, *Political Leadership in a Southern City: New Orleans in the Progressive Era, 1896–1902* (Ruston, LA: McGinty Publications, 1988); William Ivy Hair, *Bourbonism and Agrarian Protest* (Baton Rouge: Louisiana State University Press, 1969); Joy J. Jackson, *New Orleans in the Gilded Age: Politics and Urban Progress, 1880–1896* (Baton Rouge: Louisiana State University Press, 1969); Laura D. Kelley, *The Irish in New Orleans* (Lafayette: University of Louisiana at Lafayette Press, 2014).

5. For a further explanation of Louisiana's three particular geographies and attendant economies (alluvial cotton plantation parishes, alluvial sugar plantations, and backland cotton parishes), see Barnes, *The Louisiana Populist Movement, 1881–1900*, 38.

6. Barnes, *The Louisiana Populist Movement, 1881–1900*, 184. When Grover Cleveland's administration abruptly repealed the sugar subsidy in 1894, Louisiana's sugar planters dramatically and officially broke with the Democratic Party and realigned their political allegiance under a new banner: the National Republican Party or the "Lily White Republicans." The sugar planters called themselves the National Republican Party because they intended to vote Democrat in state and local but vote Republican in national elections (187).

7. Hair, *Bourbonism and Agrarian Protest; Louisiana Politics, 1877–1900*, 21–31; Nystrom, *New Orleans after the Civil War: Race, Politics, and a New Birth of Freedom*, 192–93.

8. The Choctaw Club was the name that the Ring adopted in its 1897 iteration; modeling themselves after the Iroquois Club (composed of members of Tammany Hall) in New York, its members voted on a Native American name and eventually settled on Choctaw. See Edward F. Haas, "John Fitzpatrick and Political Continuity in New Orleans, 1896–1899," *Louisiana History* 22, no. 1 (1981): 7–29. For more on the nineteenth-century use of Native American names, see Ruth B. Phillips, *Trading Identities: The Souvenir in Native North American Art from the Northeast, 1700–1900* (Seattle: University of Washington Press, 1999).

9. Haas, *Political Leadership in a Southern City*, 5; Scarpaci, *Italian Immigrants in Louisiana's Sugar Parishes*; Kelley, *The Irish in New Orleans*; Jackson, *New Orleans in the Gilded Age*; Germany, *New Orleans after the Promises*.

10. Despite the multiplicity of these names and their occasional interchangeability, I will refer to the political divisions within the Democratic Party by their most common usage during the 1890s: the Ring/Regulars and the Citizens' League/Reformers.

11. Hair, *Bourbonism and Agrarian Protest*, 21–31; Nystrom, *New Orleans after the Civil War*, 192–93.

12. Haas, *Political Leadership in a Southern City*; Kelley, *The Irish in New Orleans 168*; Brian Gary Ettinger, "John Fitzpatrick and the Limits of Working-Class Politics in New Orleans, 1892–1896," *Louisiana History* 26, no. 4 (1985): 344–45.

13. Hair, *Bourbonism and Agrarian Protest*, 115 and 237.

14. Barnes, *The Louisiana Populist Movement, 1881–1900*, 51 and 183.

15. Scarpaci, *Italian Immigrants in Louisiana's Sugar Parishes*, 281; Hair, *Bourbonism and Agrarian Protest*, 263; Justin Nystrom, *New Orleans After the Civil War: Race, Politics, and a New Birth of Freedom*, 235. The particularities of Louisiana's Populist Party, largely made up of northern "carpetbaggers," certain factions within the planter elite, and Louisiana's free black population, also contributed to the complicated allegiances during Louisiana's move toward disenfranchisement. For the most comprehensive history of the (failure of) Louisiana's Populist Party, see Barnes, *The Louisiana Populist Movement, 1881–1900*.

16. Nystrom, *New Orleans After the Civil War*, 236. See also Charles Vincent, "Black Constitution Makers: The Constitution of 1868," in *In Search of Fundamental Law: Louisiana's Constitutions, 1812–1974*, ed. Warren M. Billings and Edward F. Haas (Lafayette: Center for Louisiana Studies, University of Southwestern Louisiana, 1993); Labbe, "That the Reign of Robbery May Never Return to Louisiana: The Constitution of 1879"; Scarpaci, "Walking the Color Line," 60–76; "The Wrong of Negro Suffrage," *Daily Picayune*, January 1, 1898. For more on disenfranchisement efforts elsewhere in the South, see Keyssar, *The Right to Vote*, tables A.5–A.13.

17. "Constitutions Past and Present," *Daily Picayune*, February 6, 1898.

18. Labbe, "That the Reign of Robbery May Never Return to Louisiana," 85; Hair, *Bourbonism and Agrarian Protest*, 99.

19. Hair, *Bourbonism and Agrarian Protest*, 99 and 239; Nystrom, *New Orleans after the Civil War*, 215–16.

20. Barnes, *The Louisiana Populist Movement, 1881–1900*, 205.

21. "Illiterate and Pauper Immigration," *Daily Picayune*, January 28, 1896; "Constitutional Convention," *Daily Picayune*, May 4, 1896; "Vox Populi," *Daily Picayune*, February 16, 1896.

22. Outside of Louisiana, press discussions of the "declarant aliens" and immigrant franchise remained limited between 1885 and 1910. For these scarce references, see "How Foreign-Born Persons May Acquire Title to Public Land," *Delta Independent*, September 4, 1888 (Delta, CO), and "Criminal Offense to Vote without Papers," *Cañon City Record*, May 21, 1908 (Cañon City, CO). In New England states, like Rhode Island, reports appeared unconcerned with foreign-born voting so long as immigrants acquired US citizenship (Stefano Luconi, *The Italian-American Vote in Providence, Rhode Island, 1916–1948* (Cranbury, NJ.: Rosemont Publishing, 2004), 37).

23. "To Be Cured by the Suffrage Amendment," *Daily Picayune*, February 4, 1896.

24. "The Suffrage Amendment," *Times Democrat*, April 5, 1896.

25. Keyssar, *The Right to Vote: The Contested History of Democracy in the United States*, table A.12, 337–39. During the nineteenth century, "declarant aliens" were allowed to vote in the following states: Alabama, Arkansas, Colorado, Florida, Georgia, Indiana, Kansas, Louisiana, Minnesota, Missouri, Montana, Nebraska, North Dakota, Oregon, South Dakota, and

Texas; "declarant permission" was terminated in all of these states by 1926. With regard to the Gulf South states, the "declarant alien" provision was terminated in Alabama in 1901, Florida in 1895, and Louisiana in 1898.

26. These recommendations were in line with nationwide disenfranchisement efforts. Between 1870 and 1924, various states imposed literacy as a requirement for voting; most specified that a registrant must demonstrate their literacy in English, and some states like Mississippi and Virginia did not specify a language in their requirement, while Louisiana was the only state that allowed a registrant to "demonstrate [their] ability to read and write in English or mother tongue" (Keyssar, *The Right to Vote*, table A.13, 340–43). Meanwhile, all southern states imposed or authorized their legislature to impose a poll tax between 1885 and 1901 (Keyssar, *The Right to Vote*, Table A.10, 334–35).

27. "This Wilson Parish Committee," *Daily Picayune*, April 16, 1896.

28. "This Wilson Parish Committee."

29. "A Bombshell for the Boys; A Sensational Meeting of the Democratic Parish Committee," *Daily Picayune*, February 25, 1896.

30. "In the City," *Daily Picayune*, September 30, 1879; *Daily City Item*, October 28, 1891; Nystrom, *New Orleans after the Civil War*, 235.

31. "The Grand Procession," *Daily Picayune*, August 11, 1872.

32. "City Politics," *Daily Picayune*, August 27, 1876; "City Politics," *Daily Picayune*, August 31, 1876; "The Italian Legion," *Daily Picayune*, September 21, 1876.

33. "Political," *Daily Picayune*, August 26, 1876; "City Politics," *Daily Picayune*, August 27, 1876; "City Politics," *Daily Picayune*, August 31, 1876; "The Italian Legion," *Daily Picayune*, September 21, 1876.

34. Francis P. Burns, "St. Patrick's Hall and Its Predecessor, Odd Fellows Hall," *Louisiana History* 4, no. 1 (1963): 75.

35. "Italian Regulars Paraded by the Ring, After a Meeting at which No English was Spoken," *Daily Picayune*, March 23, 1896; *Biographical and Historical Memoirs of Louisiana: Embracing an Authentic and Comprehensive Account of the Chief Events in the History of the State . . .*, vol 2 (Chicago: Goodspeed Publishing, 1892).

36. "Italian Regulars Paraded by the Ring," *Daily Picayune*, March 23, 1896.

37. "Italian Regulars Paraded by the Ring," *Daily Picayune*, March 23, 1896.

38. "Mauberret's Italians: Opposed to Suffrage Amendments and Independent Movements," *Daily Picayune*, February 25, 1896.

39. Joseph di Carlo, president of the Italian Club, quoted in "Italian Regulars Paraded by the Ring," *Daily Picayune*, March 23, 1896; Scarpaci, *Italian Immigrants in Louisiana's Sugar Parishes*, 281.

40. Di Carlo, quoted in "Italian Regulars Paraded by the Ring."

41. "The March of the Regulars," *Daily Picayune*, April 19, 1896.

42. "The March of the Regulars." Dr. Bruns (an at-large delegate and local leader of "political reform associations") was responsible for drafting the suffrage amendment proposal. See Democratic Party Louisiana State Central Committee, *The Convention of '98: A Complete Work on the Greatest Political Event in Louisiana's History . . .* (New Orleans: W. E. Myers, 1898).

43. "Italian Regulars Paraded by the Ring, After a Meeting at which No English was Spoken," *Daily Picayune*, March 23, 1896.

44. "The March of the Regulars," *Daily Picayune*, April 19, 1896.

45. "Sunday's Italian Parade," *Times Democrat*, March 24, 1896.

46. "Italian Regulars Paraded by the Ring," *Daily Picayune*, March 23, 1896.

47. "The March of the Regulars," *Daily Picayune*, April 19, 1896; "Sunday's Italian Parade," *Times Democrat*, March 24, 1896; "The Late Italian Parade," *Times Democrat*, April 4, 1896.

48. "Citizens Not to Be Trusted," *Daily Picayune*, March 25, 1896.

49. "Sunday's Italian Parade," *Times Democrat*, March 24, 1896.

50. "The Late Italian Parade" *Times Democrat*, April 4, 1896; "Sunday's Italian Parade," *Times Democrat*, March 24, 1896.

51. "Sunday's Italian Parade," *Times Democrat*, March 24, 1896.

52. "The Late Italian Parade," *Times Democrat*, April 4, 1896.

53. "The Late Italian Parade," *Times Democrat*, April 4, 1896.

54. "The Late Italian Parade," *Times Democrat*, April 4, 1896; "Citizens Not to Be Trusted," *Daily Picayune*, March 25, 1896; "Italian Regulars Paraded by the Ring," *Daily Picayune*, March 23, 1896.

55. "The Late Italian Parade," *Times Democrat*, April 4, 1896.

56. This is in contrast to claims that the 1896 parade offered evidence of an Italian and African American coalition (Cunningham, "The Italian, a Hindrance to White Solidarity in Louisiana, 1890–1898," and Scarpaci, *Italian Immigrants in Louisiana's Sugar Parishes*). One sign held at the parade did allude to an interracial alliance: "We demand that the mechanic, the clerk and the laborer, white and black, have the same privilege to cast his ballot on election day as the millionaire" ("The March of the Regulars," *Daily Picayune*, April 19, 1896). Although the demand for the "same privilege" for "white and black" remains striking, considering this was a singular reference, this particular parade banner serves more as an attempt to invoke a working-class mentality and a demand for rights in contrast to the "millionaire." While the black community in New Orleans may have been aware of the parallels in their protests ("A Cage Rally: Colored Clubs Claim Kinship with the Ring's Italians Display," *Daily Picayune*, March 24, 1896), certain opinions within the black community in New Orleans actually voiced support for disenfranchising the Italians ("The Colored Vote Growing Watchful," *Daily Picayune*, April 17, 1896).

57. "Mauberret's Italians: Opposed to Suffrage Amendments and Independent Movements," *Daily Picayune*, February 25, 1896.

58. For more on the assessment that Italians practiced a form of calculated "self-sufficiency," see Scarpaci, *Italian Immigrants in Louisiana's Sugar Parishes*, 61.

59. W. Lee Hargrave, *The Louisiana State Constitution* (Oxford: Oxford University Press, 2011); Scarpaci, "Walking the Color Line: Italian Immigrants in Rural Louisiana, 1880–1910," 74.

60. Lanza, "Little More than a Family Matter: The Constitution of 1898." The four foreign-born in attendance at the convention included: Patrick Danahy (a planter born in Ireland), Thos R. Richardson (born in Ireland and moved to New Orleans in 1871; he joined the White League in 1874), I. D. Moore (a lawyer born in the British West Indies), and William

Driebholz (born in Germany in 1838 and moved to New Orleans in 1856) (Democratic Party (Louisiana) State Central Committee, *The Convention of '98*).

61. *Biographical and Historical Memoirs of Louisiana: Embracing an Authentic and Comprehensive Account of the Chief Events in the History of the State* . . . , vol. 1 (Chicago: Goodspeed Publishing, 1892).

62. "The Right of Louisiana to Reform its Suffrage," *Daily Picayune*, February 20, 1898; Letter to the Editor, *Times Democrat*, March 3, 1898; "The Suffrage," *Times Democrat*, March 11, 1898; R. B. Dawkins of Union, quoted in *Daily Picayune*, March 16, 1898. For more on the Australian ballot, see Daniel C. Reed, "Reevaluating the Vote Market Hypothesis: Effects of Australian Ballot Reform on Voter Turnout," *Social Science History* 38, no. 3-4 (Fall/Winter 2014): 277-290.

63. "Strong Defense of the Australian Ballot; Too Ignorant to Mark It Ought to be Disfranchised," *Times Democrat*, March 2, 1898.

64. *Daily Picayune*, January 23, 1898; "Constitutional Convention," *Daily Picayune*, January 23, 1898; "The Illiterate White Voter," *Times Democrat*, March 25, 1898; see also "The Wrong of Negro Suffrage Must Be Remedied," January 1, 1898, and "The Convention and the Suffrage Question," *Daily Picayune*, February 9, 1898.

65. Neither Mississippi nor South Carolina had previously permitted "declarant aliens" the right to vote. Beyond a few states in the South (Alabama, Arkansas, Georgia, Louisiana, Missouri, and Texas), only western/midwestern states (and no states on the Atlantic seaboard or in New England) granted "declarant aliens" voting rights (Keyssar, *The Right to Vote: The Contested History of Democracy in the United States*, table A.12, 337–39). Of the states that had formerly enfranchised "declarant aliens," only Louisiana provided a sustained debate regarding whether or not to overturn the provision.

66. The *Daily Picayune* referred to this foreign-born exemption, first reported in the New Orleans press on February 24, 1898, as "The Weeks Suffrage Plan," named for Edward T. Weeks, who was not actually a member of the convention or the Suffrage Committee. Weeks was a lawyer and member of a prominent family from New Iberia. See William Alexander Mabry, "Louisiana Politics and the 'Grandfather Clause,'" *North Carolina Historical Review* 13, no. 4 (October 1936): 290–320; Weeks Family Papers, 1771–1979, Louisiana Research Collection, Tulane University Special Collections.

67. "Text of the Suffrage Plan Prepared by the Sub-Committee of Six," *Daily Picayune*, March 2, 1898.

68. "Correspondence Which Speaks for Itself," *Daily Picayune*, February 24, 1898.

69. Historically, "Squaw" comes from the Algonquian term for woman and "Papoose" from the Algonquian word for child. According to the *Times Democrat* at the time, they borrowed the term from the Cherokee where "any white man who marries a full-blooded Cherokee squaw is called a Squaw Man . . . and is entitled to an interest in the Cherokee property and to vote in Cherokee elections because he is the husband of his wife" (March 6, 1898). Less clear is whether the *Times* chose to use "Squaw" because it possessed the offensive and pejorative connotation it holds today. In terms of the etymology of the terms, see Ives Goddard, "The True History of the Word Squaw," *Indian Country Today*, April 1997, 19A, and Vincent Shilling, "The Word Squaw, Offensive or Not?," *Indian Country Today*, March

23, 2017, accessed October 25, 2018, https://newsmaven.io/indiancountrytoday/archive/the-word-squaw-offensive-or-not-AOz_cjbLkEaxKaUEa6kejg/. Despite the fact that the etymology of the terms remains contested, Suzan Shown Harjo, a Cheyenne and Hodulgee Muscogee American Indian rights activist, argues that Native people refer to the term "Squaw" as the "S-word."

70. *Times Democrat,* March 6, 1898; "Insult to Native-Born Citizens," *Times Democrat,* March 5, 1898. Although they presented a less virulent critique of the provisions, the *Daily Picayune* invoked the same critical epithets "Squaw" and "Papoose" in their evaluation.

71. "Monstrous Suffrage Plan," *Times Democrat,* March 3, 1898.

72. "Monstrous Suffrage Plan," *Times Democrat,* March 3, 1898.

73. "Text of the Suffrage Plan Prepared by the Sub-Committee of Six; The Weeks Plans of Enfranchising All Who Were Voters," *Daily Picayune,* March 2, 1898.

74. Insult to Native Citizens," *Times Democrat,* March 8, 1898; Editorial, *Times Democrat,* March 7, 1898.

75. "Monstrous Suffrage Plan," *Times Democrat,* March 3, 1898; "Insult to Native-Born Citizens," *Times Democrat,* March 5, 1898; "Insult to Native Citizens," *Times Democrat,* March 6, 1898.

76. "The Debate on the Suffrage," *Times Democrat,* March 9, 1898.

77. Editorial, *Times Democrat,* March 7, 1898.

78. "Monstrous Suffrage Plan," *Times Democrat,* March 3, 1898.

79. "Monstrous Suffrage Plan," *Times Democrat,* March 9, 1898; "Our Voters," *Times Democrat,* March 6, 1898; Editorial, *Times Democrat,* March 4, 1898.

80. "Insult to Native Born," *Times Democrat,* March 5, 1898.

81. Quoted in "Insult to our Native Citizens," *Times Democrat,* March 6, 1898.

82. Quoted in *Times Democrat,* March 7, 1898.

83. "Foreign Voters," *Daily Picayune,* March 5, 1898.

84. "Popular Protests," *Times Democrat,* March 8, 1898; "More Protests," *Times Democrat,* March 9, 1898; "The Suffrage," *Times Democrat,* March 13, 1898.

85. "The Suffrage Clause Vastly Improved," *Daily Picayune,* March 8, 1898; "Strong Speeches on Suffrage Plans," *Daily Picayune,* March 11, 1898; "Section Five is Now Remodeled," *Daily Picayune,* March 15, 1898.

86. Democratic Party (La.) State Central Committee, *The Convention of '98,* 23; "The Suffrage Clause Vastly Improved," *Daily Picayune,* March 8, 1898.

87. "The Suffrage Clause Vastly Improved," *Daily Picayune,* March 8, 1898.

88. "The Suffrage Committee," *Times Democrat,* March 15, 1898.

89. "The Privileged 'Dago Voter,'" *Times Democrat,* March 8, 1898.

90. "The Tide of Opposition Rising," *Times Democrat,* March 10, 1898.

91. "Louisiana Opinions, What the Newspapers of this Great State Have Said on Subjects of Public Interest and General Importance," *Daily Picayune,* March 15, 1898.

92. "Louisiana Opinions, What the Newspapers of this Great State Have Said," *Daily Picayune,* March 15, 1898.

93. Quoted from the *Monroe News,* "Louisiana Opinions, What the Newspapers of this Great State Have Said."

94. Quoted from the *Lake Charles Press,* "Louisiana Opinions, What the Newspapers of this Great State Have Said," *Daily Picayune,* March 15, 1898.

95. "Louisiana Affairs," *Times Democrat,* March 22, 1898.

96. Quoted from the *Franklin News* in the *Times Democrat,* March 22, 1898. See also "Louisiana Opinions, What the Newspapers of this Great State Have Said," *Daily Picayune,* March 15, 1898.

97. Quoted from the *Monroe News,* "Louisiana Opinions, What the Newspapers of this Great State Have Said."

98. "Vox Populi," *Daily Picayune,* March 12, 1898; "The Suffrage Committee," *Times Democrat,* March 15, 1898; "Insult to American Manhood," *Times Democrat,* March 25, 1898; "Don't Adopt the Fifth Section," *Times Democrat,* March 22, 1898.

99. "Insult to our Native Citizens," *Times Democrat,* March 6, 1898.

100. "The Suffrage Committee," *Times Democrat,* March 15, 1898.

101. "Louisiana Opinions, What the Newspapers of this Great State Have Said," *Daily Picayune,* March 15, 1898.

102. "Louisiana Opinions, What the Newspapers of this Great State Have Said," *Daily Picayune,* March 15, 1898.

103. Democratic Party (La.) State Central Committee, *The Convention of '98,* 38. Fitzpatrick founded the Crescent Democratic Club in 1896; modeled after the Iroquois Club in New York, it took the name Choctaw Club in 1897 (Haas, "John Fitzpatrick and Political Continuity in New Orleans, 1896–1899"). This later iteration of the Ring—an alliance between the old Ring and New Orleans's business elite—was more or less the same organization under a different name (Ettinger, "John Fitzpatrick and the Limits of Working-Class Politics in New Orleans, 1892–1896").

104. "Louisiana Opinions, What the Newspapers of this Great State Have Said," *Daily Picayune,* March 15, 1898.

105. "A Poll Tax Plan Meeting," *Times Picayune,* March 17, 1898. Montgomery was also a member of the Agriculture and Immigration Committee at the convention (Democratic Party (La.) State Central Committee, *The Convention of '98,* 35).

106. "A Poll Tax Plan Meeting," *Times Picayune,* March 17, 1898.

107. "Vox Populi, Letter to the Editor," *Daily Picayune,* March 12, 1898.

108. "The Suffrage," *Times Democrat,* March 11, 1898.

109. "Poll Tax Plan Gaining Ground," *Daily Picayune,* March 16, 1898.

110. "Louisiana Opinions, What the Newspapers of this Great State Have Said on Subjects of Public Interest and General Importance," *Daily Picayune,* March 15, 1898.

111. "A Poll Tax Plan Meeting," *Times Picayune,* March 17, 1898.

112. "Suffrage Plan To Be Repaired," *Times Democrat,* March 12, 1898.

113. "Suffrage Plan To Be Repaired," *Times Democrat,* March 12, 1898.

114. Democratic Party (La.) State Central Committee, *The Convention of '98,* 30.

115. "Poll Tax Plan Gaining Ground," *Daily Picayune,* March 16, 1898.

116. Hargrave, *The Louisiana State Constitution.*

117. "Agreement Reached," *Daily Picayune* and *Times Democrat,* March 25, 1898; R. Vol-

ney Riser, *Defying Disenfranchisement: Black Voting Rights Activism in the Jim Crow South, 1890–1908* (Baton Rouge: Louisiana State University Press, 2010), 78.

118. Hargrave, *The Louisiana State Constitution*, 15.

119. "Agreement Reached," *Daily Picayune* and *Times Democrat*, March 25, 1898; Scarpaci, "Walking the Color Line."

120. "Suffrage Plan to be Repaired," *Daily Picayune*, March 12, 1898.

4. Segregating Italians, Sicilians, and Schools in Turn-of-the-Century Mississippi

1. The Friers, though not possessing a traditionally Italian surname, were recorded in a number of articles regarding the Sumrall incident. Despite additional genealogical research, the Friers (even while controlling for possible transcription errors) were not credibly traceable in the Mississippi vital and census records between 1900 and 1910.

2. "Italians in a Public School Cause a Row at Sumrall, Miss.," *Daily Picayune*, October 1, 1907.

3. "Italians in a Public School Cause a Row at Sumrall, Miss.," *Daily Picayune*, October 1, 1907; "Race Issue is Drawn Against the Italians," *Hattiesburg Daily News*, October 1, 1907 (Hattiesburg, MS); "Another Race Trouble: Report from the *Hattiesburg Daily News*," *Columbus Dispatch*, October 10, 1907 (Columbus, MS).

4. The press also alternatively recorded his name as Scagleone, Scageleoni, and Sciagaleoni; I have standardized the spelling of his surname to Scaglioni. Even while controlling for possible transcription errors or spelling variations, Scaglioni was not credibly traceable in the Mississippi vital and census records between 1900 and 1910.

5. "Another Race Trouble: Report from the *Hattiesburg Daily News*," *Columbus Dispatch*, October 10, 1907 (Columbus, MS).

6. "Trouble May Be the Result," *Detroit Free Press*, October 4, 1907.

7. For the limited scholarly treatment of the Sumrall event, see the following: Rowland T. Berthoff, "Southern Attitudes toward Immigration, 1865–1914," *Journal of Southern History* 17, no. 3 (August 1, 1951): 328–60; Guglielmo, *White on Arrival*, 27; Guglielmo, "No Color Barrier: Italians, Race, and Power in the United States," 36. There remains a dearth of historical scholarship on Italians in Mississippi; for a brief mention, see Celeste Ray, "European Mississippians," in *Ethnic Heritage in Mississippi, the Twentieth Century*, ed. Shana Walton and Barbara Carpenter (Jackson: University Press of Mississippi, 2012), 32–73. Other brief references include Paul V. Canonici, *The Delta Italians* (Madison, MS: Calo Creative Designs, 2003); Charles Reagan Wilson, "Italians in Mississippi," in *Mississippi History Now: An Online Publication of the Mississippi Historical Society* (2004), accessed April 4, 2019. http://www.mshistorynow.mdah.ms.gov/articles/88/italians-in-mississippi.

8. Charles C Bolton, *The Hardest Deal of All: The Battle over School Integration in Mississippi, 1870–1980* (Jackson: University Press of Mississippi, 2005), 7.

9. Frank Cavaioli, "Andrew Houston Longino," *Italian Americana* 11, no. 2 (1993): 171.

10. Bolton, *The Hardest Deal of All*, 10.

11. Bolton, *The Hardest Deal of All*, 10.

12. *Mississippi Constitution, 1890*, Article VIII, Section 207. Of note, in *State v. Treadaway* (1910), which evaluated whether or not Louisiana state law considered an "octoroon" (someone of one-eighth black descent) the same as a "negro," the Supreme Court of Louisiana provided an overview of the language used in segregation laws around the country, including those laws concerning school segregation. By and large, they found, southern states used the term "colored" or "colored races" in their explanation of laws regarding who should be separated from "whites" within public schools. Significantly, several states, including Mississippi, Florida, Georgia, and Alabama, used the term "colored" when referring to schools, but employed the terms "negro and mulatto" regarding their marriage laws. These states may have used the more ambiguous "colored" in their school segregation statute owing to the fact that schools were a public and visible venue, which could have been more readily regulated through public perception. A more "precise" racial category was likely chosen for marriage statutes, since miscegenation was regarded as such a subversive and enigmatic act (*State v. Treadaway*, No. 18,149, 126 La. 300; 52 So. 500 [Supreme Court of Louisiana, 1910]). For more on *State v. Treadaway*, miscegenation, and marriage laws, see chapter 5.

13. James W. Loewen, *The Mississippi Chinese: Between Black and White* (Cambridge, MA: Harvard University Press, 1971), 2.

14. Loewen, *The Mississippi Chinese*, 2 and 60. Owing to their liminal position, the Chinese operated as a sort of "middleman" between white and black communities in their roles as interpreters, creditors, and bondspersons. As part of this "middleman" position, Chinese-run grocery stores, on par with the number of Italian-run groceries and Italian-held colored saloon licenses in rural Louisiana, developed as staples in the Mississippi Delta (Jigna Desai and Khyati Y. Joshi, "Introduction: Discrepancies in Dixie: Asian Americans and the South," in *Asian Americans in Dixie: Race and Migration in the South*, ed. Jigna Desai and Khyati Y. Joshi (Urbana: University of Illinois Press, 2013), 61). For more on the Italians as southern middlemen, see Scarpaci, "Walking the Color Line: Italian Immigrants in Rural Louisiana, 1880–1910," 70.

15. "Coolie" was a nineteenth-century European term for unskilled, low-wage, and contract Asian laborers, usually from China. For more on the experience of Chinese immigrants in the Mississippi Delta, see Leslie Bow, *Partly Colored: Asian Americans and Racial Anomaly in the Segregated South* (New York: New York University Press, 2010); Leslie Bow, "Racial Interstitiality and the Anxieties of the 'Partly Colored': Representations of Asians under Jim Crow," in *Asian Americans in Dixie: Race and Migration in the South*, ed. Jigna Desai and Khyati Y. Joshi (Urbana: University of Illinois Press, 2013); Desai and Joshi, "Introduction: Discrepancies in Dixie: Asian Americans and the South," 3–13; Moon-Ho Jung, *Coolies and Cane: Race, Labor, and Sugar in the Age of Emancipation* (Baltimore: Johns Hopkins University Press, 2006); Loewen, *The Mississippi Chinese*.

16. Loewen, *The Mississippi Chinese*, 67.

17. Loewen, *The Mississippi Chinese*, 68.

18. *Gong Lum v. Rice*, 275 U.S. 78 (1927).

19. Loewen, *The Mississippi Chinese*, 68. A Chinese school briefly operated in Rosedale in 1933, but white public schools in Mississippi did not integrate Chinese students until 1950.

20. Bow, "Racial Interstitiality and the Anxieties of the 'Partly Colored.'" In this regard, Bow counters Loewen's assessment that Mississippi developed a "triply segregated school system" with different buildings for Chinese, whites, and blacks (Loewen, *The Mississippi Chinese,* 2).

21. Cavaioli, "Andrew Houston Longino," 170. As of the elections of 2018, Ron DeSantis of Florida remains the only other governor of Italian ancestry to represent a southern state. Nationwide, only thirty Italian American governors have ever been elected; five of those thirty were elected since 2010 (Frank J. Cavaioli, "Italian-American Governors," *Italian Americana* 25, no. 2 (2007): 133–59).

22. Cavaioli, "Andrew Houston Longino," 170. The Mississippi press, as well as newspapers in New Orleans and in northern cities, registered little concern regarding Longino's Italian heritage and remained silent on the subject. Even as Longino presided over the state during the Erwin lynching of 1901 and even while the Italian ancestry of the victims was a point of focus, Longino's heritage was not mentioned nor associated with his handling of the lynching.

23. Cavaioli, "Andrew Houston Longino," 174. Longino's antilynching stand remains rather progressive for the time period, and it could be interpreted that his Italian ancestry, in the face of the lynchings of Italians and Italian Americans, influenced his stance. However, given Longino's background and identity, it remains unlikely that he felt solidarity with the newly arrived immigrant or Sicilian populations. Ultimately, the Mississippi legislature rejected Longino's proposal, and lynching numbers remained steady over the course of his gubernatorial tenure (Cavaioli, "Andrew Houston Longino," 174).

24. Governor Longino, quoted in J. L. Power, "The Political, Educational and Social Status of the Negro in Mississippi," *Macon Beacon,* February 16, 1901 (Macon, MS).

25. Bolton, *The Hardest Deal of All,* 13.

26. Quoted in Bolton, *The Hardest Deal of All,* 15.

27. Percy, *Lanterns on the Levee: Recollections of a Planter's Son,* 144–47.

28. Benjamin E. Wise, *William Alexander Percy: The Curious Life of a Mississippi Planter and Sexual Freethinker* (Chapel Hill: University of North Carolina Press, 2012), 183. Nationwide, membership of the Catholic Church more than doubled between 1890 and 1915 (Wise, *William Alexander Percy,* 183).

29. For the recruitment of Italian laborers in Mississippi, see Bertram Wyatt-Brown, "LeRoy Percy and Sunnyside: Planter Mentality and Italian Peonage in the Mississippi Delta," in *Shadows over Sunnyside: An Arkansas Plantation in Transition, 1830–1945,* ed. Jeannie M. Whayne (Fayetteville: University of Arkansas Press, 1992), 77–94; James C. Cobb, *The Most Southern Place on Earth: The Mississippi Delta and the Roots of Regional Identity* (New York: Oxford University Press, 1992).

30. Percy, *Lanterns on the Levee,* 143–44. The Reconstruction Klan disbanded in 1869; the second Klan reformed in 1915 and arrived in the Delta in 1921 (Wise, *William Alexander Percy,* 173).

31. "All Flag and Liberty Loving, Law Abiding Citizens," *Leland Enterprise,* March 18, 1921, quoted in Wise, *William Alexander Percy,* 184.

32. "Address by Senator LeRoy Percy, Greenville, Miss., March 18, 1922." See also Wise, *William Alexander Percy*, 185–88.

33. By 1910, the Diocese of Natchez (which comprised the entire state of Mississippi until 1977) had seventy-five churches, thirty-one stations, eighteen chapels, an increase from 68 churches in 1900 (Mary Woodward, Chancellor, Diocese of Jackson). For more on early twentieth-century anti-Catholicism in the South, see Kenneth C. Barnes, *Anti-Catholicism in Arkansas: How Politicians, the Press, the Klan, and Religious Leaders Imagined an Enemy, 1910–1960* (Fayetteville: University of Arkansas Press, 2016); Justin Nordstrom, *Danger on the Doorstep: Anti-Catholicism and American Print Culture in the Progressive Era* (Notre Dame, IN: University of Notre Dame Press, 2006); Percy, *Lanterns on the Levy*, 234; Philip N. Racine, "The Ku Klux Klan, Anti-Catholicism, and Atlanta's Board of Education, 1916–1927," *Georgia Historical Quarterly* 57, no. 1 (1973): 63–75.

34. For more on the political and class context of turn-of-the-century Mississippi, see Cobb, *The Most Southern Place on Earth*; Percy, *Lanterns on the Levee*, chapters 15 and 18; Wise, *William Alexander Percy*.

35. Department of Commerce and Labor, Bureau of the Census, *Twelfth Census of the United States, 1900*, clxxiv; Bureau of the Census, *Thirteenth Census of the United States, 1910*, 1039.

36. Bureau of the Census, *Thirteenth Census of the United States, 1910*, 813.

37. Bureau of the Census, *Thirteenth Census of the United States*, Volume 2: *Population* (Washington, DC: Government Printing Office, 1913), 1044–58.

38. "A Reception at the Italian School," *Daily Picayune*, May 27, 1902; "A Word about the Italian School," *St. Bernard Voice*, September 13, 1902; "Concordia Colony of Italian Immigrants," *Daily Picayune*, December 15, 1907; "Latest News in all Louisiana," *Daily Picayune*, July 29, 1910.

39. "Captain Pizzati's Gift Creates Enthusiasm," *Daily Picayune*, June 25, 1904; "Salesian Sisters' Sicilian Schools," *Daily Picayune*, May 31, 1900; "Little Italians," *Daily Picayune*, June 28, 1901; "Bishop Scalabrini Coming to This City," *Daily Picayune*, September 2, 1901; "Bishop Blenk's Stay Comes to a Close; Distinguished Louisiana Prelate Leaving this Morning," *Daily Picayune*, May 27, 1902.

40. "Italian in Schools," *Times Picayune*, December 29, 1908.

41. "Latest News in All Louisiana," *Daily Picayune*, December 19, 1908; "Two Italian Children Attend Same School as Negroes," *Chalmette St. Bernard Voice*, December 19, 1908, quoted in Gauthreaux, "An Inhospitable Land," 52; Scarpaci, *Italian Immigrants in Louisiana's Sugar Parishes*, 266.

42. "Latest News in All Louisiana," *Daily Picayune*, December 19, 1908.

43. Quoted in Rhoda Coleman Ellison, "Little Italy in Rural Alabama," *Alabama Heritage* 2 (Fall 1986): 34–47.

44. "Italians Are Not Desirable," *Tupelo Journal*, October 19, 1906 (Tupelo, MS). Bolivar County, a mainly agricultural and farming community, accommodated an unusually diverse demographic. Owing to the 1887 founding of Mound Bayou as an independent black community, the population of Bolivar County in 1910 (49,000) was 87 percent black; Italians

made up nearly three-quarters of the county's 576 foreign-born white population (Bureau of the Census, *Thirteenth Census of the United States, 1910*, 1044).

45. "Italian School Children," *Lexington-Advisor*, October 18, 1906 (Lexington, MS); "Italians Are Not Desirable," *Tupelo Journal*, October 19, 1906 (Tupelo, MS); "A Hurtful Cry," *Tupelo Journal*, October 19, 1906; "A Hurtful Cry," *Columbus Commercial*, October 30, 1906 (Columbus, MS); "Candidates for Governor," *Grenada Sentinel*, February 2, 1907 (Grenada, MS).

46. "A Hurtful Cry," *Tupelo Journal*, October 19, 1906 (Tupelo, MS); "A Hurtful Cry," *Columbus Commercial*, October 30, 1906 (Columbus, MS).

47. "Italian School Children," *Lexington-Advisor*, October 18, 1906 (Lexington, MS). See also "It Can't Be Divided: Italians and Natives Must Attend Same Schools," *Jackson Evening News*, October 13, 1906.

48. "Italians Are Not Desirable," *Tupelo Journal*, October 19, 1906 (Tupelo, MS).

49. "A Hurtful Cry," *Tupelo Journal*, October 19, 1906 (Tupelo, MS); "A Hurtful Cry," *Columbus Commercial*, October 30, 1906 (Columbus, MS); "Italian School Children," *Lexington-Advisor*, October 18, 1906 (Lexington, MS).

50. Quoted from the *Commercial Appeal* (Jackson, MS) in "A Hurtful Cry," *Tupelo Journal*, October 19, 1906 (Tupelo, MS).

51. Bob Pittman, *Lamar County: The Land and the People* (Jackson, MS: Pittman Enterprises LLC, 2004), 85; "J. J. Newman Lumber Company Records," December 16, 2004 (University of Southern Mississippi Libraries Special Collections, Hattiesburg, MS).

52. Pittman, *Lamar County*, 87.

53. Bureau of the Census, *Thirteenth Census of the United States, 1910*, 1050.

54. "Italians in a Public School Cause a Row at Sumrall, Miss.," *Daily Picayune*, October 1, 1907; "Objected to the Italians," *The Times-Promoter*, October 4, 1907 (Hernando, MS).

55. "Italians in a Public School Cause a Row at Sumrall, Miss.," *Daily Picayune*, October 1, 1907.

56. "Race Issue is Drawn Against the Italians," *Hattiesburg Daily News*, October 1, 1907 (Hattiesburg, MS); "Another Race Trouble: Report from the *Hattiesburg Daily News*," *The Columbus Dispatch*, October 10, 1907.

57. "Another Version of the Sumrall Case," *Hattiesburg Daily News*, October 9, 1907 (Hattiesburg, MS).

58. "Another Race Trouble: Report from the *Hattiesburg Daily News*," *Columbus Dispatch*, October 10, 1907 (Columbus, MS); "Race Issue Is Drawn Against the Italians," *Hattiesburg Daily News*, October 1, 1907 (Hattiesburg, MS).

59. Charles Wollenberg, "'Yellow Peril' in the Schools (II)," in *The Asian American Educational Experience: A Source Book for Teachers and Students*, ed. Don T. Nakanishi and Tina Yamano Nishida (New York: Routledge, 1995), 15–16.

60. For more on the Gentleman's Agreement, see Meyer Weinberg, *Asian-American Education: Historical Background and Current Realities* (Mahwah, NJ: Lawrence Erlbaum Associates, 1997), 58; Charles Wollenberg, *All Deliberate Speed: Segregation and Exclusion in California Schools, 1855–1975* (Berkeley: University of California Press, 1976), chapter 3.

61. Elsewhere on the Pacific Coast, anti-Asian violence escalated in Bellingham, Washington, as 125 South Asians, believed to be taking "white" jobs and driving down wages, were

driven from the town (Erika Lee, "Hemispheric Orientalism and the 1907 Pacific Coast Race Riots," *Amerasia Journal* 33, no. 2 (2007): 19–48).

62. "Aliens in the Schools," *Washington Post,* October 9, 1907.

63. "Trouble May Be the Result," *Detroit Free Press,* October 4, 1907; "Aliens in the Schools," *Washington Post,* October 9, 1907; "Aliens in Danger in Mississippi," *Chicago Daily Tribune,* November 28, 1907.

64. "The South Wants Italians," *The Outlook,* November 16, 1907. *The Outlook* was a weekly magazine based in New York. Originally begun as a Baptist paper with a religious and moral emphasis, the magazine shifted in 1893 to "family general" with a focus on sociological and political issues. Circulation in the early 1900s was more than 100,000 (Hazel Dicken Garcia, *Journalistic Standards in Nineteenth-Century America* (Madison: University of Wisconsin Press, 1989), 253). I turn to *The Outlook* because of its comparatively extensive reporting on the Sumrall incident.

65. "Aliens in Danger in Mississippi," *Chicago Daily Tribune,* November 28, 1907.

66. "Italians in a Public School Cause a Row at Sumrall, Miss.," *Daily Picayune,* October 1, 1907.

67. "Another Version of the Sumrall Case," *Hattiesburg Daily News,* October 9, 1907 (Hattiesburg, MS).

68. "Remarkable Race Prejudice," *Columbus Dispatch,* October 17, 1907 (Columbus, MS); "Italians in a Public School Cause a Row at Sumrall, Miss.," *Daily Picayune,* October 1, 1907.

69. "Another Version of the Sumrall Case," *Hattiesburg Daily News,* October 9, 1907 (Hattiesburg, MS).

70. "Race Issue Is Drawn Against the Italians," *Hattiesburg Daily News,* October 1, 1907 (Hattiesburg, MS).

71. "Trouble May Be the Result"; *Detroit Free Press,* October 4, 1907; "Aliens in Danger in Mississippi," *Chicago Daily Tribune,* November 28, 1907.

72. "Aliens in Danger in Mississippi," *Chicago Daily Tribune,* November 28, 1907; "Italians in the South," *The Outlook,* November 16, 1907.

73. "Objected to the Italians," *Macon Beacon,* October 5, 1907 (Macon, MS); "Italians Removed to Hattiesburg," *Daily States,* October 5, 1907; "Italians in a Public School Cause a Row at Sumrall, Miss.," *Daily Picayune,* October 1, 1907; "Whipped Italian for Pernicious Activity," *Daily States,* October 1, 1907.

74. "Trouble May Be the Result," *Detroit Free Press,* October 4, 1907; "State Department not Apprised of Whipping of Italian," *Washington Post,* October 5, 1907; "Consul Investigating Charges of Cruelty," *Atlanta Constitution,* October 3, 1907.

75. "Race Issue Is Drawn Against the Italians," *Hattiesburg Daily News,* October 1, 1907 (Hattiesburg, MS).

76. "Race Issue Is Drawn Against the Italians," *Hattiesburg Daily News,* October 1, 1907.

77. "Italians Removed to Hattiesburg," *Daily States,* October 5, 1907. The population of Hattiesburg, in Forrest County, was greater than that of Lamar County and included a proportionally higher number of black residents. That being said, non-native whites made up less than 5 percent of the county's white population, with Italians representing less than 12

percent of the foreign-born/foreign-parentage demographic (Bureau of the Census, *Thirteenth Census of the United States, 1910,* 1046).

78. "Italians in a Public School Cause a Row at Sumrall, Miss.," *Daily Picayune,* October 1, 1907.

79. "Italians in a Public School Cause a Row at Sumrall, Miss.," *Daily Picayune,* October 1, 1907.

80. *Greenville Times,* October 6, 1907 (Washington County, MS).

81. "Italians are Aroused," *Daily Picayune,* October 6, 1907; "Details Aren't Fit to Print," *Daily States,* October 3, 1907.

82. *Greenville Times,* October 6, 1907 (Washington County, MS).

83. "Italians at Sumrall. Result of Investigation Sent to Ambassador at Washington," *Daily Picayune,* October 4, 1907; "Trouble May be the Result," *Detroit Free Press,* October 4, 1907.

84. "Details Aren't Fit to Print," *Daily States,* October 3, 1907; "Italians at Sumrall. Result of Investigation Sent to Ambassador at Washington," *Daily Picayune,* October 4, 1907.

85. "Labor Troubles in Mississippi: Special Report from *Times Democrat,*" *Macon Beacon,* October 5, 1907 (Macon, MS).

86. "Remarkable Race Prejudice," *Columbus Dispatch,* October 17, 1907 (Columbus, MS).

87. "Details Aren't Fit to Print," *Daily States,* October 3, 1907.

88. "Italians at Sumrall. Result of Investigation Sent to Ambassador at Washington," *Daily Picayune,* October 4, 1907; "Labor Troubles in Mississippi: Special Report from *Times Democrat,*" *Macon Beacon,* October 5, 1907 (Macon, MS).

89. "Details Aren't Fit to Print," *Daily States,* October 3, 1907; "Italians at Sumrall. Result of Investigation Sent to Ambassador at Washington," *Daily Picayune,* October 4, 1907; "Labor Troubles in Mississippi: Special Report from *Times Democrat,*" *Macon Beacon,* October 5, 1907 (Macon, MS); "The South Wants Italians," *The Outlook,* November 16, 1907.

90. "Labor Troubles in Mississippi: Special Report from *Times Democrat,*" *Macon Beacon,* October 5, 1907 (Macon, MS).

91. C. Vann Woodward, *Origins of the New South, 1877–1913* (Baton Rouge: Louisiana State University Press, 1951), 265.

92. "Importation is Costly," *The Caucasian* (Shreveport, LA), December 17, 1907. See also "Around the State," *The Donaldsonville Chief* (Donaldsonville, LA), December 21, 1907; "News from All Over the State," *St. Landry Clarion* (Opelousas, LA), December 21, 1907.

93. "Guide to the News," *Daily Picayune,* December 17, 1907.

94. *Daily Picayune,* December 16–17, 1907, cited in Webb, "The Lynching of Sicilian Immigrants in the American South, 1886–1910," 175–204.

95. Berthoff, "Southern Attitudes Toward Immigration, 1865–1914," 328.

96. "Italians in the South," *The Outlook,* November 16, 1907.

97. "Quiet at Sumrall. Nearly All of the Italians Transferred to Hattiesburg. Negroes Sent to Sumrall to work the Newman Lumber Company's Mill," *Daily Picayune,* October 3, 1907.

98. "Another Race Trouble," *Columbus Dispatch,* October 10, 1907 (Columbus, MS); "Details Aren't Fit to Print," *Daily States,* October 3, 1907.

99. "Italians in a Public School Cause a Row at Sumrall, Miss.," *Daily Picayune,* October

1, 1907; *Times Democrat* quoted in "The South Wants Italians," *The Outlook,* November 16, 1907; "Remarkable Race Prejudice," *Columbus Dispatch,* October 17, 1907 (Columbus, MS).

100. "Labor Troubles in Mississippi: Special Report from *Times Democrat*," *Macon Beacon,* October 5, 1907 (Macon, MS); "The South Wants Italians," *The Outlook,* November 16, 1907.

101. "Likes Italian Labor," *Daily States,* October 4, 1907.

102. "Labor Troubles in Mississippi: Special Report from *Times Democrat*," *Macon Beacon,* October 5, 1907 (Macon, MS).

103. "Labor Troubles in Mississippi."

104. "Guide to the News," *Daily Picayune,* December 17, 1907; "Current Comment in Mississippi," *Daily Picayune,* December 17, 1907; "Gov. Vardaman Denies the Story," *Biloxi Daily Herald,* December 31, 1907 (Biloxi, MS).

105. "Guide to the News," *Daily Picayune,* December 17, 1907.

106. "Italians in the South," *The Outlook,* November 16, 1907; "Gov. Vardaman Denies the Story," *Biloxi Daily Herald,* December 31, 1907.

107. "Current Comment in Mississippi," *Daily Picayune,* December 17, 1907.

108. "Gov. Vardaman Denies the Story," *Biloxi Daily Herald,* December 31, 1907 (Biloxi, MS); "Were Undesirable," *The Greenville Times,* January 5, 1908 (Washington County, MS).

109. "Gov. Vardaman Denies the Story," *Biloxi Daily Herald,* December 31, 1907 (Biloxi, MS).

110. "Were Undesirable," *The Greenville Times,* January 5, 1908 (Washington County, MS).

111. "Gov. Vardaman Denies the Story," *Biloxi Daily Herald,* December 31, 1907 (Biloxi, MS).

112. Woodward, *Origins of the New South, 1877–1913,* 375; Percy, *Lanterns on the Levy,* 143–49.

113. "Quiet At Sumrall," *Daily Picayune,* October 3, 1907.

114. "Remarkable Race Prejudice," *Columbus Dispatch,* October 17, 1907 (Columbus, MS).

115. "Remarkable Race Prejudice," *Columbus Dispatch,* October 17, 1907 (Columbus, MS).

116. Quoted in "Remarkable Race Prejudice," *Columbus Dispatch,* October 17, 1907 (Columbus, MS).

117. "Remarkable Race Prejudice," *Columbus Dispatch,* October 17, 1907 (Columbus, MS).

118. "Remarkable Race Prejudice," *Columbus Dispatch,* October 17, 1907 (Columbus, MS).

5. Legislating Miscegenation, Marriages, Whiteness, and Italians in Louisiana and Alabama

1. Orleans Parish Marriage Records (1890), Louisiana Department of State Vital Records Registry, accessed May 2015, https://www.sos.la.gov/HistoricalResources/ResearchHistoricalRecords/LocateHistoricalRecords/Pages/OrleansParishMarriageRecords.aspx; Bureau of the Census, *Eleventh Census of the United States, 1890* (Washington, DC: Government Printing Office, 1890), Orleans Parish, Louisiana Population Schedule.

2. "A Miscegenation Mess," *Daily Picayune*, December 15, 1896; "Both Willing," *Daily States*, December 14, 1896.

3. *Rollins v. State*, 6 Div. 927, Vol. 278 Transcript (Court of Appeals of Alabama 1921).

4. *Rollins v. State*, 6 Div. 927, 18 Ala. App. 354; 92 So. 35 (Court of Appeals of Alabama 1922).

5. For more on the (limited) histories of Italians in Alabama, see the following: Jeff Norrell, *The Italians from Bisacquino to Birmingham* (Birmingham, AL: Birmingfind, 1982); *La Storia: Birmingham's Italian Community*, exhibition (Vulcan Park and Museum, Birmingham, AL), visited December 18, 2014.

6. Department of Commerce and Labor, Bureau of the Census, *Thirteenth Census of the United States Taken in the Year 1910, Vol. 2: Population*, 1044–58.

7. Between 1883 and 1938, 343 individuals were charged and 177 convicted for violating Alabama's antimiscegenation law; between 1865 and 1967, Alabama's appellate courts ruled in thirty-eight miscegenation cases, more than any other state (Julie Novkov, "Racial Constructions: The Legal Regulation of Miscegenation in Alabama, 1890–1934," *Law and History Review* 20, no. 2 (2002): 227). Louisiana's Supreme Court heard nineteen cases related to miscegenation between 1868 and 1967, more than any other southern state (Michelle Brattain, "Miscegenation and Competing Definitions of Race in Twentieth-Century Louisiana," *Journal of Southern History* 71, no. 3 (2005): 633).

8. Since Louisianans historically recognized a third or intermediate racial category that challenged the endorsement and regulation of miscegenation law, Louisiana has been specifically omitted from studies of miscegenation (Pascoe, *What Comes Naturally: Miscegenation Law and the Making of Race in America* (Oxford: Oxford University Press, 2009); Martha Elizabeth Hodes, *White Women, Black Men: Illicit Sex in the Nineteenth-Century South* (New Haven, CT: Yale University Press, 1997), 12). While recognizing this complicated fluidity, I work to bring Louisiana more fully into the miscegenation historiography by demonstrating that Louisiana was connected to the larger web of both intraregional and interregional southern influences. Furthermore, despite the presumption that Louisiana adhered to a more fluid set of racial categories than neighboring southern states, a comparative analysis of the treatment of Sicilians and other Italians within miscegenation statutes in Louisiana and Alabama shows that legal racial categories within the Gulf South were steadily bifurcating by the turn of the century.

9. For more on this gendered pattern and the intersectionality of race and gender in marking certain interracial relationships as particularly conspicuous in the antebellum and postbellum eras, see Peter Bardaglio, "'Shamefull Matches': The Regulation of Interracial Sex and Marriage in the South before 1900," in *Sex, Love, Race: Crossing Boundaries in North America*, ed. Martha Hodes (New York: New York University Press, 1999), 112–40; Pascoe, *What Comes Naturally*, 44; Robinson, *Forsaking All Others*, chapter 3. For more on the toleration of certain interracial relationships, see Martha Hodes, ed., *Sex, Love, Race: Crossing Boundaries in North American History* (New York: New York University Press, 1999); Joshua D. Rothman, *Notorious in the Neighborhood: Sex and Families Across the Color Line in Virginia, 1787–1861* (Chapel Hill: University of North Carolina Press, 2003).

10. For a clear map of the existing miscegenation laws in 1865, see Pascoe, *What Comes Naturally*, 42.

11. Scholars like Jennifer Spear choose to use the term "racially exogamous" rather than designating a relationship as "miscegenation" or even "interracial." Spear's choice rests on the fact that in her discussion of colonial New Orleans, she refrains from imposing racial categorizations that were not used at the time; because New Orleanians did not have a single word that defined racially mixed (as perceived at the time) relationships, Spear suggests that this was indicative of the fact that they did not define such relationships as belonging to a separate category (Spear, *Race, Sex, and Social Order in Early New Orleans*). However, because the term "miscegenation" marks the particular historical moment under investigation here, I do make use of this term.

12. For more on the distinction between the "intimacy color line" and the "sexual color line," see Charles F. Robinson, "What's Sex Got to Do with It? Antimiscegenation Law and Southern White Rhetoric," in *Manners and Southern History*, ed. Ted Ownby (Jackson: University Press of Mississippi, 2007), 98–104; Robinson, *Dangerous Liaisons*; Pascoe, *What Comes Naturally*, 12.

13. Pascoe, *What Comes Naturally*, 9.

14. Pascoe, *What Comes Naturally*, 13; Cott, *Public Vows: A History of Marriage and the Nation*, 4.

15. Robinson, *Dangerous Liaisons*; Cott, *Public Vows*.

16. "A Digest of the Civil Laws now in force in the Territory of Orleans," 1808, 24.

17. Brattain, "Miscegenation and Competing Definitions of Race in Twentieth-Century Louisiana," 629. Louisiana was not unique in this regard, as other Gulf South states passed similar provisions during the antebellum era. Although not a specific marriage ban, by 1822 Mississippi officials were only permitted to solemnize marriages "between any free white persons within the state," and Florida prohibited marriages between "Blacks and Whites" in 1832 (*An Act to Regulate the Solemnization of Marriages*, 1822 Mississippi Laws; Pascoe, *What Comes Naturally*, 21).

18. For more on the inconsistent enforcement of Louisiana's 1724 *Code Noir*, one of the earliest colonial bans on interracial marriage in French Louisiana, and the persistence of interracial cohabitation as common practice, see Dawdy, *Building the Devil's Empire*, 4; Hall, *Africans in Colonial Louisiana*; Gwendolyn Midlo Hall, "African Women in French and Spanish Louisiana: Origins, Roles, Family, Work, Treatment," in *The Devil's Lane: Sex and Race in the Early South*, ed. Catherine Clinton and Michele Gillespie (Oxford: Oxford University Press, 1997), 247–61; Spear, *Race, Sex, and Social Order in Early New Orleans*. For more on the extent to which Spanish officials in Louisiana tolerated the illegal practice of interracial "common-law marriages" and interracial concubinage, see Kimberly S. Hanger, *Bounded Lives, Bounded Places: Free Black Society in Colonial New Orleans, 1769–1803* (Durham, NC: Duke University Press, 1997); Kimberly S. Hanger, "Patronage, Property and Persistence," 44–64; Gould, "'A Chaos of Iniquity and Discord.'"

19. Brattain, "Miscegenation and Competing Definitions of Race in Twentieth-Century Louisiana," 630; Hodes, *White Women, Black Men: Illicit Sex in the Nineteenth-Century South*,

144; Peter Wallenstein, *Tell the Court I Love My Wife: Race, Marriage, and Law: An American History* (New York: Palgrave Macmillan, 2002), 51–52.

20. Hodes, *White Women, Black Men,* 1; Pascoe, *What Comes Naturally,* 2, 28; Robinson, *Dangerous Liaisons: Sex and Love in the Segregated South* (Fayetteville: University of Arkansas Press, 2003), 49–59. One of two states that seceded without an interracial marriage prohibition, Mississippi officially outlawed interracial marriage in 1865, making it a felony offense punishable by life in prison (Pascoe, *What Comes Naturally: Miscegenation Law and the Making of Race in America,* 30). By the end of the Civil War, twenty-eight of thirty-six US states had recorded laws to prohibit miscegenation or interracial marriage.

21. *Alabama Code,* 1852; Pascoe, *What Comes Naturally: Miscegenation Law and the Making of Race in America,* 30 and 57.

22. *Alabama Penal Code,* 1866; *Alabama Code,* 1923. Alabama was one of the few states with a miscegenation law that specifically outlawed "interracial sex" (Pascoe, *What Comes Naturally,* 135).

23. Under military rule and Radical Reconstruction, seven of the former Confederate states removed, repealed, or banned their miscegenation statutes; the seven included Arkansas and the original Confederate states (except for Georgia): Alabama, Florida, Louisiana, Mississippi, South Carolina, and Texas; Mississippi repealed its marriage ban in 1870, just as Florida omitted its ban from the state code passed in the early 1870s (Pascoe, *What Comes Naturally,* 41; Wallenstein, *Tell the Court I Love My Wife,* 80). For more on how personnel changes created this discontinuity in the legal responses to interracial marriages in post–Civil War Alabama, see Wallenstein, *Tell the Court I Love My Wife,* 71.

24. Pascoe, *What Comes Naturally,* 42–45.

25. Pascoe, *What Comes Naturally,* 63. South Carolina reinstated its miscegenation statute in 1879, Mississippi in 1880, Florida in 1881, and Louisiana in 1894 (Fay Botham, *Almighty God Created the Races: Christianity, Interracial Marriage, and American Law* (Chapel Hill: University of North Carolina Press, 2009), 152). In the Reconstruction/post-Reconstruction eras, interracial marriage bans were added to the following state constitutions: North Carolina (1876), Florida (1885), Mississippi (1890), South Carolina (1895), and Alabama (1901) (Pascoe, *What Comes Naturally,* 63).

26. *Constitution of Alabama,* 1901. After the Supreme Court ruling in *Loving v. Virginia* in 1967, which outlawed interracial marriage bans, Alabama's prohibition was no longer constitutional or enforceable. However, the language remained on the books, and Alabama owned the infamous title of being the last state in the nation with a constitutional edict outlawing interracial marriage. Alabama voters did not officially repeal the language until the year 2000.

27. Rosen, *Terror in the Heart of Freedom,* 136.

28. Hannah Rosen, "The Rhetoric of Miscegenation and the Reconstruction of Race: Debating Marriage, Sex, and Citizenship in Postemancipation Arkansas," in *Gender and Slave Emancipation in the Atlantic World,* ed. Pamela Scully and Diana Paton (Durham, NC: Duke University Press, 2005), 303–4.

29. The decision in *State v. Gibson* (Indiana, 1871) conferred the supremacy of state's rights concerning marriage laws over federal civil rights; as a result, the court established a

precedent that defined marriage as more than a contract (moving it beyond the protection of the Fourteenth Amendment) and under the jurisdiction of the state police (and outside of federal control) (*State v. Gibson*, 36 Ind. 389 (Supreme Court of Indiana 1871); Pascoe, *What Comes Naturally*, 56).

30. *Pace & Cox v. the State*, 69 Ala. 231 (Supreme Court of Alabama 1881).

31. *Pace v. State of Alabama*, 106 U.S. 583 (U.S. Supreme Court 1883).

32. Gross, *What Blood Won't Tell*, 9.

33. Gross, *What Blood Won't Tell*, 8 and 104.

34. *Louisiana Civil Code*, Amd. Act 54, 1894, 63.

35. *Acts Passed by the General Assembly of the State of Louisiana*, Act No. 87, 1908.

36. *State v. Treadaway*, No. 18,149, 126 La. 300; 52 So. 500 (Supreme Court of Louisiana 1910). Treadaway had been indicted and acquitted of violating the aforementioned Act No. 87 of 1908.

37. *State v. Treadaway*, No. 18,149, 126 La. 300; 52 So. 500 (Supreme Court of Louisiana 1910).

38. *Acts Passed by the General Assembly of the State of Louisiana*, Act No. 206, 1910. Louisiana's *Acts Passed by the General Assembly* in 1920 expanded the categories of exclusion by "prohibiting marriage between persons of the Indian race and persons of the colored or black race."

39. Pascoe, *What Comes Naturally*, 136; Charles F. Robinson, *Forsaking All Others: A True Story of Interracial Sex and Revenge in the 1880s South* (Knoxville: University of Tennessee Press, 2010), 44.

40. Between 1894 and 1967, only five criminal cases explicitly involved the legality of marriage within the confines of Louisiana's miscegenation statutes; between 1915 and 1934, the years of the greatest frequency of litigation, Alabama's appellate court only heard twelve miscegenation cases (Brattain, "Miscegenation and Competing Definitions of Race in Twentieth-Century Louisiana," 632–33; Novkov, "Racial Constructions: The Legal Regulation of Miscegenation in Alabama, 1890–1934," 233). Part of these calculations is the question of which cases count as miscegenation cases, since some cases involving inheritances, estates, wills, and even divorce may have involved an evaluation of a marriage's legality but may not have made an explicit reference to miscegenation (Gross, *What Blood Won't Tell*, 77; Pascoe, *What Comes Naturally*, 11). The number of criminal cases cited above does not account for the number of civil suits or local regulatory actions, nor does it necessarily correlate with the prevalence of interracial sex (Brattain, "Miscegenation and Competing Definitions of Race in Twentieth-Century Louisiana," 632).

41. Pascoe, *What Comes Naturally*, 9, and chapter 5, especially 138–39.

42. *State v. Treadaway* (Supreme Court of Louisiana, 1910).

43. Pascoe, *What Comes Naturally: Miscegenation Law and the Making of Race in America*, 139.

44. Christine B. Hickman, "The Devil and the One Drop Rule: Racial Categories, African Americans, and the U.S. Census," *Michigan Law Review* 95, no. 5 (1997): 1185; Aliya Saperstein and Aaron Gullickson, "A 'Mulatto Escape Hatch' in the United States? Examining Evidence of Racial and Social Mobility During the Jim Crow Era," *Demography* 50, no. 5

(2013): 1921–42. Additionally, because census enumerators were generally procured from within the local community, that means that even though the census was a federal form, racial determinations made within the census provide on-the-ground insight into local racial assessments and determinations.

45. While enumerators were given specific definitions for determining an individual's racial category, they were not given explicit guidance for how to apply those definitions. For example, according to the 1890 instructions for census enumerators, they were required to categorize individuals, based on a visual inspection, into a number of constructed blood quantums: "Be particularly careful to distinguish between blacks, mulattos, quadroons, and octoroons. The word "black" should be used to describe those persons who have three-fourths or more black blood; "mulatto," those persons who have from three-eighths to five-eighths black blood; "quadroon," those persons who have one-fourth black blood; and "octoroon," those persons who have one-eighth or any trace of black blood."

46. Bureau of the Census, *Ninth Census of the United States, 1870* (Washington, DC: Government Printing Office, 1870), Orleans Parish, Louisiana Population Schedule. Throughout, I have retained the capitalization for those racial categories specified by the census schedules.

47. Bureau of the Census, *Ninth Census of the United States, 1870* (Washington, DC: Government Printing Office, 1870), vol. 1, 341; Bureau of the Census, *Ninth Census of the United States, 1870,* Orleans Parish, Louisiana Population Schedule.

48. What follows is an overview of Italian marriages in Orleans Parish between 1890 and 1915, including instances of "interracial" relationships that have been otherwise unreported or unnoticed in the historical record. In order to gauge whether or not marriage patterns changed along with the passage of increasingly restrictive miscegenation statutes, I began by surveying the Orleans Parish Marriage Records for the years 1890, 1900, and 1915; the marriage licensing records from 1910 and 1914 remain incomplete, which precluded an assessment of 1910. (Orleans Parish Marriage Records, Louisiana Department of State Vital Records Registry, accessed May 2015, https://www.sos.la.gov/HistoricalResources/ResearchHistoricalRecords/LocateHistoricalRecords/Pages/OrleansParishMarriageRecords.aspx). While browsing, I took note of Italian surnames, accounting for those instances when Italian surnames were linked with other Italian surnames (thus denoting an Italian/Italian marriage); I also took note of moments when Italian surnames (or surnames that could possibly or plausibly be Italian) were linked with non-Italian surnames. Upon compiling this list, I performed a genealogical investigation of those possible intermarriages; using marriage records, birth and death certificates, voting and draft registrations, and US census schedules, I tracked race, birthplace, and parentage in order to determine the best approximation of the ancestral background of these marriage contracts. My underlying questions remained: To what extent did Italians and black southerners intermarry, and were these marriages considered to be in violation of miscegenation laws?

49. Bureau of the Census, *Twelfth Census of the United States, 1900* (Washington, DC: Government Printing Office, 1900), Orleans Parish, Louisiana Population Schedule.

50. The Italian foreign-born population between 1890 and 1900 doubled in Mississippi and nearly tripled in Alabama (Bureau of the Census, *Eleventh Census of the United States,*

1890, vol. 1, part 1, 689; Bureau of the Census, *Twelfth Census of the United States, 1900*, vol. 1, part 1, clxxiv).

51. Bureau of the Census, *Twelfth Census of the United States, 1900*, 773. In 1890, there were more than twice as many foreign-born Italians as native-born Italians in Louisiana (Bureau of the Census, *Eleventh Census of the United States, 1890*, 687 and 691; Bureau of the Census, *Thirteenth Census of the United States, 1910*, 3:773), yet by 1910, 20,233 foreign-born Italians and 22,678 native-born Italians resided in the state.

52. *Louisiana Civil Code*, Amd. Act 54, 1894, 63.

53. Bureau of the Census, *Twelfth Census of the United States, 1900*; Orleans Parish Marriage Records (1896), Louisiana Department of State Vital Records Registry, accessed May 2015, https://www.sos.la.gov/HistoricalResources/ResearchHistoricalRecords/LocateHistoricalRecords/Pages/OrleansParishMarriageRecords.aspx.

54. Census enumerators reported the birthplace of Amerigo's mother as Spain in 1880, Cuba in 1900, and Spain/Cuba in 1910; while Amerigo's mother may have been born in Cuba, I reason that she was of Spanish ancestry given Amerigo's earliest reporting of his mother's birthplace as Spain.

55. Bureau of the Census, *Tenth Census of the United States, 1880* (Washington, DC: Government Printing Office, 1880), Orleans Parish, Louisiana Population Schedule.

56. Bureau of the Census, *Twelfth Census of the United States, 1900*. By 1900, bureaucrats—census takers and marriage licensing agents alike—steadily denaturalized interracial marriages and families; despite a person's ancestry, official designations assigned a couple or family living under the same roof (or presumed the couple or family to be) the same race.

57. For historical discussions of passing, beyond those found in literature and literary criticism, see the following: Gross, *What Blood Won't Tell*; Allyson Vanessa Hobbs, *A Chosen Exile: A History of Racial Passing in American Life* (Cambridge, MA: Harvard University Press, 2014); Pascoe, *What Comes Naturally*; Martha A. Sandweiss, *Passing Strange: A Gilded Age Tale of Love and Deception across the Color Line* (New York: Penguin Press, 2009).

58. Hobbs, *A Chosen Exile: A History of Racial Passing in American Life*, 6.

59. *Acts Passed by the General Assembly of the State of Louisiana*, Act No. 87, 1908.

60. Despite the surname "Pizero," census enumerators consistently read both Leonie and August as either "Black" or "Mulatto" between 1880 and 1930. Alternatively, census enumerators read Agnes Reggio as "White" throughout records between 1900 and 1920, even though her grandfather was recorded as "Mulatto" in 1870.

61. "A Miscegenation Mess," *Daily Picayune*, December 15, 1896.

62. "A Miscegenation Mess," *Daily Picayune*, December 15, 1896.

63. "Both Willing," *Daily States*, December 14, 1896.

64. "Both Willing," *Daily States*, December 14, 1896.

65. "A Miscegenation Mess," *Daily Picayune*, December 15, 1896. Thompson was charged as a "juvenile vagrant."

66. "Both Willing," *Daily States*, December 14, 1896.

67. Martin, "Plaçage and the Louisiana *Gens de Couleur Libre*," 57–70.

68. "Both Willing," *Daily States*, December 14, 1896.

69. Certainly, had the genders been reversed, meaning, had this been a relationship be-

tween an Italian girl and an African American man, it is likely that this relationship may not have received the same social sanction within the press.

70. "Henry Johnson Turned Loose," *Birmingham Age Herald*, January 24, 1901 (Birmingham, AL); "A Negro in Luck," *Biloxi Daily Herald*, January 27, 1901 (Biloxi, MS).

71. "Henry Johnson Turned Loose," *Birmingham Age Herald*, January 24, 1901 (Birmingham, AL).

72. "A Negro in Luck," *Biloxi Daily Herald*, January 27, 1901 (Biloxi, MS).

73. "Henry Johnson Turned Loose," *Birmingham Age Herald*, January 24, 1901 (Birmingham, AL).

74. "A Negro in Luck," *Biloxi Daily Herald*, January 27, 1901 (Biloxi, MS).

75. "A Negro in Luck," *Biloxi Daily Herald*, January 27, 1901.

76. Within the historiography of *Rollins v State*, differing interpretations prevail depending on the sources consulted: the appeals summary (Gross, *What Blood Won't Tell*, 230; Jacobson, *Whiteness of a Different Color*, 4), or the actual court transcripts (Robinson, *Dangerous Liaisons*; Robinson, "What's Sex Got to Do with It?"; Julie Novkov, *Racial Union Law, Intimacy, and the White State in Alabama, 1865–1954* (Ann Arbor: University of Michigan Press, 2008). My reading of *Rollins v. State* employs both the court transcripts and the appeals summary.

77. According to the court transcript, Labue testified to being a taxicab driver and mechanic, although various census records list Labue as a musician and a member of an orchestra and band. Perhaps this is evidence of gendered coaching, since a mechanic may have been seen as more believable and trustworthy than a musician.

78. *Rollins v. State*, Transcript (Court of Appeals of Alabama 1921).

79. *Rollins v. State*, Transcript (Court of Appeals of Alabama 1921), emphasis mine.

80. *Rollins v. State*, Transcript (Court of Appeals of Alabama 1921).

81. *Rollins v. State*, Transcript (Court of Appeals of Alabama 1921).

82. Alabama Convict Records; Mrs. Nesbitt's identity and relationship to Labue remains unknown. After this point, Edith Labue disappears from the historical record, although it does not seem that Edith and Joe Labue ever lived together again after Edith's arrest and Joe's court testimony.

83. *Rollins v. State* (Court of Appeals of Alabama 1922).

84. *Rollins v. State* (Court of Appeals of Alabama 1922).

85. Novkov, *Racial Union Law, Intimacy, and the White State in Alabama, 1865–1954*, 125.

86. *Rollins v. State* (Court of Appeals of Alabama 1922).

87. *Rollins v. State* (Court of Appeals of Alabama 1922).

88. Robinson, "What's Sex Got to Do with It?," 111.

89. Later that same year, the Alabama Appeals Court confirmed in *Lewis v. State* that a child was sufficient evidence to prove miscegenation. Hint Lewis, a white man, and Bess Adams, a black woman, were convicted of "felonious fornication." The court ulitmately ruled that the existence of the child was sufficient to sustain a conviction for felonious fornication. It was not necessary for someone to have witnessed the parties engaged in sexual intercourse (*Lewis v. State*, No. 4 Div. 723, 18 Ala. App. 263; 89 So. 904 [Court of Appeals of Alabama 1921]).

90. *Rollins v. State*, Transcript (Court of Appeals of Alabama 1921).

91. *Wilson v. State*, No. 1 Div. 527, 20 Ala. App. 137; 101 So. 417 (Court of Appeals of Alabama 1924).

92. *Wilson v. State*, No. 1 Div. 527, 20 Ala. App. 137; 101 So. 417 (Court of Appeals of Alabama 1924).

93. Additionally, in contrast with Louisiana's 1910 ruling in *State v. Treadaway*, Alabama courts by the 1920s had concluded that the terms "negro" and "colored" were interchangeable.

94. For other miscegenation cases where race was determined by association, see the following: *Weaver et al. v. State*, No. 1 Div. 756, 757, 22 Ala. App. 469; 116 So. 893 (Court of Appeals of Alabama 1928); *Wilson v State*, No. 1 Div. 527, 20 Ala. App. 137; 101 So. 417 (Court of Appeals of Alabama 1924); *Tyson et al. v. Raines* (No. 27126, 165 La. 625; 115 So. 803 (Supreme Court of Louisiana 1928).

95. *Jackson v. State*, No. 6 Div. 769, 23 Ala. App. 555; 129 So. 306 (Court of Appeals of Alabama 1930).

96. *Jackson v. State*, No. 6 Div. 769, 23 Ala. App. 555; 129 So. 306 (Court of Appeals of Alabama 1930).

97. The Supreme Court had determined as much in 1923 in *Thind v. United States*, where Bhagat Singh Thind, as a "high caste Hindu of full Indian blood," had petitioned the court for his right to naturalize based on his Caucasian ancestry (*U.S. v. Bhagat Singh Thind*, No. 202, 261 U.S. 204, 205 [United States Supreme Court, 1923]). Despite the 1790 Naturalization Law that granted the right of naturalization to "free white persons" and a recognition that the terms "white" and Caucasian were synonymous, the court concluded, "'Free white persons' are words of common speech, to be interpreted in accordance with the understanding of the common man, synonymous with the word 'Caucasian' only as the word is popularly understood." Consequently, Thind was denied the right to naturalize on the grounds that he phenotypically diverged from the "common man's" definition of whiteness. Thus "public imagination," "common knowledge," and a concept of race as determined by the "average man" were all becoming legally admissible within courts of law (Ian Haney-López, *White by Law: The Legal Construction of Race* [New York: New York University Press, 2006]).

Epilogue: Italian Citizenship and Immigration Legislation in the Gulf South to 1924 and Beyond

1. "Editorial," *New York Times*, April 26, 1891; "Sifting Immigration," *New York Times*, April 27, 1891; "Restricting Immigration," *New York Times*, March 6, 1892.

2. "The Press is With Us," *Daily States*, March 20, 1891.

3. "Expressions of the Louisiana Press on the New Orleans Lynching: Popular Justice," *Daily Picayune*, April 1, 1891; *Weekly Messenger*, March 21, 1891 (St. Martinsville, LA); "To Restrict Foreign Immigration," *Daily Picayune*, March 5, 1895; "Outbreak of the Mafia," *Daily Picayune*, July 24, 1895.

4. "Italy and the United States," *New York Times*, May 16, 1891.

5. "Report of the Citizens Committee," *Daily Picayune*, May 15, 1891. See also "The Lynch-

ers Justified: Report of the Grand Jury of New Orleans," *New York Times*, May 6, 1891; "They Are Not Good Citizens," *New York Times*, March 23, 1891; "Foreign Immigration," *Daily Picayune*, November 9, 1896.

6. *Daily Picayune*, December 4, 1897; *Weekly Messenger*, March 21, 1891.

7. "The Immigration Season Started," *Daily Picayune*, October 19, 1901.

8. "Must Guard Our Gates: The Necessity of Restricting Immigration to Our Shores," *New York Times*, March 17, 1896.

9. "Must Guard Our Gates," *New York Times*, March 17, 1896.

10. Henry Cabot Lodge, "Lynch Law and Unrestricted Immigration," *North American Review* 152.414 (May 1891): 605.

11. Immigration Restriction League, "Immigration Restriction League Outlines the 'Immigration Problem,'" 1894.

12. Lodge, "Lynch Law and Unrestricted Immigration," 612.

13. "Illiteracy Among Immigrants," *Daily Picayune*, May 4, 1896.

14. "Immigration Bill Finally Passed," *Daily Picayune*, February 18, 1897. Although it was passed by Congress, President Cleveland vetoed the bill.

15. "Immigration Bill Finally Passed," *Daily Picayune*, February 18, 1897; "Illiteracy Among Immigrants," *Daily Picayune*, May 4, 1896.

16. Berthoff, "Southern Attitudes Toward Immigration, 1865–1914," 360.

17. Quoted in Berthoff, "Southern Attitudes Toward Immigration, 1865–1914," 349.

18. Quoted in Berthoff, 349.

19. *Manufacturers Record* 48 (1905), 5–13.

20. Berthoff, "Southern Attitudes Toward Immigration, 1865–1914," 360.

21. Berthoff, 360. Although the bill again passed both houses of Congress, it was again defeated by presidential veto; this pattern repeated for a third time in 1915.

22. Jager, "The Worst 'White Lynching' in American History: Elites vs. Italians in New Orleans 1891," 177; Nystrom, *Creole Italian: Sicilian Immigrants and the Shaping of New Orleans Food Culture*, 88; Nystrom, *New Orleans After the Civil War: Race, Politics, and a New Birth of Freedom*, 211.

23. For more on the Gay-Shattuck Liquor Law, see Long, *The Great Southern Babylon: Sex, Race, and Respectability in New Orleans*, 181; Nystrom, *Creole Italian*, chapter 4.

24. Nystrom, *Creole Italian*, 90.

25. Nystrom, *Creole Italian*, 92; Records of the New Orleans District Criminal Court, City Archives, New Orleans Public Library.

26. Charles A. O'Neill, "Editorial: Foreigners Are Not Forbidden Privileges of Selling Liquors," *Daily Picayune*, January 26, 1909.

27. O'Neill, "Editorial," *Daily Picayune*, January 26, 1909.

28. Stefano Luconi, "Tampa's 1910 Lynching: The Italian-American Perspective and Its Implications," *The Florida Historical Quarterly* 88, no. 1 (Summer 2009): 36. For more on the Italian experience in Florida, see Gary Ross Mormino and George E. Pozzetta, *The Immigrant World of Ybor City: Italians and Their Latin Neighbors in Tampa, 1885–1985* (Urbana and Chicago: University of Illinois Press, 1987); Ilaria Serra, "A Story Never Told: An Italian Immigrant in South Florida," in Gary R. Mormino and Ilaria Serra, *Italian Americans & Flor-*

ida (Boca Raton: Center for Interdisciplinary Studies at Florida Atlantic University, 2003).

29. Luconi, "Tampa's 1910 Lynching," 30. For more on the Tampa lynching, see Salvetti, *Rope and Soap*, chapter 6; Stahle, *The Italian Emigration of Modern Times*, 93–106.

30. *Tampa Morning Tribune*, September 21, 1910; see also Luconi, "Tampa's 1910 Lynching," 31. Photographs-turned-postcards of the lynched victims included the caption, "Labor agitators lynched during the cigar makers' strike." James Allen, ed., *Without Sanctuary: Lynching Photography in America* (Santa Fe, NM: Twin Palms, 2000), 167–68).

31. "Lynchings During 1913," *Journal of the American Institute of Criminal Law and Criminology* 4, no. 6 (March 1914): 927–30.

32. "Negro Shot After Striking Merchant who Dirtied Him," *Montgomery Advertiser*, August 28, 1913; "Lynchings During 1913," 927–30.

33. "Negro Shot After Striking Merchant who Dirtied Him," *Montgomery Advertiser*, August 28, 1913.

34. "Father R. Carra May Be Soldier in Italy's Army," *Times-Picayune*, September 22, 1914; "American Citizens Forced into Army," *Times-Picayune*, October 15, 1914; "Naturalization Does Not Protect," *Times-Picayune*, June 5, 1915.

35. "American Citizens Forced into Army," *Times-Picayune*, October 15, 1914.

36. "American Citizens Forced into Army," *Times-Picayune*, October 15, 1914.

37. "Italy Disclaims Children Born Here," *Times-Picayune*, August 24, 1915; "Italo-American Will Not Be Conscripted While Visiting in Italy During Peace Time," *State Times Advocate*, November 5, 1929 (Baton Rouge, LA).

38. "Foreign Born Told the Advantages of Citizenship," *Times-Picayune*, October 12, 1917; Frederic J. Haskin, "The Alien Again," *Times-Picayune*, January 14, 1918.

39. "Guide Designed to Pave Way for Aliens Desiring Citizenship," *Times-Picayune*, July 3, 1916; "Italian, German Take Papers for Naturalization," *State Times Advocate*, March 26, 1917 (Baton Rouge, LA); "19 Naturalized in U.S. Court Monday Session," *Miami Herald*, May 1, 1917; "Five Admitted to Citizenship," *Times-Picayune*, January 15, 1918; "Aliens to Study at Night School for Examination," *Times-Picayune*, October 29, 1929.

40. Frederic J. Haskin, "The Alien Again," *Times-Picayune*, January 14, 1918.

41. Haskin, "The Alien Again," *Times-Picayune*, January 14, 1918.

42. "Foreign Born Told the Advantages of Citizenship," *Times-Picayune*, October 12, 1917.

43. "Naturalization of Aliens," *Times-Picayune*, August 7, 1915; "Naturalization," *Times-Picayune*, November 27, 1919; "The Making of a Citizen," *Miami Herald*, March 21, 1920.

44. "Naturalization of Aliens," *Times-Picayune*, August 7, 1915.

45. "Foreign Born Told the Advantages of Citizenship," *Times-Picayune*, October 12, 1917.

46. "Foreign Born Told the Advantages of Citizenship," *Times-Picayune*, October 12, 1917.

47. "To Pass H.R. 10384, (39 Stat. 874, 2–5-17), of the President, a Bill Regulating the Immigration of Aliens to and the Residence of Aliens in the US—Senate Vote #324—Feb 5, 1917," *GovTrack.us*, accessed March 14, 2017, https://www.govtrack.us/congress/votes/64-2/s324; "To Pass H.R. 10384 (39 Stat. 874, Feb. 5, 1917), over President's Veto, a Bill to Regulate the Immigration of Aliens to and the Residence of Aliens in the US —House Vote #121—Feb 1, 1917," *GovTrack.us*, accessed March 14, 2017, https://www.govtrack.us/congress/votes/64-2/h121.

48. "To Pass H.R. 10384, (39 Stat. 874, 2–5-17), of the President, a Bill Regulating the Immigration of Aliens to and the Residence of Aliens in the US—Senate Vote #324—Feb 5, 1917," *GovTrack.us*, accessed March 14, 2017, https://www.govtrack.us/congress/votes/64-2/s324; "To Pass H.R. 10384 (39 Stat. 874, Feb. 5, 1917), over President's Veto, a Bill to Regulate the Immigration of Aliens to and the Residence of Aliens in the US —House Vote #121—Feb 1, 1917," *GovTrack.us*, accessed March 14, 2017, https://www.govtrack.us/congress/votes/64-2/h121.

49. "To Agree to the Report of Conference Committee on H.R. 7995, to Limit the Immigration of Aliens into the United States (P. 8651-1)—House Vote #90—May 15, 1924," *GovTrack.us*, accessed March 14, 2017, https://www.govtrack.us/congress/votes/68-1/h90; "To Agree to Report of Conference Committee on H.R. 7995, (App. 5/26/1924, 43 Stat. L. 153), A Bill to Limit the Immigration of Aliens into the United States—Senate Vote #126—May 15, 1924," *GovTrack.us*, accessed March 14, 2017, https://www.govtrack.us/congress/votes/68-1/s126.

50. This refers to the US Bureau of Immigration practice that recorded "North Italians" and "South Italians" as different "races" since 1899, a classification practice that officials nationwide selectively continued at least through the late 1930s. See, for example, Giovanni Egizio Lenci entry, "Manifests of Alien Arrivals at Calexico, California, March 1907–December 1952," March 24, 1937, Records of the Immigration and Naturalization Service, 1787–2004, NA; Victoria Rose Myers entry, "Manifests of Alien Arrivals at Blaine, Washington, 1924–1956," July 30, 1936, Records of the Immigration and Naturalization Service, 1787–2004, NA; Rose Sherolla entry, "Manifests of Alien Arrivals at Eastport, Idaho, 1924–1956," August 9, 1936, Records of the Immigration and Naturalization Service, 1787–2004, NA. See also "Manifests of Alien Arrivals at Ranier and International Falls, Minnesota, January 1909–December 1952," Records of the Immigration and Naturalization Service, 1787–2004, NA; "Manifests of Passengers Arriving at St. Albans, VT, District through Canadian Pacific and Atlantic Ports, 1895–1954," Records of the Immigration and Naturalization Service, 1787–2004, NA; "Passenger Lists of Vessels Arriving at Boston, Massachusetts, 1891–1943," Records of the Immigration and Naturalization Service, 1787–2004, NA; "Passenger Lists of Vessels Arriving at New York, New York, 1820–1897," Records of the US Customs Service, NA.

51. Scarpaci, "Walking the Color Line," 60–76.

52. John V. Baiamonte, *Spirit of Vengeance: Nativism and Louisiana Justice, 1921–1924* (Baton Rouge: Louisiana State University Press, 1986).

53. Margavio and Salomone, *Bread and Respect*, 266.

54. *Daily States*, July 24, 1899; *Daily States*, July 27, 1899.

55. Jessica Williams, "Mayor Cantrell apologizes for 1891 Italian-American lynchings in New Orleans: 'What happened was wrong,'" *New Orleans Advocate* (April 12, 2019), accessed May 2, 2019, https://www.theadvocate.com/new_orleans/news/article_6262f734–5d5d-11e9-b3ab-ff791456d518.html.

Bibliography

ARCHIVAL/MANUSCRIPT COLLECTIONS

American Italian Research Library, East Bank Regional Library, Metairie, Louisiana. Benevolent Society Papers.

Archivio del Consolato D'italia in New Orleans (1879–1961), Ministero Degli Affari Esteri, Rome, Italy.

Catholic Diocese of Jackson, Mississippi. Chancellor's Office, Mary Woodward, Chancellor.

The Historic New Orleans Collection, Williams Research Center, New Orleans, Louisiana. Alessandra/Marchese Family Papers, Black Soldiers in Louisiana Collection, and Gustavo Mazzei letters.

Immigration History Research Center Archives, University of Minnesota, Minneapolis. Notes from the Italian Legation in the U.S. to the Department of State.

Samford University Library, Birmingham, Alabama. Italians in Birmingham, Theresa Beavers Papers, Special Collection.

COURT CASES

Jackson v. State, No. 6 Div. 769, 23 Ala. App. 555; 129 So. 306 (Court of Appeals of Alabama 1930).

Lewis v. State, No. 4 Div. 723, 18 Ala. App. 263; 89 So. 904 (Court of Appeals of Alabama 1921).

Pace v. State of Alabama, 106 U.S. 583 (U.S. Supreme Court 1883).

Pace & Cox v. the State, 69 Ala. 231 (Supreme Court of Alabama 1881).

Rollins v. State, 6 Div. 927, Vol. 278 Transcript (Court of Appeals of Alabama 1921).

Rollins v. State, No. 6 Div. 927, 18 Ala. App. 354; 92 So. 35 (Court of Appeals of Alabama 1922).

State v. Gibson, 36 Ind. 389 (Supreme Court of Indiana 1871).

State v. Treadaway, No. 18,149, 126 La. 300; 52 So. 500 (Supreme Court of Louisiana 1910).

Tyson et al. v. Raines, No. 27126, 165 La. 625; 115 So. 803 (Supreme Court of Louisiana 1928).

U.S. v. Bhagat Singh Thind, No. 202, 261 U.S. 204, 205 (United States Supreme Court, 1923).

Weaver et al. v. State, No. 1 Div. 756, 757, 22 Ala. App. 469; 116 So. 893 (Court of Appeals of Alabama 1928).

Wilson v. State, No. 1 Div. 527, 20 Ala. App. 137; 101 So. 417 (Court of Appeals of Alabama 1924).

GOVERNMENT DOCUMENTS AND RECORDS

Acts Passed by the General Assembly of the State of Louisiana, 1908, Louisiana Law Library, Louisiana Supreme Court (New Orleans, Louisiana).

Acts Passed by the General Assembly of the State of Louisiana, 1910, Louisiana Law Library, Louisiana Supreme Court (New Orleans, Louisiana).

Acts Passed by the General Assembly of the State of Louisiana, 1920, Louisiana Law Library, Louisiana Supreme Court (New Orleans, Louisiana).

Bureau of the Census, *Ninth Census of the United States, 1870*. Washington, DC: Government Printing Office, 1870.

Bureau of the Census, *Tenth Census of the United States, 1880*. Washington, DC: Government Printing Office, 1880.

Bureau of the Census, *Eleventh Census of the United States, 1890*. Washington, DC: Government Printing Office, 1890.

Bureau of the Census, *Thirteenth Census of the United States, 1910*. Washington, DC: Government Printing Office, 1910.

Bureau of the Census, *Fourteenth Census of the United States, 1920*. Washington, DC: Government Printing Office, 1920.

Bureau of the Census, *Fifteenth Census of the United States, 1930*. Washington, DC: Government Printing Office, 1930.

Bureau of the Census, *Sixteenth Census of the United States, 1940*. Washington, DC: Government Printing Office, 1940.

Criminal District Court Records Docket Numbers 14220–14415, 1890. *David Hennessy Murder Trial Documents*, New Orleans Public Library.

Department of Commerce and Labor, Bureau of the Census, *Thirteenth Census of the United States Taken in the Year 1910, Volume 2: Population*. Washington, DC: Government Printing Office, 1913.

"A Digest of the Civil Laws now in force in the Territory of Orleans," 1808, Louisiana Law Library, Louisiana Supreme Court (New Orleans, Louisiana).

Louisiana Civil Code, Amd. Act 54, 1894, Louisiana Law Library, Louisiana Supreme Court (New Orleans, Louisiana).

"Manifests of Alien Arrivals at Blaine, Washington, 1924–1956." Records of the Immigration and Naturalization Service, 1787–2004. National Archives, Washington, DC.

"Manifests of Alien Arrivals at Calexico, California, March 1907–December 1952." Records of the Immigration and Naturalization Service, 1787–2004. National Archives, Washington, DC.

"Manifests of Alien Arrivals at Eastport, Idaho, 1924–1956." Records of the Immigration and Naturalization Service, 1787–2004. National Archives, Washington, DC.

"Manifests of Alien Arrivals at Ranier and International Falls, Minnesota, January 1909–December 1952." Records of the Immigration and Naturalization Service, 1787–2004. National Archives, Washington, DC.

"Manifests of Passengers Arriving at St. Albans, VT, District through Canadian Pacific and Atlantic Ports, 1895–1954." Records of the Immigration and Naturalization Service, 1787–2004. National Archives, Washington, DC.

Orleans Parish Marriage Records (1870–1968), Vital Records Registry, Louisiana Department of State (Baton Rouge, Louisiana). https://www.sos.la.gov/HistoricalResources/ResearchHistoricalRecords/LocateHistoricalRecords/Pages/OrleansParishMarriageRecords.aspx

Papers Relating to the Foreign Relations of the United States, Transmitted to Congress, With the Annual Message of the President, December 9, 1891. Washington, DC: Government Printing Office, 1892.

Papers Relating to the Foreign Relations of the United States, Transmitted to Congress, With the Annual Message of the President, December 7, 1896. Washington, DC: Government Printing Office, 1897.

Papers Relating to the Foreign Relations of the United States, Transmitted to Congress, With the Annual Message of the President, December 5, 1899. Washington, DC: Government Printing Office, 1901.

Papers Relating to the Foreign Relations of the United States, Transmitted to Congress, With the Annual Message of the President, December 3, 1901. Washington, DC: Government Printing Office, 1902.

"Passenger Lists of Vessels Arriving at Boston, Massachusetts, 1891–1943." Records of the Immigration and Naturalization Service, 1787–2004. National Archives, Washington, DC.

"Passenger Lists of Vessels Arriving at New Orleans, Louisiana, 1820–1902." Records of the Immigration and Naturalization Service. National Archives, Washington, DC.

"Passenger Lists of Vessels Arriving at New York, New York, 1820–1897." Records of the US Customs Service. National Archives, Washington, DC.

NEWSPAPERS AND PERIODICALS

Biloxi Daily Herald

Birmingham Age Herald

Broad Ax (Chicago, IL)

Cañon City Record (Cañon City, CO)

The Caucasian (Shreveport, LA)

Cheyenne Record (Cheyenne County, CO)

Chicago Daily Tribune

Cleveland Gazette

Colfax Chronicle (Colfax, LA)

Columbus Commercial (Columbus, MS)

Columbus Dispatch (Columbus, MS)

Cristoforo Colombo (New York)

Daily Advocate (Baton Rouge, LA)

Daily Capitolian-Advocate (Baton Rouge, LA)

Daily Crusader (New Orleans)

Daily Inter Ocean (Chicago)

Daily Picayune (New Orleans)

Daily States (New Orleans)

Daily Telegraph (Monroe, LA)

Delta Independent (Delta County, CO)

Donaldsonville Chief (Donaldsonville, LA)

Fort Worth Daily Gazette (Fort Worth, TX)

Freeman's Lance (Peru, KS)

Galveston Daily News (Houston)

Greenville Times (Washington County, MS)

Grenada Sentinel (Grenada, MS)

Hattiesburg Daily News (Hattiesburg, MS)

Huntsville Gazette (Huntsville, AL)

Indian Country Today (online)

Jackson Evening News (Jackson, MS)

Lafayette Gazette (Lafayette, LA)

Lexington-Advisor (Lexington, MS)

Los Angeles Times

Louisiana Democrat (Alexandria)

Macon Beacon (Macon, MS)

The Mascot (New Orleans)

Memphis Daily Appeal

Le Meschacebe (Lucy, LA)
Miami Herald
Milan Exchange (Milan, TN)
Montgomery Advertiser (Montgomery, AL)
National Republican (Washington, DC)
National Tribune (Washington, DC)
New Delta (New Orleans)
New Orleans Item (New Orleans)
New York Sun
New York Times
New York Tribune
The Outlook (New York)
Pascagoula Democrat-Star (Pascagoula, MS)
Plaindealer (Detroit)
Il Progresso (New York)
Richland Beacon (Rayville, LA)
Rocky Mountain News (Denver)
San Francisco Chronicle
State Times Advocate (Baton Rouge, LA)
St. Landry Clarion (Opelousas, LA)
St. Louis Globe Democrat
Times Democrat (New Orleans)
Times-Picayune (New Orleans)
Tupelo Journal (Tupelo, MS)
Washington Bee
Washington Post
Weekly Commercial Herald (Vicksburg, MS)
Weekly Messenger (St. Martinsville, LA)

PUBLISHED PRIMARY WORKS

American Newspaper Directory. 19th ed. New York: Geo. P. Rowell & Company, 1887.
American Newspaper Directory. 32nd ed. New York: Geo. P. Rowell & Company, 1900.
Biographical and Historical Memoirs of Louisiana: Embracing an Authentic and Comprehensive Account of the Chief Events in the History of the State. . . . Vols. 1 and 2. Chicago: Goodspeed Publishing Company, 1892.
Blumenbach, Johann Friedrich. *The Elements of Physiology.* Translated by John Elliotson. London: A. & R. Spottiswoode, 1828.

D'Azeglio, Massimo. *I Miei Ricordi*. Firenze, Italia: G. Barbera, 1867.

Democratic Party (LA) State Central Committee. *The Convention of '98: A Complete Work on the Greatest Political Event in Louisiana's History. . . .* New Orleans: W. E. Myers, 1898.

Dillingham, William Paul, and U.S. Immigration Commission 1907–10. *Reports of the Immigration Commission: Dictionary of Races or Peoples*. Washington, DC: Government Printing Office, 1911.

———. *Reports of the Immigration Commission: Emigration Conditions in Europe*. Washington, DC: Government Printing Office, 1911.

Grant, Madison. *The Passing of the Great Race: The Racial Basis of European History*. New York: Charles Scribner's Sons, 1916.

Levi, Carlo. *Cristo si é fermato a Eboli*. 1945. Translated by Frances Frenaye as *Christ Stopped at Eboli: The Story of a Year*. New York: Noonday Press, 1963.

Lombroso, Cesare. *Criminal Man*. 1876. Translated by Mary Gibson and Nicole Hahn Rafer. Durham, NC: Duke University Press, 2006.

"Lynchings During 1913." *Journal of the American Institute of Criminal Law and Criminology* 4, no. 6 (March 1914): 927–930.

Lodge, Henry Cabot. "Lynch Law and Unrestricted Immigration." *North American Review* 152, no. 414 (May 1891): 602–12.

Morgan, Appleton. "What Shall We Do with the 'Dago'?" *Popular Science Monthly* 38 (December 1890): 172–79.

Morton, Samuel George. *Crania Americana: A Comparative View of the Skulls of Various Aboriginal Nations of North and South America*. Philadelphia: J. Dobson, 1839.

Ripley, William Zebina. "The Racial Geography of Europe: A Sociological Study." *Popular Science Monthly* 51 (June 1897): 17–33.

Ross, Edward Alsworth. "Italians in America." *Century Magazine* 87 (July 1914): 439–45.

Wells-Barnett, Ida B. *On Lynchings: Southern Horrors; A Red Record; Mob Rule in New Orleans*. 1892. Reprint, New York: Arno Press, 1969.

Works Progress Administration. "WPA History of Lamar County, Mississippi." From Pamela J. Gibbs, *Lamar County, Mississippi Genealogy and History*, 2007.

STATISTICAL DIRECTORIES AND DATABASES

GovTrack.us, Civic Impulse, LLC.

Historical Statistics of the United States Millennial Edition Online. Edited by Susan B. Carter, Scott Sigmund Gartner, Michael R. Haines, Alan L. Olmstead, Richard Sutch, and Gavin Wright. Cambridge: Cambridge University Press, 2016.

Project HAL: Historical American Lynching Data Collection, University of North Carolina Wilmington, http://people.uncw.edu/hinese/HAL/HAL%20Web%20 Page.htm.

SECONDARY SOURCES

Allen, James, ed. *Without Sanctuary: Lynching Photography in America.* Santa Fe, NM: Twin Palms Publishers, 2000.

Anderson, Bridget. *Us and Them? The Dangerous Politics of Immigration Control.* Oxford: Oxford University Press, 2013.

Arellano, Lisa. *Vigilantes and Lynch Mobs: Narratives of Community and Nation.* Philadelphia: Temple University Press, 2012.

Arnesen, Eric. "Whiteness and the Historians' Imagination." *International Labor and Working-Class History* 60 (2001): 3–32.

Baiamonte, John V. *Spirit of Vengeance: Nativism and Louisiana Justice, 1921–1924.* Baton Rouge: Louisiana State University Press, 1986.

———. "'Who Killa de Chief' Revisited: The Hennessey Assassination and Its Aftermath,1890– 1991." *Louisiana History* 33, no. 2 (1992): 117–46.

Bailey, Amy Kate, and Stewart Tolnay. *Lynched: The Victims of Southern Mob Violence.* Chapel Hill: University of North Carolina Press, 2015.

Bailey, Amy Kate, Stewart E. Tolnay, E. M. Beck, Alison Renee Roberts, and Nicholas H. Wong. "Personalizing Lynch Victims: A New Database to Support the Study of Mob Violence." *Historical Methods: A Journal of Quantitative and Interdisciplinary History* 41, no. 1 (2008): 47–64.

Bailey, Amy, Stewart Tolnay, E. Beck, and Jennifer Laird. "Targeting Lynch Victims: Social Marginality or Status Transgressions?" *American Sociological Review* 76, no. 3 (2011): 412–36.

Bald, Vivek. *Bengali Harlem and the Lost Histories of South Asian America.* Cambridge, MA: Harvard University Press, 2012.

———. "Selling the East in the American South: Bengali Muslim Peddlers in New Orleans and Beyond, 1880–1920." In *Asian Americans in Dixie: Race and Migration in the South.* Edited by Jigna Desai and Khyati Y. Joshi, 33–53. Urbana: University of Illinois Press, 2013.

Bardaglio, Peter Winthrop. *Reconstructing the Household: Families, Sex, and the Law in the Nineteenth-Century South.* Chapel Hill: University of North Carolina Press, 1995.

———. "'Shamefull Matches': The Regulation of Interracial Sex and Marriage in the South Before 1900." In *Sex, Love, Race: Crossing Boundaries in North Amer-*

ica. Edited by Martha Hodes, 112–40. New York: New York University Press, 1999.

Barnes, Donna A. *The Louisiana Populist Movement, 1881–1900*. Baton Rouge: Louisiana State University Press, 2011.

Barnes, Kenneth C. *Anti-Catholicism in Arkansas: How Politicians, the Press, the Klan, and Religious Leaders Imagined an Enemy, 1910–1960*. Fayetteville: University of Arkansas Press, 2016.

Barrett, James R., and David Roediger. "Inbetween Peoples: Race, Nationality and the 'New Immigrant' Working Class." *Journal of American Ethnic History* 16, no. 3 (Spring 1997): 3–44.

Beales, Derek Edward Dawson, and Eugenio F. Biagini. *The Risorgimento and the Unification of Italy*. New York: Routledge, 2013.

Beck, E. M., and Timothy Clark. "Strangers, Community Miscreants, or Locals: Who Were the Black Victims of Mob Violence?" *Historical Methods: A Journal of Quantitative and Interdisciplinary History* 35, no. 2 (2002): 77–83.

Berthoff, Rowland T. "Southern Attitudes Toward Immigration, 1865–1914." *Journal of Southern History* 17, no. 3 (August 1, 1951): 328–60.

Bolton, Charles C. *The Hardest Deal of All: The Battle over School Integration in Mississippi, 1870–1980*. Jackson: University Press of Mississippi, 2005.

Bonacich, Edna. "A Theory of Middleman Minorities." *American Sociological Review* 38, no. 5 (1973): 583–94.

Botein, Barbara. "The Hennessy Case: An Episode in Anti-Italian Nativism." *Louisiana History* 20, no. 3 (1979): 261–79.

Botham, Fay. *Almighty God Created the Races: Christianity, Interracial Marriage, and American Law*. Chapel Hill: University of North Carolina Press, 2009.

Bow, Leslie. *Partly Colored: Asian Americans and Racial Anomaly in the Segregated South*. New York: New York University Press, 2010.

———. "Racial Interstitiality and the Anxieties of the 'Partly Colored': Representations of Asians under Jim Crow." In *Asian Americans in Dixie: Race and Migration in the South*. Edited by Jigna Desai and Khyati Y Joshi, 54–76. Urbana: University of Illinois Press, 2013.

Brattain, Michelle. "Miscegenation and Competing Definitions of Race in Twentieth-Century Louisiana." *Journal of Southern History* 71, no. 3 (2005): 621–58.

Brodkin, Karen. *How Jews Became White Folks and What That Says about Race in America*. New Brunswick, NJ: Rutgers University Press, 1998.

Brundage, W. Fitzhugh. *Lynching in the New South: Georgia and Virginia, 1880–1930*. Urbana: University of Illinois Press, 1993.

———. *Under Sentence of Death: Lynching in the South*. Chapel Hill: University of North Carolina Press, 1997.

Burns, Francis P. "St. Patrick's Hall and Its Predecessor, Odd Fellows Hall." *Louisiana History* 4, no. 1 (1963): 73–84.

Campanella, Richard. "An Ethnic Geography of New Orleans." *Journal of American History* 94, no. 3 (2007): 704–15.

———. *Time and Place in New Orleans: Past Geographies in the Present Day.* Gretna, LA: Pelican Publishing, 2002.

Canaday, Margot. *The Straight State: Sexuality and Citizenship in Twentieth-Century America.* Princeton, NJ: Princeton University Press, 2009.

Carrigan, William D., ed. *Lynching Reconsidered: New Perspectives in the Study of Mob Violence.* New York: Routledge, 2008.

———. *The Making of a Lynching Culture: Violence and Vigilantism in Central Texas, 1836–1916.* Urbana: University of Illinois Press, 2004.

Carrigan, William D., and Clive Webb. *Forgotten Dead Mob Violence against Mexicans in the United States, 1848–1928.* Oxford: Oxford University Press, 2013.

Cavaioli, Frank. "Andrew Houston Longino." *Italian Americana* 11, no. 2 (1993): 170–78.

———. "Italian-American Governors." *Italian Americana* 25, no. 2 (2007): 133–59.

Choate, Mark. *Emigrant Nation: The Making of Italy Abroad.* Cambridge, MA: Harvard University Press, 2008.

Clark, Emily. *Masterless Mistresses: The New Orleans Ursulines and the Development of a New World Society, 1727–1834.* Chapel Hill: University of North Carolina Press, 2007.

Clark, Martin. *Modern Italy, 1871 to the Present.* New York: Pearson Longman, 2008.

Cobb, James C. *The Most Southern Place on Earth: The Mississippi Delta and the Roots of Regional Identity.* Oxford: Oxford University Press, 1992.

Connell, William J., and Stanislao G. Pugliese. *The Routledge History of Italian Americans.* New York: Routledge, 2018.

Conzen, Kathleen Neils. "Immigrants, Immigrant Neighborhoods, and Ethnic Identity: Historical Issues." *Journal of American History* 66, no. 3 (1979): 603–15.

Cook, Lisa D. "Converging to a National Lynching Database: Recent Developments and the Way Forward." *Historical Methods: A Journal of Quantitative and Interdisciplinary History* 45, no. 2 (2012): 55–63.

Cordasco, Francesco. "Bollettino Dell'Emigrazione (1902–1927): A Guide to the Chronicles of Italian Mass Migration." In *The Columbus People: Perspectives in Italian Immigration to the Americas and Australia.* Edited by Lydio F. Tomasi, 499–508. New York: Center for Migration Studies, 1994.

Cott, Nancy F. *Public Vows: A History of Marriage and the Nation.* Cambridge, MA: Harvard University Press, 2000.

Coxe, John E. "The New Orleans Mafia Incident." *Louisiana Historical Quarterly* 20 (1937): 1067–1110.

Cunningham, George. "The Italian, a Hindrance to White Solidarity in Louisiana, 1890–1898." *Journal of Negro History* 50, no. 1 (January 1965): 22–36.

Dabney, Thomas Ewing. *One Hundred Great Years; The Story of the Times-Picayune from Its Founding to 1940.* Baton Rouge: Louisiana State University Press, 1944.

Davis, John A. "Italy, 1796–1870: The Age of the Risorgimento," in *The Oxford Illustrated History of Italy.* Edited by George Holmes, 177–209. Oxford: Oxford University Press, 1997.

D'Agostino, Peter. "Craniums, Criminals, and the 'Cursed Race': Italian Anthropology in American Racial Thought, 1861–1924." *Comparative Studies in Society and History* 44, no. 2 (April 2002): 319–43.

Dawdy, Shannon Lee. *Building the Devil's Empire: French Colonial New Orleans.* Chicago: University of Chicago Press, 2008.

Desai, Jigna, and Khyati Y. Joshi. "Introduction: Discrepancies in Dixie: Asian Americans and the South." In *Asian Americans in Dixie: Race and Migration in the South.* Edited by Jigna Desai and Khyati Y Joshi, 1–33. Urbana: University of Illinois Press, 2013.

DeSalvo, Louise. "Color: White/Complexion: Dark." In *Are Italians White? How Race Is Made in America.* Edited by Jennifer Guglielmo and Salvatore Salerno, 17–28. New York: Routledge, 2003.

Dickie, John. *Cosa Nostra: A History of the Sicilian Mafia.* New York: Palgrave Macmillan, 2004.

Di Scala, Spencer. *Italy from Revolution to Republic: 1700 to the Present.* Boulder, CO: Westview Press, 2004.

Dittmer, John. *Black Georgia in the Progressive Era, 1900–1920.* Urbana: University of Illinois Press, 1977.

Domínguez, Virginia R. *White by Definition: Social Classification in Creole Louisiana.* New Brunswick, NJ: Rutgers University Press, 1986.

Ellison, Rhoda Coleman. "Little Italy in Rural Alabama." *Alabama Heritage*, no. 2 (Fall 1986): 34–47.

Equal Justice Initiative. *Lynching in America: Confronting the Legacy of Racial Terror.* 3rd edition. Montgomery, AL: Equal Justice Initiative, 2017, accessed April 14, 2019, https://lynchinginamerica.eji.org/report/.

Fahrmeir, Andreas. *Citizenship: The Rise and Fall of a Modern Concept.* New Haven, CT: Yale University Press, 2007.

Feimster, Crystal N. *Southern Horrors: Women and the Politics of Rape and Lynching.* Cambridge, MA: Harvard University Press, 2009.

Fields, Barbara J. "Slavery, Race and Ideology in the United States." *New Left Review* 181 (May 1, 1990): 95–118.

———. "Whiteness, Racism, and Identity." *International Labor and Working-Class History* 60 (2001): 48–56.

Gabaccia, Donna R. *From Sicily to Elizabeth Street: Housing and Social Change among Italian Immigrants, 1880–1930.* Albany: State University of New York Press, 1984.

———. "Is Everyone Nowhere? Nomads, Nations, and the Immigrant Paradigm of United States History." *Journal of American History* 86, no. 3 (December 1999): 1115–37.

———. *Italy's Many Diasporas.* Seattle: University of Washington Press, 2000.

———. *Militants and Migrants: Rural Sicilians Become American Workers.* New Brunswick, NJ: Rutgers University Press, 1988.

Gambino, Richard. *Vendetta: The True Story of the Largest Lynching in U.S. History.* Garden City, NY: Doubleday, 1977.

Garcia, Hazel Dicken. *Journalistic Standards in Nineteenth-Century America.* Madison: University of Wisconsin Press, 1989.

Gauthreaux, Alan G. "An Inhospitable Land: Anti-Italian Sentiment and Violence in Louisiana, 1891–1924." *Louisiana History* 51, no. 1 (2010): 41–68.

Germany, Kent B. *New Orleans after the Promises: Poverty, Citizenship, and the Search for the Great Society.* Athens: University of Georgia Press, 2007.

Giordano, Paolo. "Italian Immigration in the State of Louisiana: Its Causes, Effects, and Results." *Italian Americana* 5, no. 2 (1979): 160–77.

Gomez, Michael Angelo. *Exchanging Our Country Marks: The Transformation of African Identities in the Colonial and Antebellum South.* Chapel Hill: University of North Carolina Press, 1998.

Gonzales-Day, Ken. *Lynching in the West, 1850–1935.* Durham: Duke University Press, 2006.

Gould, Virginia Meacham. "'A Chaos of Iniquity and Discord': Slave and Free Women of Color in the Spanish Ports of New Orleans, Mobile, and Pensacola." In *The Devil's Lane: Sex and Race in the Early South.* Edited by Catherine Clinton and Michele Gillespie, 232–46. Oxford: Oxford University Press, 1997.

Gross, Ariela Julie. *What Blood Won't Tell: A History of Race on Trial in America.* Cambridge, MA: Harvard University Press, 2008.

Guglielmo, Jennifer. *Living the Revolution: Italian Women's Resistance and Radicalism in New York City, 1880–1945.* Chapel Hill: University of North Carolina Press, 2010.

Guglielmo, Jennifer, and Salvatore Salerno, eds. *Are Italians White? How Race Is Made in America*. New York: Routledge, 2003.

Guglielmo, Thomas. "No Color Barrier: Italians, Race, and Power in the United States." In *Are Italians White? How Race Is Made in America*. Edited by Jennifer Guglielmo and Salvatore Salerno, 29–43. New York: Routledge, 2003.

———. *White on Arrival: Italians, Race, Color, and Power in Chicago, 1890–1945*. New York: Oxford University Press, 2003.

Guterl, Matthew. *The Color of Race in America, 1900–1940*. Cambridge, MA: Harvard University Press, 2001.

Haas, Edward F. "Guns, Goats, and Italians: The Tallulah Lynching of 1899." *North Louisiana Historical Association* 13, no. 2 (1982): 45–58.

———. *Political Leadership in a Southern City: New Orleans in the Progressive Era, 1896–1902*. Ruston: McGinty Publications, Louisiana Tech University, 1988.

Hair, William Ivy. *Bourbonism and Agrarian Protest; Louisiana Politics, 1877–1900*. Baton Rouge: Louisiana State University Press, 1969.

Hale, Grace Elizabeth. *Making Whiteness: The Culture of Segregation in the South, 1890–1940*. New York: Vintage Books, 1999.

Hall, Gwendolyn Midlo. *Africans in Colonial Louisiana: The Development of Afro-Creole Culture in the Eighteenth Century*. Baton Rouge: Louisiana State University Press, 1992.

———. "African Women in French and Spanish Louisiana: Origins, Roles, Family, Work, Treatment." In *The Devil's Lane: Sex and Race in the Early South*. Edited by Catherine Clinton and Michele Gillespie, 247–61. Oxford: Oxford University Press, 1997.

Haney-López, Ian. *White by Law: The Legal Construction of Race*. New York: New York University Press, 2006.

Hanger, Kimberly S. *Bounded Lives, Bounded Places: Free Black Society in Colonial New Orleans, 1769–1803*. Durham: Duke University Press, 1997.

———. "Coping in a Complex World: Free Black Women in Colonial New Orleans." In *The Devil's Lane: Sex and Race in the Early South*. Edited by Catherine Clinton and Michele Gillespie, 218–31. Oxford: Oxford University Press, 1997.

———. "Patronage, Property and Persistence: The Emergence of a Free Black Elite in Spanish New Orleans." *Slavery and Abolition* 17, no. 1 (1996): 44–64.

Hargrave, W. Lee. *The Louisiana State Constitution*. Oxford: Oxford University Press, 2011.

Harris, Cheryl I. "Whiteness as Property." *Harvard Law Review* 106, no. 8 (June 1993): 1707–1791.

Hickman, Christine B. "The Devil and the One Drop Rule: Racial Categories, African Americans, and the U.S. Census." *Michigan Law Review* 95, no. 5 (1997): 1161–1265.

Higham, John. *Strangers in the Land: Patterns of American Nativism, 1860–1925*. New York: Atheneum, 1963.

Hobbs, Allyson Vanessa. *A Chosen Exile: A History of Racial Passing in American Life*. Cambridge, MA: Harvard University Press, 2014.

Hodes, Martha Elizabeth, ed. *Sex, Love, Race: Crossing Boundaries in North American History*. New York: New York University Press, 1999.

———. *White Women, Black Men: Illicit Sex in the Nineteenth-Century South*. New Haven, CT: Yale University Press, 1997.

Hunt, Thomas, and Martha Macheca Sheldon. *Deep Water: Joseph P. Macheca and the Birth of the American Mafia*. New York: iUniverse, 2007.

Hyde, Samuel C. *Sunbelt Revolution: The Historical Progression of the Civil Rights Struggle in the Gulf South, 1866–2000*. Gainesville: University Press of Florida, 2003.

Iorizzo, Luciano J., and Salvatore Mondello. *The Italian Americans*. Boston: G. K. Hall, 1980.

Jackson, Jessica Barbata. "Before the Lynching: Reconsidering the Experience of Italians and Sicilians in Louisiana, 1870s–1890s." *Louisiana History* 58, no. 3 (2017): 300–338.

Jackson, Joy J. *New Orleans in the Gilded Age: Politics and Urban Progress, 1880–1896*. Baton Rouge: Louisiana State University Press, 1969.

Jacobson, Matthew Frye. *Whiteness of a Different Color: European Immigrants and the Alchemy of Race*. Cambridge, MA: Harvard University Press, 1998.

Jäger, Daniela G. "The Worst 'White Lynching' in American History: Elites vs. Italians in New Orleans, 1891." *AAA: Arbeiten Aus Anglistik Und Amerikanistik* 27, no. 2 (2002): 161–79.

Johnson, Walter. *River of Dark Dreams: Slavery and Empire in the Cotton Kingdom*. Cambridge, MA: Belknap Press of Harvard University Press, 2013.

———. *Soul by Soul: Life Inside the Antebellum Slave Market*. Cambridge, MA: Harvard University Press, 1999.

Jones, Edgar Malcolm, and H. G. Lewis. *Soil Survey of Lamar County, Mississippi*. Washington, DC: Government Printing Office, 1922.

Jung, Moon-Ho. *Coolies and Cane: Race, Labor, and Sugar in the Age of Emancipation*. Baltimore: Johns Hopkins University Press, 2006.

Kelley, Laura D. *The Irish in New Orleans*. Lafayette: University of Louisiana at Lafayette Press, 2014.

Kendall, John S. *History of New Orleans*. Chicago: Lewis Publishing, 1922.

———. "Who Killa de Chief?" *Louisiana Historical Quarterly* 22, no. 2 (1939): 492–530.

Kessner, Thomas. *The Golden Door: Italian and Jewish Immigrant Mobility in New York City, 1880–1915*. New York: Oxford University Press, 1977.

Keyssar, Alexander. *The Right to Vote: The Contested History of Democracy in the United States*. New York: Basic Books, 2000.

Kurtz, Michael L. "Organized Crime in Louisiana History: Myth and Reality." *Louisiana History* 24, no. 4 (1983): 355–76.

Labbe, Ronald M. "That the Reign of Robbery May Never Return to Louisiana: The Constitution of 1879." In *In Search of Fundamental Law: Louisiana's Constitutions, 1812–1974*. Edited by Warren M. Billings and Edward F. Haas. Lafayette: Center for Louisiana Studies, University of Southwestern Louisiana, 1993.

LaGumina, Salvatore John. "Discrimination, Prejudice and Italian American History." In *The Routledge History of Americans*. Edited by William J. Connell and Stanislao G. Pugliese, 223–38. New York: Routledge, 2018.

———. *Wop!: A Documentary History of Anti-Italian Discrimination in the United States*. Toronto: Guernica, 1999.

Lampedusa, Giuseppe Tomasi di. *Il Gattopardo*. 1958. Translated by Archibald Colquhoun as *The Leopard*. New York: Pantheon Books, 2007.

Lanza, Michael. "Little More than a Family Matter: The Constitution of 1898." In *In Search of Fundamental Law: Louisiana's Constitutions, 1812–1974*. Edited by Warren M. Billings and Edward F. Haas. Lafayette: Center for Louisiana Studies, University of Southwestern Louisiana, 1993.

La Storia: Birmingham's Italian Community. Exhibition. Vulcan Park and Museum, Birmingham, AL, visited December 18, 2014.

Lee, Erika. "Hemispheric Orientalism and the 1907 Pacific Coast Race Riots." *Amerasia Journal* 33, no. 2 (2007): 19–48.

Leonard, Stephen J. *Lynching in Colorado, 1859–1919*. Boulder: University Press of Colorado, 2002.

Loewen, James W. *The Mississippi Chinese: Between Black and White*. Cambridge, MA: Harvard University Press, 1971.

Long, Alecia P. *The Great Southern Babylon: Sex, Race, and Respectability in New Orleans, 1865–1920*. Baton Rouge: Louisiana State University Press, 2004.

Lopez, Ian Haney. *White by Law: The Legal Construction of Race*. New York: New York University Press, 1996.

Lopreato, Joseph. *Italian Americans*. New York: Random House, 1970.

Louisiana Writers' Project, Lyle Saxon, Edward Dreyer, and Robert Tallant. *Gumbo Ya-Ya*. Boston: Houghton Mifflin, 1945.

Luconi, Stefano. "Black Dagoes? Italian Immigrants' Racial Status in the United

States: An Ecological View." *Journal of Transatlantic Studies* 14, no. 2 (2016): 188–99.

———. *The Italian-American Vote in Providence, Rhode Island, 1916–1948.* Cranbury, NJ.: Rosemont Publishing, 2004.

———. "The Lynching of Italian Americans: A Reassessment." In *Selected Essays from the 42nd Annual Conference of the American Italian Historical Association, Held October 29–31, 2009, in Baton Rouge, Louisiana.* Edited by Alan J. Gravano, Ilaria Serra, and the American Italian Historical Association, 58–78. New York: John D. Calandra Italian-American Institute, 2013.

———. "Tampa's 1910 Lynching: The Italian-American Perspective and its Implications." *Florida Historical Quarterly* 88, no. 1 (Summer 2009): 30–53.

Lumley, Robert, and Jonathan Morris, eds. *The New History of the Italian South: The Mezzogiorno Revisited.* Exeter: Exeter University Press, 1997.

Mabry, William Alexander. "Louisiana Politics and the 'Grandfather Clause.'" *North Carolina Historical Review* 13, no. 4 (October 1936): 290–320.

Mangione, Jerre, and Ben Morreale. *La Storia: Five Centuries of the Italian American Experience.* New York: Harper Collins, 1992.

Margavio, Anthony V., and Jerome J. Salomone. *Bread and Respect: The Italians of Louisiana.* Gretna, LA: Pelican Publishing, 2002.

Martin, Joan M. "Plaçage and the Louisiana *Gens de Couleur Libre:* How Race and Sex Defined the Lifestyles of Free Women of Color." In *Creole: The History and Legacy of Louisiana's Free People of Color.* Edited by Sybil Kein, 57–70. Baton Rouge: Louisiana State University Press, 2000.

McClean, Nancy. "Gender, Sexuality, and the Politics of Lynching: The Leo Frank Case Revisited." In *Under Sentence of Death: Lynching in the South.* Edited by W. Fitzhugh Brundage. Chapel Hill: University of North Carolina Press, 1997.

Moe, Nelson. *The View from Vesuvius: Italian Culture and the Southern Question.* Berkeley: University of California Press, 2002.

Molina, Natalia. *How Race Is Made in America: Immigration, Citizenship, and the Historical Power of Racial Scripts.* Berkeley: University of California Press, 2014.

Moloney, Deirdre M. *National Insecurities: Immigrants and U.S. Deportation Policy since 1882.* Chapel Hill: University of North Carolina Press, 2012.

Morris, Benjamin. *Hattiesburg, Mississippi: A History of the Hub City.* Charleston, SC: The History Press, 2014.

Nelli, Humbert S. *The Business of Crime: Italians and Syndicate Crime in the United States.* New York: Oxford University Press, 1976.

———. *From Immigrants to Ethnics: The Italian Americans.* New York: Oxford University Press, 1983.

———. *Italians in Chicago, 1880–1930: A Study in Ethnic Mobility*. New York: Oxford University Press, 1970.

Ngai, Mae M. *Impossible Subjects: Illegal Aliens and the Making of Modern America*. Princeton, NJ: Princeton University Press, 2004.

Nordstrom, Justin. *Danger on the Doorstep: Anti-Catholicism and American Print Culture in the Progressive Era*. Notre Dame, IN: University of Notre Dame Press, 2006.

Norrell, Jeff. *The Italians from Bisacquino to Birmingham*. Birmingham, AL: Birmingfind, 1982.

Novak, William J. "The Legal Transformation of Citizenship in Nineteenth-Century America." In *The Democratic Experiment: New Directions in American Political History*. Edited by Meg Jacobs, William J. Novak, and Julian E. Zelizer, 85–119. Princeton, NJ: Princeton University Press, 2003.

Novkov, Julie. "Racial Constructions: The Legal Regulation of Miscegenation in Alabama, 1890–1934." *Law and History Review* 20, no. 2 (2002): 225–77.

———. *Racial Union Law, Intimacy, and the White State in Alabama, 1865–1954*. Ann Arbor: University of Michigan Press, 2008.

Nystrom, Justin A. *Creole Italian: Sicilian Immigrants and the Shaping of New Orleans Food Culture*. Athens: University of Georgia Press, 2018.

———. *New Orleans after the Civil War: Race, Politics, and a New Birth of Freedom*. Baltimore: Johns Hopkins University Press, 2010.

Parker, Kunal. *Making Foreigners: Immigration and Citizenship Law in America, 1600–2000*. Cambridge: Cambridge University Press, 2015.

Pascoe, Peggy. "Miscegenation Law, Court Cases, and Ideologies of 'Race' in Twentieth-Century America. In *Sex, Love, Race: Crossing Boundaries in North America*. Edited by Martha Hodes, 464–91. New York: New York University Press, 1999.

———. *What Comes Naturally: Miscegenation Law and the Making of Race in America*. Oxford: Oxford University Press, 2009.

Percy, William Alexander. *Lanterns on the Levee: Recollections of a Planter's Son*. New York: Alfred Knopf, 1941.

Perlman, Joel. *America Classifies the Immigrants: From Ellis Island to the 2020 Census*. Cambridge, MA: Harvard University Press, 2018.

Pfeifer, Michael J. *The Roots of Rough Justice: Origins of American Lynching*. Urbana: University of Illinois Press, 2011.

———. *Rough Justice: Lynching and American Society, 1874–1947*. Urbana: University of Illinois Press, 2004.

Phillips, Ruth B. *Trading Identities: The Souvenir in Native North American Art from the Northeast, 1700–1900*. Seattle: University of Washington Press, 1999.

Pittman, Bob. *Lamar County: The Land and the People.* Jackson, MS: Pittman Enterprises, 2004.

Racine, Philip N. "The Ku Klux Klan, Anti-Catholicism, and Atlanta's Board of Education, 1916–1927." *Georgia Historical Quarterly* 57, no. 1 (1973): 63–75.

Ray, Celeste. "European Mississippians." In *Ethnic Heritage in Mississippi, the Twentieth Century.* Edited by Shana Walton and Barbara Carpenter, 32–73. Jackson: University Press of Mississippi, 2012.

Reed, *Daniel* C. "Reevaluating the Vote Market Hypothesis: Effects of Australian Ballot Reform on Voter Turnout." *Social Science History* 38, no. 3–4 (Fall/Winter 2014): 277–290.

Rimanelli, Giose. "The 1891 New Orleans Lynching: Southern Politics, Mafia, Immigration and the American Press." In *The 1891 New Orleans Lynching and U.S.–Italian Relations: A Look Back.* Edited by Marco Rimanelli and Sheryl L. Postman, 53–105. New York: P. Lang, 1992.

Rimanelli, Marco. "The 1891–92 U.S.–Italian Crisis and War-Scare: Foreign and Domestic Policies of the Harrison and Di Rudini Governments." In *The 1891 New Orleans Lynching and U.S.–Italian Relations: A Look Back.* Edited by Marco Rimanelli and Sheryl L. Postman, 183–285. New York: P. Lang, 1992.

———. "The New Orleans Lynching & US–Italian Relations from Harmony to War-Scare: Immigration, Mafia, Diplomacy." In *The 1891 New Orleans Lynching and U.S.–Italian Relations: A Look Back.* Edited by Marco Rimanelli and Sheryl L. Postman, 106–82. New York: P. Lang, 1992.

Rimanelli, Marco, and Sheryl L. Postman, eds. *The 1891 New Orleans Lynching and U.S.–Italian Relations: A Look Back.* New York: P. Lang, 1992.

Riser, R. Volney. *Defying Disfranchisement: Black Voting Rights Activism in the Jim Crow South, 1890–1908.* Baton Rouge: Louisiana State University Press, 2010.

Robinson, Charles F. *Dangerous Liaisons: Sex and Love in the Segregated South.* Fayetteville: University of Arkansas Press, 2003.

———. *Forsaking All Others: A True Story of Interracial Sex and Revenge in the 1880s South.* Knoxville: University of Tennessee Press, 2010.

———. "What's Sex Got to Do with It? Antimiscegenation Law and Southern White Rhetoric." In *Manners and Southern History.* Edited by Ted Ownby, 97–113. Jackson: University Press of Mississippi, 2007.

Rodrigue, John C. *Reconstruction in the Cane Fields: From Slavery to Free Labor in Louisiana's Sugar Parishes, 1862–1880.* Baton Rouge: Louisiana State University Press, 2001.

Roediger, David R. The Wages of Whiteness: Race and the Making of the American Working Class, rev. ed. London: Verso, 2007.

———. *Working Towards Whiteness: How America's Immigrants Became White. The*

Strange Journey form Ellis Island to the Suburbs. New York: Basic Books, 2005.

Rosaldo, Renato. "Cultural Citizenship and Educational Democracy." *Cultural Anthropology* 9, no. 3 (August 1, 1994): 402–11.

Rosen, Hannah. "The Rhetoric of Miscegenation and the Reconstruction of Race: Debating Marriage, Sex, and Citizenship in Postemancipation Arkansas." In *Gender and Slave Emancipation in the Atlantic World*. Edited by Pamela Scully and Diana Paton, 289–309. Durham, NC: Duke University Press, 2005.

———. *Terror in the Heart of Freedom: Citizenship, Sexual Violence, and the Meaning of Race in the Postemancipation South*. Chapel Hill: University of North Carolina Press, 2009.

Rothman, Adam. *Slave Country: American Expansion and the Origins of the Deep South*. Cambridge, MA: Harvard University Press, 2005.

Rothman, Joshua. *Notorious in the Neighborhood: Sex and Families across the Color Line in Virginia, 1787–1861*. Chapel Hill: University of North Carolina Press, 2003.

Rushdy, Ashraf H. A. *The End of American Lynching*. New Brunswick, NJ: Rutgers University Press, 2012.

Salvetti, Patrizia. *Rope and Soap: Lynchings of Italians in the United States*. Translated by Fabio Girelli-Carasi. New York: Bordighera Press, John D. Calandra Italian-American Institute, 2017.

Sandweiss, Martha A. *Passing Strange: A Gilded Age Tale of Love and Deception across the Color Line*. New York: Penguin Press, 2009.

Santore, John. *Modern Naples: A Documentary History, 1799–1999*. New York: Italica Press, 2001.

Saperstein, Aliya, and Aaron Gullickson. "A 'Mulatto Escape Hatch' in the United States? Examining Evidence of Racial and Social Mobility During the Jim Crow Era." *Demography* 50, no. 5 (2013): 1921–42.

Scarpaci, Vincenza. *Italian Immigrants in Louisiana's Sugar Parishes: Recruitment, Labor Conditions, and Community Relations, 1880–1910*. New York: Arno Press, 1980.

———. "Walking the Color Line: Italian Immigrants in Rural Louisiana, 1880–1910." In *Are Italians White? How Race Is Made in America*. Edited by Jennifer Guglielmo and Salvatore Salerno, 60–76. New York: Routledge, 2003.

Schneider, Jane, ed. *Italy's "Southern Question": Orientalism in One Country*. New York: Berg, 1998.

Smith, Rogers M. *Civic Ideals: Conflicting Visions of Citizenship in U.S. History*. New Haven, CT: Yale University Press, 1997.

Smith, Tom. *The Crescent City Lynchings: The Murder of Chief Hennessy, the New*

Orleans "Mafia" Trials, and the Parish Prison Mob. Guilford, CT: Lyons Press, 2007.

Snowden, Frank M. *Naples in the Time of Cholera, 1884–1911*. Cambridge: Cambridge University Press, 1995.

Spear, Jennifer M. *Race, Sex, and Social Order in Early New Orleans*. Baltimore: Johns Hopkins University Press, 2009.

Stahle, Patrizia Famá. *The Italian Emigration of Modern Times: Relations between Italy and the United States concerning Emigration Policy, Diplomacy and Anti-Immigrant Sentiment, 1870–1927*. Newcastle, UK: Cambridge Scholars Publishing, 2016.

Sweet, Frank W. *Legal History of the Color Line: The Rise and Triumph of the One-Drop Rule*. Palm Coast, FL: Backintyme, 2000.

Thomas, Teresa Fava. *The Reluctant Migrants: Migration from the Veneto to Central Massachusetts 1880–1920*. Amherst, NY: Teneo Press, 2015.

Tolnay, Stewart Emory, and E. M. Beck. *A Festival of Violence: An Analysis of Southern Lynchings, 1882–1930*. Urbana: University of Illinois Press, 1995.

Topp, Michael M. *The Sacco and Vanzetti Case: A Brief History with Documents*. Bedford, MA: Palgrave MacMillian, 2005.

———. "The Sacco and Vanzetti Case and the Psychology of Political Violence." In *The Routledge History of Italian Americans*. Edited by William J. Connell and Stanislao G. Pugliese, 286–304. New York: Routledge, 2018.

Usner, Daniel H. *Indians, Settlers & Slaves in a Frontier Exchange Economy: The Lower Mississippi Valley Before 1783*. Chapel Hill: University of North Carolina Press, 1992.

Vecoli, Rudolph. "Are Italian Americans Just White Folks?" *Italian Americana* 13 (1995): 149–61.

———. "Contadini in Chicago: A Critique of *The Uprooted*." *Journal of American History* 51, no. 3 (December 1964): 404–17.

Vellon, Peter G. "'Between White Men and Negroes': The Perception of Southern Italian Immigrants through the Lens of Italian Lynchings." In *Anti-Italianism: Essays on a Prejudice*. Edited by William J. Connell and Fred Gardaphé. Basingstoke, UK: Palgrave Macmillan, 2010.

———. *A Great Conspiracy against Our Race: Italian Immigrant Newspapers and the Construction of Whiteness in the Early Twentieth Century*. New York: New York University Press, 2014.

Vyhnanek, Louis Andrew. *Unorganized Crime: New Orleans in the 1920s*. Lafayette: Center for Louisiana Studies, University of Southwestern Louisiana, 1998.

Vincent, Charles. "Black Constitution Makers: The Constitution of 1868." In *In*

Search of Fundamental Law: Louisiana's Constitutions, 1812–1974. Edited by Warren M. Billings and Edward F. Haas. Lafayette: Center for Louisiana Studies, University of Southwestern Louisiana, 1993.

Waldrep, Christopher. *The Many Faces of Judge Lynch: Extralegal Violence and Punishment in America*. New York: Palgrave, 2002.

Wallenstein, Peter. *Tell the Court I Love My Wife: Race, Marriage, and Law: An American History*. New York: Palgrave Macmillan, 2002.

Walton, Shana, and Barbara Carpenter, eds. *Ethnic Heritage in Mississippi, the Twentieth Century*. Jackson: University Press of Mississippi, 2012.

Webb, Clive. "The Lynching of Sicilian Immigrants in the American South, 1886–1910." In *Lynching Reconsidered: New Perspectives in the Study of Mob Violence*. Edited by William D. Carrigan, 175–204. New York: Routledge, 2008.

Weinberg, Meyer. *Asian-American Education: Historical Background and Current Realities*. Mahwah, NJ: Lawrence Erlbaum Associates, 1997.

Weise, Julie M. *Corazon De Dixie: Mexicanos in the U.S. South since 1910*. Chapel Hill: University of North Carolina Press, 2015.

Welke, Barbara Young. *Law and the Borders of Belonging in the Long Nineteenth Century United States*. Cambridge: Cambridge University Press, 2010.

Whayne, Jeannie M., ed. *Shadows Over Sunnyside: An Arkansas Plantation in Transition, 1830–1945*. Fayetteville: University of Arkansas Press, 1993.

Wilds, John. *Afternoon Story: A Century of the New Orleans States-Item*. Baton Rouge: Louisiana State University Press, 1976.

Williams, Jessica. "Mayor Cantrell Apologizes for 1891 Italian-American Lynchings in New Orleans: 'What Happened was Wrong.'" *New Orleans Advocate* (April 12, 2019), accessed May 2, 2019, https://www.theadvocate.com/new_orleans/news/article_6262f734-5d5d-11e9-b3ab-ff791456d518.html.

Willoughby, Urmi Engineer. *Yellow Fever, Race, and Ecology in Nineteenth-Century New Orleans*. Baton Rouge: Louisiana State University Press, 2017.

Wise, Benjamin E. *William Alexander Percy: The Curious Life of a Mississippi Planter and Sexual Freethinker*. Chapel Hill: University of North Carolina Press, 2012.

Wollenberg, Charles. *All Deliberate Speed: Segregation and Exclusion in California Schools, 1855–1975*. Berkeley: University of California Press, 1976.

——. "'Yellow Peril' in the Schools (II)." In *The Asian American Educational Experience: A Source Book for Teachers and Students*. Edited by Don T. Nakanishi and Tina Yamano Nishida, 13–29. New York: Routledge, 1995.

Wood, Amy Louise. *Lynching and Spectacle: Witnessing Racial Violence in America, 1890–1940*. Chapel Hill: University of North Carolina Press, 2009.

Woodward, C. Vann. *Origins of the New South, 1877–1913*. Baton Rouge: Louisiana State University Press, 1951.

Wyatt-Brown, Bertram. "LeRoy Percy and Sunnyside: Planter Mentality and Italian Peonage in the Mississippi Delta." In *Shadows over Sunnyside: An Arkansas Plantation in Transition, 1830–1945*. Edited by Jeannie M. Whayne, 77–94. Fayetteville: University of Arkansas Press, 1992.

Wyman, Mark. *Round-Trip to America: The Immigrants Return to Europe, 1880–1930*. Ithaca, NY: Cornell University Press, 1993.

Yans-McLaughlin, Virginia. *Family and Community: Italian Immigrants in Buffalo, 1880–1930*. Ithaca, NY: Cornell University Press, 1977.

Zolberg, Aristide R. "The Great Wall Against China: Responses to the First Immigration Crisis, 1885–1925." In *How Many Exceptionalisms? Explorations in Comparative Macroanalysis*. Philadelphia: Temple University Press, 2008.

Index

culture of, 12; geography of, 12–13; Gulf
States, 13–14
Gulfport, MS, 106

Hahnville, LA, 18, 32–33, 35–37, 45–46,
57–59, 62
Harbert, Principal, 98, 107
Harjo, Suzan Shown, 183–84n69
Haskin, Frederic J., 152
Hattiesburg, MS, 106, 110, 115–16
Hattiesburg Daily News, 106–7, 109
Hawkins, Elizabeth, 126
Haynes, Walter, 56
Hearsey, Maj. Henry James, 14
Hennessy, David, 50, 78; assassination of,
17, 33, 43–44, 49–52, 54; spelling of
name, 163n1
Higham, John, 160n32
Hodge, Dr. J. Ford, 60–62
Hubbard, Detective, 135

Iberic (race), 5
Il Progresso (New York), 64
Illinois, 19
illiterate voters, 71, 75–76, 85–86, 88–92,
95, 148
immigrants, 148–49, 152–55; Asian, 153,
187n15, 190n61; Assyrian, 115; Caribbean,
12, 31; European, 1, 5, 7, 31, 93, 128, 130,
144; French, 94, 127–29; German, 20, 62,
127, 130; Greek, 115; in the Gulf South,
104, 116; Irish, 74, 94, 127, 167–68n63;
Japanese, 108; Latin American, 31, 47,
120; in Louisiana, 5, 12, 23, 25–27, 48,
72, 76, 78, 87; in Mississippi, 103, 114–15;
Russian Jews, 115; Southern and Eastern
Europeans, 4, 153. *See also* Chinese; Italians; Sicilians
immigration, 5, 12, 27, 40; bureau in South
Carolina, 149; of Italians/Sicilians,
18–20, 22, 27, 30, 33, 93, 105, 116, 128; to

Louisiana, 5, 23–25, 28–29; restrictions
against, 5, 7, 11, 20, 24, 107, 147–49, 153–
54; restrictions against Sicilians/South-
ern Italians, 65, 146–47, 154
Immigration Commission, US, 5, 149
Immigration Restriction League, 148–49
inbetween/inbetweenness: Barrett and Roediger on, 7; Chinese as inbetween, 101;
Guglielmo on, 7; Higham on, 160n32;
Italians as inbetween, 7–8, 76, 104. *See
also* racial transiency
Incardona, Bastian, 44, 54, 174n30
indemnity: debates, 18, 38, 42, 69, 108, 110,
152; payments/indemnities, 18, 34–35,
37–38, 41–42, 169n91. *See also* citizenship, US
indigenous, 120; anti-indigenous rhetoric,
110; as lynching victims, 47. *See also* Native Americans
Innocenti, 50
Irish immigrants, 74, 94, 127, 167–68n63;
anti-Irish rhetoric, 91; Catholics, 31
Iroquois Club, 179n8, 185n103
Italian Club, 77–78, 82
Italian Colony, 22, 24, 38, 40, 52
Italian consulate, in New Orleans, 13, 42,
98, 107, 110
Italian Guards Battalion, 126
Italian Legion, 77
Italian Parade. *See* "Dago Parade"
Italianità, 11, 19, 40–42, 70, 73, 77–78, 96,
154; Italian-ness, 11, 19, 54–57, 70, 82,
127–29, 132, 140–41, 144, 151, 155; Ital-
ianization, 4, 21
Italian-language newspapers, 14, 41, 64
Italians: and African Americans, 32–33,
82–83; in Alabama, 2, 12–13, 118–19; and
anti-Italian rhetoric, 4, 9, 10, 14, 17, 18,
20, 26, 28, 30, 32, 42, 106, 113–14, 146,
149, 167n52; citizenship of, 9–10, 18–19,
34–38, 89–90, 92, 152, 154; in the Gulf
South, 2, 6, 11–14, 18, 31, 33, 42, 100, 104,